# ROYAL INDIAN COOKERY

### A TASTE OF PALACE LIFE

# ROYAL INDIAN COOKERY

## A TASTE OF PALACE LIFE

## MANJU SHIVRAJ SINGH

### McGraw-Hill Book Company

New York · St. Louis · San Francisco
Bogotá · Guatemala · Hamburg · Lisbon · Madrid
Mexico · Montreal · Panama · Paris · San Juan
São Paulo · Tokyo · Toronto

DEDICATED TO MY HUSBAND SHIVRAJ,
MY SON-IN-LAW BHAWANI,
AND MY GRANDSON DHRUV.

1 2 3 4 5 6 7 8 9 9 8 7

ISBN 0-07-057534-7

Editor: Sally Taylor
Designer: Carole Thomas
Home Economist: Anne Hildyard
Production: Richard Churchill

This edition published 1987 for
McGraw-Hill Book Company.

I am often reminded of the vast amount of entertaining of international visitors that my husband and I have done here at the Rambagh and City Palaces in Jaipur. Great care and time was always given to the selection of menus in order to give our guests a taste of the varied and exciting Jaipur cuisine.

Although Manju was only young during that time, her natural enthusiasm gave her an early insight and awareness of the importance of color in our culture – whether in the choice of clothes or presentation of food. This beautiful book of recipes and the glimpse it gives into the life at the Palace is, in its way, a tribute to the people of Jaipur who want to share the tastes of India with the rest of the world.

My own favorite recipe is the Rajasthani Sulaas which I remember tasting at a dinner party at Manju's home. I'm sure, however, that all the dishes are equally delicious and that you will enjoy the opportunity to celebrate with us the festivities and wonderful food of Rajasthan.

*Gayatri Devi of Jaipur.*

HER HIGHNESS THE RAJ MATA OF JAIPUR

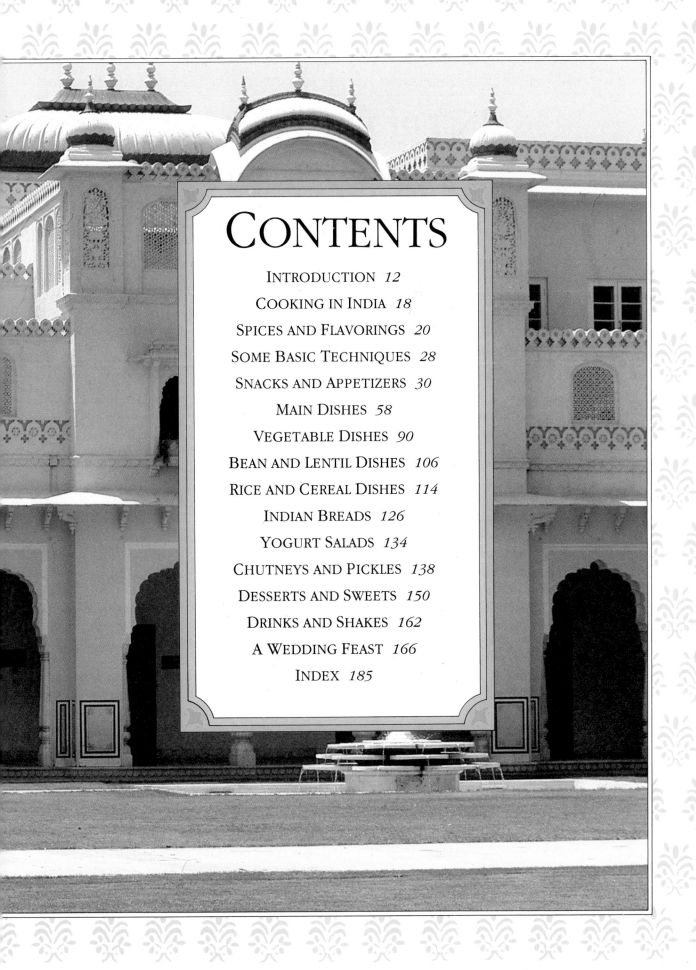

# CONTENTS

# INTRODUCTION

Jaipur, named the Pink City because of the pretty pink color painted onto its magnificent buildings, is the capital of Rajasthan, the one-time "Land of the Kings". Here the real romance of India lies, in this land that was once the home of warrior princes, wealthy beyond all dreams, whose every wish and whim was obeyed by their subjects, and who continually sought to outshine one another through the splendor of their palaces.

Rajasthan is still viewed as the princely state of India, and it lies in the extreme north-west of the country, bordering Pakistan. Jaipur is situated in a wide valley surrounded by desert plains and rocky dry hills, once the location of wild boar hunts and tiger shoots. It was built in 1727 by the warrior, astronomer and politician Maharaja Jai Singh II, when he moved his capital from the inhospitable hill site of Amber to the valley below. His ambition was to make Jaipur one of the best cities of his time and he was clearly successful.

In her book, *A Princess Remembers*, Her Highness Gayatri Devi of Jaipur, wife of the last Maharaja, describes Jaipur as lying "on a plain, encircled by brown desert hills with fortifications and walls snaking over their contours. The capital itself was the prettiest I had ever seen – an intricacy of domes and towers, lattices and verandas, with all the buildings colored a deep oleander pink. In the wide well-planned streets the women wore skirts, bodices and shawls instead of saris, and all the men wore gloriously colored turbans – red, magenta, daffodil yellow and an indescribable pink that was both pale and piercing. It was an incredible effect, this pink against the background of desert and sky."

Outside the walls of the old city, there is now a spreading mass of new buildings, but the wonderful old palaces – many now turned into luxury hotels – remain the city's center of attraction. The Rambagh Palace, for example, once the home of Her Highness Gayatri Devi and the late Maharaja, is now one of the finest hotels in the world. People wishing to stay here in the height of the tourist season from October to March, find they have to book their rooms at least one year in advance. The City Palace, the home of the Maharaja and Maharani covers nearly one-seventh of the area of the old city.

Rajasthan's people, the Rajputs, are of Aryan origin, claiming their descent from the *Kshatriyas*. Hindus are born into one of four castes, the *Brahmins*, *Kshatriyas*, *Vaisyas* and *Sudras*. The *Kshatriyas* are a martial race and often, as a result of skill in conquest or a reward for success, also rulers and landowners. Thus most of the princely families belonged to the *Kshatriya* caste, and it is certainly as warriors that the Rajputs have long been renowned, fighting bravely and fiercely through Moslem and Mogul invasions over the years.

When one considers the brave and daring feats of the Rajput warriors, however, one should remember their womenfolk, too, for they are imbued with the same great courage and a high sense of honor and duty to their men. It was this that drove thousands of young women to become *sati*, that is to dress themselves in their wedding finery in order to sit on the funeral pyres of their dead husbands to be burnt alive with his body. My grandmother has told me stories of watching this horrific, but enormously brave, event.

In the days of fierce and frequent fighting, funeral pyres would be kept burning day and night, so that when news of the warriors' deaths reached the wives, they would throw themselves into the fire, again to be burnt alive. This is the tradition of *jauhar*, a ritual mass suicide in anticipation of capture by the enemy when one no longer had the protection of a husband. Today, of course, such events are happily no more than part of history, but the women of Rajasthan still maintain this high sense of duty and fidelity. We continually pray and fast in order to promote the long life and good health of our husbands and the glass bangles that we wear as a sign of our married status are ceremonially broken on the death of our husbands.

Under British Rule, the proud Rajputs maintained a measure of independence. The State had its own laws, courts of justice, tax system and even its own military forces, so that the people naturally looked towards the Maharaja or prince as the real governmental authority in their lives. The term

THIS IMAGE OF A RAJPUT PRINCESS IS A COPY OF THE FAMOUS RAJASTHANI PAINTING CALLED "BANI THANI." IT WAS PRESENTED TO MANJU ON HER WEDDING DAY.

"Maharaja," incidentally, means "Great King;" "Rajah" is more simply "Ruler" or "King" and "Kumari" denotes the daughter of a noble man.

When independence for India came in 1947, Rajasthan, like all other States, acceded to the Indian Union. This meant the dissolution of the kingdoms, for the loss of which the Royal Families received privy purses. In 1970, Congress abolished the privy purses, and with their major source of income lost, the princely rulers were reduced to ordinary Indian citizens in all but title. Today it is these titles and the remnants of Royal tradition that survive as reminders of the former glories – of the times when the State's anthem would be played whenever a member of the Maharaja's family passed in or out of the front gates of the Royal Palace. But still there are prestigious tea parties on the lawns of the City Palace where guests are served wafer-thin cucumber sandwiches, tiny samosas and kabobs, and the sweet toffee known as *barfi*, and still the Maharaja receives people in his office at the Raj Mahal palace every morning between the hours of ten and one o'clock. His guests may be visiting foreign dignitaries or they may be local people with a grievance to air. At night-time, he hosts sumptuous dinners in the magnificent banquet hall of the opulent palace.

An aspect of life in Jaipur in which the Maharaja and Maharani are still greatly involved is during the celebrations of the many festivals that occur throughout the year. Festivals are an important and integral part of Indian life, whether they signify a great religious feast or some formal occasion of state. The celebrations have always been led by the Maharaja, with the townspeople and villagers from the surrounding countryside participating. Parades and processions pass through the city streets, followed by celebrations and feastings inside private homes and the Royal Palace. Many of these festivals are celebrated throughout India, but Rajasthan has a few extra of its own – indeed every month sees some occasion to celebrate in traditional style.

One of the most important festivals is that of *Divali* or *Deepavali*. This is the Hindu festival of lights that signifies the Hindu New Year and, according to the lunar calendar, it falls in November. In Jaipur, the whole of the city and the palace is lit with little oil lamps or tiny colored bulbs placed on walls, balconies and terraces and their twinkling lights are reflected in the city's many ponds and water tanks. In accordance with tradition we spring-clean our houses and white-wash them, to welcome *Lakshmi*, the goddess and giver of wealth. Sweets are prepared and exchanged as gifts between friends and relatives and new clothes are purchased especially for the festivities, this being the only day we are traditionally allowed to wear the colors of navy blue and black. The Maharaja invites us, as his relatives, to the Palace in the evening and entertains us on the topmost floor of the palace in a beautiful room called the "Sheesh Mahal," the walls of which are made entirely of semi-precious stones and mirrors. It is quite exquisite. Drinks and snacks are served on the terrace outside this room so that we can watch the firework display staged on the Palace lawns. Then we go down to the large hall to chance our luck at roulette. Gambling with small stakes is allowed on this day as *Lakshmi* has visited all the homes.

The festival of *Divali* goes on for three days. Following the cleaning of our homes we all perform our own *poojas* (prayers) at home in our small prayer rooms. The day after the celebrations at the Palace, everybody visits their relatives with the gifts of home-made sweets, and on the third day, known as *Bhaiya Dooj*, we worship our brothers, giving them more gifts. We really do spoil our men!

Another great occasion at the Palace is the festival of *Dashera* in October. On this day, remembering their warring past, the Rajputs worship their swords and guns, but it is also the official birthday of Maharaja Bhawani Singh of Jaipur, so we go to the Palace in the morning to wish him a happy birthday and to attend the *pooja* that is performed in his honor. We have to be formally dressed in our traditional Rajasthani *poshaks* (these are dresses – or ankle-length full skirts – worn with a long bodice and a shawl or veil), together with our finest gold jewelry. Everyone dresses in their very best clothes.

On this day only the ladies are allowed into the wing of the palace where the *pooja* is being performed and the men wait outside. They, too, are formally dressed in their finery, wearing *achkans* (long coats) with breeches and brightly colored *safaas* (turbans). The auspicious color to wear for the Royal birthday is red, so we women wear red *poshaks* and the men – red turbans. In the evening Maharaja "Bubbles" (so nick-named by his English nanny because of the huge amount of champagne that flowed at his christening as he was the first male heir to be born to a ruling Maharaja of Jaipur for two generations!) invites his close friends and relatives to a grand dinner on the terrace of his Royal apartments. We dine under the stars on small round tables scattered over the terrace. The tables are covered with pale pink organdy tablecloths and we eat off silver *thaalis* (platters). The wonderful buffet is laid out on a Lalique glass dining table. It is a truly romantic occasion.

A gentle and lovely festival for the ladies is celebrated on the lawns of the Palace in August. This is *Teej* or the Swing Festival, dedicated to the goddess *Parvati*, to celebrate the day when she was reunited with her consort Lord *Shiva*. Her Highness Gayatri Devi describes this as being a festival "of particular significance . . . in the stories of Hindu Mythology. Parvati had meditated for years and years in order to win Lord Shiva as husband. Accordingly, the unmarried women (today) prayed to Parvati to endow them with a husband as good as Shiva, while the married women begged that their husbands should be granted many more years of life so that they could 'always be dressed in red' – rather than the unrelieved white clothes of widows."

The Maharani invites her relatives to the Palace for *Teej* and performs the special ceremonies of prayers and offerings to the image of *Parvati* in the Palace's shrine. We wear *poshaks* of two different colors, with red or green striped chiffon or georgette veils. A swing is erected in the gardens of the Palace and we take it in turns to swing on it, during which time we must compose four lines of poetry about our husbands! Then tea is served in the Maharani's apartments.

*Raksha Bandhan* or *Raakhi* is also celebrated in August. On this day the womenfolk tie a silk thread around the right wrists of their brothers, thereby signifying that they are seeking their brothers' protection. Wherever a sister is, she will always make an effort to visit her brother on this day, bringing with her a large *thaal* piled high with sweets, fruit and a coconut. The brother returns the gesture by giving his sister a gift. My daughters, having no brother, rather miss out on this day, but they more than make up for it by going to the Palace and tying a *raakhi* on the Maharaja, whom they know as "Bubbles Mama" – meaning Uncle. He gives each of them a gift, and they are well pleased!

*Holi* – the festival of color that is an "exuberant celebration of Spring" – is a great Hindu festival and occurs in March. In Jaipur, we dress up in village dresses and assemble to sing and dance to the beat of the *chang* – a flat drum – on the lawns of the house belonging to one of my uncles. Then we burn the wicked *Holika*, whose

ABOVE: MANJU'S SISTER HELPS THE MAHARANI PADMINI DEVI PERFORM A LIGHT-HEARTED CUSTOM DURING THE TEEJ FESTIVAL. CELEBRATED BY THE WOMENFOLK, THE TEEJ FESTIVAL OCCURS IN AUGUST. ACCORDING TO RITUAL, THE MARRIED WOMEN TAKE IT IN TURN TO SIT ON A SWING AND COMPOSE SHORT POEMS ABOUT THEIR HUSBANDS. STRIPED *POSHAKS* ARE TRADITIONALLY WORN.

RIGHT: MANJU'S ELDEST DAUGHTER, SHIVINA, DANCING AT THE HOLI FESTIVAL WHICH CELEBRATES THE ARRIVAL OF SPRING. IT IS CUSTOMARY FOR THE DANCERS TO WEAR YELLOW AT THIS FESTIVAL.

ABOVE: MAHARAJA BHAWANI SINGH – KNOWN TO HIS FRIENDS AND RELATIVES AS "BUBBLES" – IS ENJOYING HIS LUNCH, WHICH IS SET OUT ON THE TRADITIONAL *THAALI*.

LEFT: THE CITY PALACE IN JAIPUR, THE HOME OF THE MAHARAJA AND MAHARANI, IS ONE OF THE MAGNIFICENT SIGHTS OF THE OLD CITY. PRESTIGIOUS TEA PARTIES ARE STILL HELD ON THE MAGNIFICENT LAWNS OF THE CITY PALACE.

effigy is made from sticks. The next day is called *Dulandi* and, dressed in our oldest clothes, we visit each other's houses to throw colored powders and water at one another. It is a very colorful and fun affair, but a very messy one!

At about eleven in the morning, our family gathers to wish Her Highness Gayatri Devi a happy *Holi* day at her residence – the Lilypool. Again we throw colored powders and water at one another and then snacks and drinks are served on the lawns. After this, we go to the Palace to pass on the same good wishes to the Maharaja and Maharani, and here the pool is filled with colored water. Most people end up in it! At two or three in the afternoon, we return home for a thorough wash before falling asleep, absolutely exhausted. The traditional fare on this day is a special sweet called *gujiya*. It is a sweet samosa made with a filling of semolina, sugar, coconut and dried fruits.

Food, of course, plays an important part in all these festivals and the food of Jaipur is, in my opinion, among the best in India. Some people might think me biased, I suppose, as I am a staunch Jaipurite, but I think we have a fair claim. We love a good curry, marinating the meat in yogurt, garlic, onion and freshly ground chili paste, before cooking it gently so that the spices are absorbed into the meat which is meltingly tender. The staple food is *maas* and *roti* – that is meat curry which is red and hot and fresh home-made bread. This is all washed down with lots of *daroo* (booze!). A wedding feast in Jaipur comprises the most magnificent display of food, surely one "fit for a king."

But if food plays an important part in the lives of the Rajputs, so does fasting – particularly among the women. Once again, this fasting is undertaken in order to promote the long life and good health of our husbands, or in the case of the unmarried, to ask for a good husband. *Shivratri*, the birthday of Lord *Shiva* in February is a traditional fast day for women and girls. We visit *Shiva's* temple in the morning with offerings and to say prayers, and then we may eat only one non-cereal meal during the day. Such a meal generally consists of potatoes, milk, sweets, fruit and *puris* made with water chestnut flour. Only rock salt can be used for seasoning. In June there is a special fast day called *Nir Jala Vrat*, when no water or food is allowed at all until sunset. This is very tough to follow as it is so hot at this time of year.

Lord *Krishna's* birthday falls at the end of August and is known as *Janamashthami*. Men and women fast on this day eating fruits and drinking milk during the day but having just one meal at midnight. *Bhajans* – holy songs – are sung in all homes during the evening. In September, Lord *Ganesh* – the God of good luck – has his birthday. This marks another fasting day, and we visit the famous *Ganesh* temple at Moti Doongri in Jaipur. I believe greatly in the powers of Lord *Ganesh*, and visit his temple every Wednesday when I am in Jaipur. He always seems to answer my requests. In April and October, nine fast days – *Navratri* – are observed by all Rajputs.

Life in Jaipur, however, is by no means all fasting. The bustling and busy city has much to offer tourists as well as the inhabitants. The local people provide a splash of vivid color – the men with their orange and red turbans, and the ladies with their yellow and red veils and their brightly colored flouncy skirts. Further opulence is provided by the mass of gold and silver jewelry worn by the ladies, together with their scores of glass bangles and beads. Much of the gold jewelry is a sign of their married status – the toe rings being the wedding bands and the gold anklets, the chains of matrimony. Architectural delights abound in the city, too, with such sights as the beautiful Palace of Winds – the *Hawa Mahal* – now no more than the breathtakingly lovely, delicately chiseled facade that looks onto a bustling thoroughfare. At one time the Royal ladies would look down from here onto the Royal processions and busy everyday life, neither of which they were allowed to join in.

Seven miles outside of Jaipur is the much visited old capital of Amber, set in a gorge among the hills which dominate the pass to the north. Here you can ride on an elephant to see the palaces of a bygone era and the Temple of the Goddess *Shila Mata* the Royal Deity, which is situated on top of a hill. The Maharaja visits this temple daily during the nine days of *Navratri*. In October there is a big *mela* (fair) at Amber on the seventh day of *Navratri*, and then on the ninth day the Maharaja performs a *pooja* at the temple and a small buffalo is slaughtered as a sacrifice. The cool marble floors inside the temple seem to invade your very soul, making you feel both clean and sacred. Beyond Amber and into the countryside of Rajasthan, there are huge areas of arid, daunting desert and forests full of *chinkara* and cheetals (types of deer), blackbuck and tigers. The sprawling sanctuary areas boast birds of rare origin including migrating Siberian ducks.

And a word should be said about the handicrafts of Rajasthan, for they also are an important part of our heritage, along with the music and dancing that you will hear and see everywhere. There are tie-and-dye and beautiful hand-printed fabrics, painting, gem cutting, carpet making, gold and silver jewelry crafting, enamel ware, ivory carving, blue pottery, brasswork, paper making, leather work, stone carving – and almost any other craft activity you can think of! Jaipur can even boast a place on the fashion stage of the world for its marvelous hand-printed fabrics are designed into clothes by French and British dress designers and may be seen displayed on the catwalks of many countries.

Brave and courageous warriors the Rajputs may lay claim to be, but they are also friendly and festive, loving nothing more than to dine and dance, sing or simply chat with their friends – new and old – at their homes or on picnics and outings. So come to Jaipur and sample its many visual and edible glories. Your appetite will become a slave to its curries and you will be totally enchanted by the Pink City of India.

**"Khamaghani"**
**special greetings from Rajasthan**
Manju Shivraj Singh

# COOKING IN INDIA

Since times long past, Indian ladies have sat on the floor by a single naked flame to cook the daily meals for their families. The flame would be provided either by hot coals, firewood or a small kerosene stove. Nowadays, however, most homes sport a gas stove which will have the supreme luxury of two heat rings, and perhaps even a small grill. The type of pan most usually used over the flame is a "wok." This is favored over the flat frying-pan as the heat is distributed more evenly around the food, allowing food to be fried quickly in just a small amount of oil. A large draining spoon is most frequently used in conjunction with a wok.

Nearly all Indian dishes are cooked over this small source of heat, the most notable exception being the spicy, red *tandoori* dishes, popular throughout the world. Meat and fish can be cooked *tandoor*-style, but by far and away the most popular dish in this type of cooking is *tandoori* chicken. After being marinated in spices, the food is cooked in a *tandoor* which is a very large earthenware pot, generally about 3 feet long and half as wide. In the old style of *tandoor*, the pot would be buried underground, wedged around by clay to keep it firm, and with a bed of burning charcoal inside to give an even heat throughout. The meat is cooked speared on long skewers which sit vertically in the pot. The *naan* or *roti* generally served with *tandoori* meat is cooked in the pot too. It is dampened on one side and stuck to the inside walls of the pot.

Not all homes will have a *tandoor*, of course, and in these days, hotels and restaurants, in particular, will have portable *tandoors*. In these, the clay pot is encased in an iron drum, held firm

SOME OF THE MOST FREQUENTLY USED COOKING UTENSILS IN RAJASTHANI COOKING. CLOCKWISE FROM LEFT THEY ARE, A WOK (*KARACHI*), A ROLLING PIN AND BOARD (*BELAN* AND *CHAKLA*) AND A GRIDDLE (*TAWA*).

**A**BOVE: A CLOSE-UP VIEW OF THE INSIDE OF THE EARTHENWARE COOKING POT KNOWN AS A *TANDOOR*. MEAT PIECES ARE SPEARED ONTO LONG SKEWERS AND PLACED VERTICALLY OVER THE BURNING CHARCOAL INSIDE THE POT.

**R**IGHT: FROM TIME TO TIME DURING THE COOKING PROCESS, THE MEAT IS LIFTED FROM THE *TANDOOR* AND BASTED WITH A MARINADE.

with clay and ash. The drum itself is on wheels, so that the whole contraption can be pushed around – even used outside for garden banquets and parties. They have such a *tandoor* at the Royal Palace in Jaipur, and I have enjoyed some delicious *tandoori* dishes from it!

As well as a wok, heavy-based saucepans are used frequently in Indian cookery. Many of the dishes have to be cooked for a long time over a low heat, often without a lot of liquid. The heavy-based types of pan are essential if food is not to stick and burn during cooking. Because of these long cooking times, many people like to use pressure cookers, particularly to cook the various *dal* dishes (see pages 106–113). Breads and some snacks – notably the *dosas* (pancakes) – are cooked on a heavy cast-iron griddle known as a *tawa*. If you have not got one of these a heavy, cast-iron frying-pan will do just as well. You will find tongs are a useful item of equipment for turning breads, *poppadums*, etc.

Indian cookery relies heavily on the use of spices (see pages 20–25) and it is the combination of these that gives Indian food its unique and many different flavors. Everyday the spices wanted for the day's meals will be freshly ground,

so as to give the very best and freshest flavor. Grinding the spices is traditionally done with a pestle and mortar or with a stone, ground against another flatter stone. You can buy a pestle and mortar in most specialist kitchen shops, but the job of grinding dry spices is less arduously – and more effectively – done in a coffee or spice grinder. Wipe it out well with paper towels before and after grinding the spices. Ingredients such as onions, garlic and ginger, which are used in nearly all curries, have also to be finely ground to form the base of the curry and this can be done in a food processor or blender.

By and large, the use of freezers is not part of Indian life to the extent it is in the west. Instead food is purchased and cooked daily – the idea that curries are best cooked on one day, then left to "stew" overnight before being eaten the following day, is not one that is given much credence in India. Shopping is often a much simpler business in India than it is here, for butchers and grocers all bring their wares to the individual houses. However, you will find that many of the dishes in this book – the meat and vegetable curries in particular – can be prepared and cooked and then frozen for future use very successfully.

# SPICES AND FLAVORINGS

The use of spices in Indian cooking is of very great importance, both to give the dish a characteristic flavor and to balance the various ingredients, helping to make indigestible ingredients easy to digest, for example. Spices have an effect on our general well-being – turmeric is an anti-convulsant, ginger contributes to the working of the intestines and can help in easing chest complaints, while chilies – taken in moderate quantity at least – can aid the digestion.

Most spices used in this book you will find on the spice racks at your local supermarkets; a few you might only be able to get at specialist Indian shops. However, when a ground spice is called for, whenever possible, buy the spice whole and grind your own – the flavor is incomparable to those you buy ready-ground. Grind the spices in a spice or coffee grinder or a pestle and mortar (see page 18). If you grind too much for one recipe, put the excess in a small screwtop jar, but be sure to label it; you'll soon forget what it is and it is hard to tell one spice from another until you are really familiar with them. When in Britain, I tend to buy spices in bulk and then freeze them, as this helps to retain their flavor.

If you buy spices ready-ground, buy them in the smallest quantities possible and keep them in screw-top jars in a cool, dark place. Then use them as quickly as possible – the flavors do quickly deteriorate.

A description of the various spices follows, with the English name followed by the Indian name. Some specialist Indian shops may only know these ingredients by the Indian name, so include both on your shopping list to be sure of buying the right one!

## ANISE SEED
### Sonf

This looks quite similar to cumin seed, but has a sweet, somewhat numbing taste. It can be used in snacks, sweets and curries, but perhaps more usually it is roasted and cooled, then eaten after a curry meal to aid digestion.

## ASAFETIDA
### Heeng

This is a resin and is generally only found at specialist Indian food shops, sold either as a rock or powdered (it is sold in small flat boxes – make sure it remains tightly covered wherever you store it). An aid to digestion, it has a peculiar, rather penetrating smell, which seems to stay in the kitchen and house for some time after it has been used. Its flavor is very strong, so only a small pinch is ever used – either in a *baghar* (see page 28) or sometimes it is added to hot oil to flavor a vegetable dish.

## BAY
### Tej patta

Bay leaves are frequently used in meat and rice dishes, added to hot oil to flavor it before any other ingredients are added. As in Western cuisines, the bay leaves should always be discarded before serving.

## BLACK SALT
### Kaala namak

This salt is used in spicy vegetable dishes and in some spice mixtures. It can be bought from specialist Indian stores in powdered form in small packets. An aid to digestion and stomach disorders, it has a very strong pungent smell.

## CARDAMOM
### Elaichi

There are two types of cardamom pods – green and black. The green one is very small and is used to flavor all sorts of dishes; sweet and savory, or as an after-dinner digestive. It is said to help prevent nausea, and may be used whole or in powdered form. Black cardamoms are double the size and used to flavor rice and meat dishes. Inside the cardamom pods are small seeds, which can be bought in this form – that is, without the pods. Black cardamoms are crushed and used in a *garam masala* mixture (see page 29) or to flavor curries.

## CAROM SEED
*Ajwain*

Known also as lovage, this piquant-flavored seed is used mainly to flavor vegetables and pickles. You will find it at specialist Indian shops, probably called only by its Indian name.

## CHILI PEPPERS, GREEN
*Hari mirch*

Fresh hot green chili peppers are used in chutneys, vegetables, snacks, curries, etc. and are a vital ingredient in Indian cooking. The hot chili peppers used in India are available from specialist Indian and Asian shops, but jalapeño and serrano chili peppers or any other small hot green chili peppers make perfectly good substitutes. Keep fresh green chilies in the refrigerator in a plastic box or bag and use quickly.

## CHILI PEPPERS, RED
*Lal mirch*

Red chili peppers are just the same as green chili peppers – they have just been allowed to ripen on the plant. Most usually however, red chilies are sold dried.

The most distinctive flavor of a curry comes from the dried red chilies; they should be soaked in water for about 30 minutes, then ground. Use them carefully as they are very, very hot and while they aid digestion if used moderately, they can cause stomach disorders if used in large quantities. Discard the seeds from dried chilies before using in any dish.

When handling fresh chilies, green or red, either do so wearing rubber gloves, or make sure you wash your hands thoroughly immediately afterwards, particularly before touching your face. They contain an irritant which can burn.

## CINNAMON
*Dalcheeni*

The familiar sticks are pieces of dried young bark and have a sweet aromatic flavor. They are used for flavoring meats and rice dishes, and also in a *garam masala* mixture (see page 29). Like bay leaves, cinnamon sticks should be discarded before serving.

## CITRIC ACID
*Neebu ka sat*

This is available in specialist Indian shops and many druggists. It is a lemon powder which has a very tangy taste and it is used in *chaats* and Bombay savory mixes (see page 52).

## CLOVES
*Long*

Cloves are often used to give flavor and aroma to meat and rice dishes. Like cinnamon sticks, they should be discarded before serving.

## COCONUT
*Nariyal* or *Khopra*

Coconut plays an important part in Indian cooking, particularly in the southern coastal towns. You can buy it dried in flakes, in tiny shreds, or fresh and its prime use is to be made into coconut milk (see page 28 – note, this is not the liquid contained in the coconut). Coconut milk made from fresh coconut will have the best flavor, and many supermarkets as well as specialist Indian shops sell fresh coconuts. This milk helps to enrich the sauces in all types of dishes – meat, chicken, fish, vegetables and chutneys. Coconut will also be used in many sweets.

If you buy a coconut, grate all the flesh and use what you need. Freeze the remainder in a small plastic container.

## CORIANDER
*Dhania*

There are three types of coriander – seeds, powdered and fresh leaves. The seeds are little, light brown balls and are widely available. You can crush these to form the powdered coriander or sow them in window boxes in the summer to give fresh coriander leaves. Ground coriander is a very commonly used spice in all sorts of Indian dishes.

Fresh coriander, or cilantro, is used in Indian cooking rather like parsley is in Western cuisines. Very popular as a garnish, it can also be ground to go into fresh chutneys. You will often find it among the fresh herbs in the vegetable section of supermarkets. Or try growing your own – it does have the most lovely, delicate flavor.

SPICES AND FLAVORINGS COMMONLY USED IN INDIAN COOKING. CLOCKWISE FROM TOP LEFT: FRESH CORIANDER (CILANTRO), WHOLE CINNAMON STICKS, DRIED RED CHILI PEPPERS, TURMERIC, GARLIC, CINNAMON STICK PIECES (ON THE STONE), FRESH CHILI PEPPERS, FRESH GINGER ROOT, NUTMEGS, SAFFRON STRANDS, AND CORIANDER SEEDS.

PICTURED IN THE SPICE BOX, CLOCKWISE FROM TOP LEFT: PEPPERCORNS, TURMERIC POWDER, CARDAMOM PODS, PAPRIKA, SALT, GROUND CHILI PEPPERS AND CUMIN SEEDS (IN CENTER).

## CUMIN
### Zeera

Cumin can be bought whole – in tiny seeds – or powdered. Always pick through seeds to clean them before using as they tend to contain all sorts of little bits of grit etc. Whole seeds are added to hot oil to flavor vegetable and rice dishes.

Roasted cumin seeds (see page 28) are widely used, either left whole or ground to a powder. They are an essential part of a *raita* (see pages 134–137).

At specialist Indian shops you may also find a type of black cumin, called *shahi zeera*. This is sometimes used in *garam masala* mixtures and is more expensive than the commoner type.

## CURRY LEAVES
### Kari patta

The leaves of the curry plant are similar to those of the bay leaf, but smaller. You can buy them fresh or dried at specialist Indian stores. As you might imagine, they have a distinctive aroma, and are used to flavor rice, curries and chutney.

## CURRY POWDER

This is a blend of many of the spices listed here, usually prepared commercially to save you time and trouble. You can make your own (see page 29); keep in a screw-top jar and use quickly.

## FENUGREEK
### Maithi

It is the seeds of fenugreek that are most commonly used. They are small, very hard and flat, pale brown in color and very bitter, so use only in small quantities. They are used to flavor vegetables and pickles rather than meats. In India a drink made by boiling fenugreek seeds in water and straining them is often given to mothers after childbirth as a purgative.

## GARLIC
### Lahsun

This is very important in Indian cookery and in Rajasthan we use more of it than anywhere else in India! We buy it in huge quantities – enough for a month, then have a big session peeling the cloves, cutting them up and freezing them. It is best to wear rubber gloves for this as the smell is hard to remove from your hands. It is believed that garlic helps to remove cholesterol from the body and we take garlic pills as digestive aids. Besides the fresh bulbs you can buy garlic in granules or as a purée in tubes. These do not have such a good flavor as the fresh cloves but can be useful as emergency stand-bys.

## GINGER, FRESH AND DRIED
### *Adrak* and *Sonth*

The knobbly fresh ginger we use in cooking can be found in the vegetable sections of many supermarkets as well as in specialist Asian and Indian stores. The light brown skin must first always be peeled away with a potato peeler and the ginger can then be finely sliced, grated, ground or crushed through a garlic press. It has a wonderful, pungent, hot flavor and is widely used in curries. If you buy more than you need (which you generally will as most recipes call for a piece only about 1 inch big), peel and cut it into small pieces, then freeze it.

To get dried ground ginger, fresh ginger is dried in the sun and then ground. It is available in powdered form in all supermarkets and is useful to have on hand in the kitchen, but do try to use fresh ginger whenever possible.

## HOT SPICE
### *Garam masala*

*Masala* is the word for spice and *garam masala* is a mixture of many spices used to flavor curry dishes. You can buy it commercially prepared or make your own. The latter is the most satisfactory as you can blend the spices to suit your taste. Every housewife in India will have her own recipe for *garam masala* and I have given you mine on page 29, but adapt this to your own liking. It may be ground or left whole – that is all the spices remain whole and are not ground together. In this form it is used to flavor meat curries and rice dishes. In its ground form it is generally added to a dish towards the end of cooking time, or sprinkled over it as a garnish.

## JAGGERY
### *Gur*

This is like molasses and can be bought in specialist Indian stores. It is used in chutneys, vegetable dishes and sweets.

## MACE AND NUTMEG
### *Javitri* and *Jaiphal*

These two spices are formed on the same plant, the wispy mace strands encompassing the nutmeg. Their flavors are quite similar and they are used mostly in rich meat curries and sweets. You can buy both spices powdered, but with nutmeg in particular, buy whole nutmegs and grate them on the smallest holes of a grater when required.

## MANGO POWDER
### *Amchur*

This is a sour powder made by drying the flesh of green mangoes in the sun and then grinding it. You have to buy it in powdered form and you will only find it in specialist Indian stores. It is used in vegetable dishes when a somewhat sour taste is wanted.

## MINT
### *Podina*

Mint comes fresh, dried or bottled as mint sauce or jelly. Fresh mint is a favorite garnish in Indian cuisine, or it can be chopped and added to curries while they are cooking. Mint sauce mixed with tomato ketchup gives a tasty instant chutney or dip to go with snacks. Mint is an important ingredient in many *raitas* (see pages 134–137).

## MUSTARD SEED
### *Rai*

Mustard seeds come in three colors – yellow, brown and black. It is the black ones that are most commonly used whole in cookery and they are generally put into hot oil to give flavor to vegetable curries, *dals* and chutneys – never meat curries. Yellow mustard seeds ground into a paste are used in fish curries. Mustard oil is an oil made from mustard seeds and is a favorite one for cooking fish in particular. Look for it in specialist Indian stores.

## NIGELLA OR ONION SEEDS
*Kalonji* or *Mangrail*

These dark black, oval-shaped seeds are similar in size and shape to sesame seeds and are used in vegetable dishes and pickles, or sprinkled on top of *naans* – the unleavened bread served with *tandoori* dishes.

## ONIONS
*Pyaaz*

I've included onions here because they are such an important ingredient in a curry. Generally they are ground almost to a paste in a food processor, cooked in hot oil and then simmered with water to make the base sauce of the curry. They determine the thickness of the sauce. Scallions are often used as a garnish.

## POMEGRANATE SEEDS
*Anaardaana*

These are the dried seeds of pomegranates, found only in specialist Indian stores. They have a tart and tangy flavor and are used in *pakoras*, chutneys and *raitas*. They can also be crushed and used in chutneys. Always wash the seeds before using them.

## POPPY SEEDS
*Khus khus*

Poppy seeds are tiny granular seeds which are usually roasted in a dry pan (see page 28) and then ground either in a coffee grinder or with a little water in a food processor. This paste is used to enrich curries (it also helps to thicken the sauce) and in sweets.

## ROCK SALT
*Saindha namak*

This is bought in rock form (from specialist Indian stores) and is then crushed in a pestle and mortar. Its most common use is in fasting when ordinary salt is not permitted.

## SAFFRON
*Kaiser*

Saffron is an expensive, delicately-flavored spice which is grown in the northern state of Kashmir. The strands which look like shreds of tobacco are a deep orange color and impart a lovely yellow hue and wonderful flavor to rice dishes and sweets. Spanish saffron is also available and will be a little cheaper than that from Kashmir. Turmeric (see below) can be used to color food yellow, but the flavor is not nearly as delicate.

## SESAME SEEDS
*Til*

The oval-shaped, flattish sesame seeds vary in color from almost white to dark brown. Generally they are roasted (see page 28) and then ground into a paste which is added to curries, rice dishes, sweets, pickles and chutneys.

## TAMARIND
*Imli*

This is the fruit of the tamarind tree, sold as a "lump" or paste in specialist Indian shops. From this, tamarind water (*imli paani*) is made – the instructions for this are on page 29 – and the tangy-tasting water is used to flavor curries, rice dishes and chutneys.

## TURMERIC
*Haldi*

Fresh turmeric is similar in appearance to fresh ginger. In Rajasthan where most people have their own farms, they will grow turmeric, along with many other spices, but in the US it is mainly only available in its powdered form. It is turmeric that gives the characteristic yellow hue to many Indian dishes, and it can be used as a cheaper substitute (although not with the same delicate flavor) for saffron to color rice. Use it carefully; it is quite a powerful dye.

## VINEGAR
*Sirka*

Vinegar is used in pickles and *vindaloos* and the type used is always the dark malt vinegar. When I was a child, I remember the cook would always give the chickens a swig of vinegar half an hour or so before he planned to slaughter them. It made them drowsy. The smell of vinegar always brings this vividly into my mind!

FAR LEFT: STREET VENDORS IN JAIPUR SELLING DRIED CHILI PEPPERS AND GARLIC.

ABOVE: A SNACK STALL OUTSIDE THE AMBER FORT IN JAIPUR. ON SALE ARE VARIOUS NUTS AND THE INGREDIENTS FOR SPICY BOMBAY MIX (SEE PAGE 52). THESE ARE SOLD SEPARATELY SO THAT THE MIX CAN BE MADE TO INDIVIDUAL TASTES.

LEFT: A STREET VENDOR WEIGHS OUT *DAL* – THE SPLIT PEAS AND LENTILS THAT ARE A MAINSTAY OF THE INDIAN DIET.

# Some Basic Techniques

Many of the recipes in this book call for certain ingredients, other than the spices already discussed, which are not widely used in other cuisines. By and large these are prepared in the kitchen at the start of the cooking. How to make each one is described below.

## Buttermilk
### *Chaach*

Dilute one part plain yogurt to three parts water and mix together in a blender. With salt and roasted cumin seed powder (see right) added, this makes a cooling drink in the summer.

## Coconut Milk
### *Nariyal doodh*

Break open a small fresh coconut and strain off the liquid (drink this!). Prise the white flesh away from the shell with a knife, then peel off the brown skin with a sharp knife or a potato peeler. Grate the flesh, put in a measuring cup and add about 2 cups of boiling water. Leave to infuse for at least 20 minutes, then strain off the liquid, pressing the coconut to remove as much liquid as possible. The soaked coconut is discarded.

To make coconut milk using dried coconut, pour 2 cups boiling water onto 6 tablespoons dried shredded coconut. Leave to infuse and strain as outlined above.

## Ghee

This is clarified butter which is widely (although not exclusively) used to fry ingredients in Indian cookery. In some recipes, vegetable oil is used instead of *ghee*. You can buy *ghee* in specialist Indian shops, or you can make it yourself. To do this melt $\frac{1}{2}$ pound (2 sticks) butter in a small saucepan and let it simmer *very* gently until all the water evaporates. This has happened when the white, milky particles at the top of the butter turn golden. It takes anything from 20–45 minutes. Remove the pan from the heat and strain the butter through several layers of cheesecloth. Pour into a clean jar when cool and keep covered.

## Indian Cheese
### *Paneer*

Bring $7\frac{1}{2}$ cups milk to a boil and add the juice of 2 lemons. Stir until the milk curdles, then set aside for about half an hour. Strain into a bowl through wet cheesecloth and squeeze out all the excess liquid. Tie the ends of the cheesecloth securely in a knot around the cheese and put under a heavy weight for at least 3 hours. Cut the resulting cheese into small squares.

## Khoa

This is a form of dried liquid milk, sold in some specialist Indian shops, but you can make your own. Put $2\frac{1}{2}$ quarts milk into a heavy-based pan or wok, bring to a boil over a very low heat, then simmer *very* gently for 1–2 hours until the liquid has evaporated and there is a substance like scrambled egg left in the pan. Let this cool and keep refrigerated until required.

## Roasting Spices

Many recipes call for spices – cumin seeds, poppy seeds, etc. – to be roasted. To do this heat a heavy-based frying-pan or iron griddle until quite hot, then add the spice. Keep shaking the pan until the spice turns dark (or a deeper) brown and is giving off a strong aroma. Remove from the heat and leave to cool, then grind to a fine powder in a spice or coffee grinder or pestle and mortar. Keep in a screw-top jar. When the spice is required for sprinkling over a *raita* – usually this applies to roasted cumin seeds – put it into a salt shaker and just shake it over the surface of the chilled *raita* before serving.

## Seasoning
### *Baghar* or *Tarka*

These are often included as sort of flavorsome garnishes to savory dishes – particularly *dals*. Heat some oil or *ghee* in a small pan and add some cumin or mustard seeds, chopped garlic and crumbled dried chili peppers. Cook for about 1 minute. Pour over the dish before serving.

# SPICE MIXTURES

As mentioned previously, many shops sell ready made mixtures of spice powders under their various names – curry powder, *garam masala* and so on. In all cases, it is best to make your own from fresh spices. Here are some basic mixtures for you to try, but remember to adapt them to suit your own tastes. Never make more than the amounts given in these recipes; it is better to make small quantities and use them quickly.

## CHAAT MASALA

Mix together the following and keep in a screw-top jar in a cool place.

1 teaspoon black pepper
1 teaspoon cumin seeds, roasted and ground (see left)
1 teaspoon ground ginger
1 teaspoon cardamom powder
1 teaspoon rock salt
1 teaspoon black salt
1 teaspoon cinnamon powder
1 teaspoon brown sugar
1 teaspoon red chili powder

## CURRY POWDER

Mix together the following and keep in a screw-top jar in a cool place.

1 tablespoon turmeric powder
2 tablespoons cumin powder
2 tablespoons red chili powder
$\frac{1}{4}$ cup coriander powder

## GARAM MASALA
*Whole*

Mix together the following and keep in a screw-top jar in a cool place.

2 teaspoons cumin seeds
2 teaspoons black peppercorns
2 teaspoons cloves
2 teaspoons green cardamoms
2 teaspoons black cumin seeds
4 1-inch pieces cinnamon stick
2 teaspoons coriander seeds
2 teaspoons black cardamoms
6 bay leaves

## GARAM MASALA
*Powdered*

Grind together the following in a spice or coffee grinder. Keep refrigerated in a screw-top jar.

1 teaspoon black peppercorns
1 teaspoon cloves
2-inch piece cinnamon stick
1 teaspoon green cardamoms
2 black cardamoms
1 teaspoon black cumin seeds

## SAMBHAR
*Powdered*

Roast each of these ingredients separately in a dry frying-pan or griddle as described under ROASTING SPICES on the opposite page. Let each one cool completely, then grind each one separately in a spice or coffee grinder. Mix together and keep in a screw-top jar in the refrigerator.

1 tablespoon coriander seeds
1 teaspoon cumin seeds
1 teaspoon split yellow chickpeas (*chana dal*)
1 teaspoon black beans or grams (*urad dal*)
a pinch of *asafetida*
1 stick cinnamon
1 teaspoon black peppercorns
$\frac{1}{2}$ teaspoon fenugreek seeds
4 dried hot red chili peppers
1 teaspoon dried shredded coconut

## TAMARIND WATER
*Imli paani*

Soak a walnut-size lump of tamarind in 1 cup of hot water for about 20 minutes. Squeeze the pulp to remove all the liquid and strain through a sieve before using. It will keep in the refrigerator, covered, for up to one week.

# SNACKS AND APPETIZERS

The word *Shuruaat* means the beginning, so in this case it is the beginning of a meal. The recipes in this section could be served as appetizers to a meal, or they could be served as snacks at any time. In India, most of these would be served as cocktail nibbles rather than at the start of a meal. Most Indian snacks are deep-fried and will generally be served with tomato ketchup or a chutney for dipping the snacks.

Probably the best-known Indian snacks of all are *samosas* – little pastry triangles filled with a savory stuffing and deep-fried so they puff up into a mouth-watering delicacy. They are served in Indian restaurants the world over. Next to them in popularity come *pakoras* or *bhajiyas* – deep-fried fritters made from all sorts of vegetables – sliced potatoes or onions, cauliflower florets, whole green chili peppers, sliced peppers or eggplant, folded spinach leaves and so on. They can also be made with small pieces of meat or fish, even cheese or hard-boiled eggs. Both these snacks, and the other delicious ones in this chapter are very easy to make at home – try them, the results will be delicious!

*Shorva* is the Indian word for soup. By and large, soups do not form a large or essential part of Indian cuisine. They are more popular in restaurants than as part of the daily fare in homes, although they are quite often served at dinner in the winter months. I always make myself a bowl of hot soup when I have a sore throat.

## FRITTERS
### *Pakoras* or *Bhajiyas*

*T*he batter in this recipe can be used to coat other ingredients. However, the *pakoras* are very tasty as they are served with a chutney or tomato ketchup.

2 cups chickpea flour
1 teaspoon baking powder
salt to taste
$\frac{1}{2}$ teaspoon red chili powder
1 teaspoon cumin seeds
1 teaspoon *garam masala* powder
1 teaspoon mango powder
$1\frac{1}{4}$ cups water (approx)
1 cup oil for frying

SERVES 6

1 Combine all the ingredients except the water and oil in a large bowl. Add sufficient water to make a thick batter and beat well with a wooden spoon until the mixture is smooth.
2 Heat the oil in a frying-pan or wok. When it is very hot, drop spoonfuls of the batter into it.
3 When the fritters are lightly browned on one side, turn them over and brown them on the other side. Remove with a slotted spoon and drain on paper towels. Serve hot.

NOTE Chickpea flour is available at specialist Indian shops. If you cannot find it, use $1\frac{2}{3}$ cups all-purpose flour and add 1 teaspoon turmeric powder.

FOREGROUND LEFT AND RIGHT: SAVORY MEAT TURNOVERS AND AMERICAN TOAST. A BOWL OF PLAIN YOGURT CAN ACCOMPANY EITHER DISH.

## ❧ EGGPLANT FRITTERS ❧
### Baigan pakoras

*E*ggplants are a very popular vegetable in Indian cooking. They are cooked in all sorts of different ways to make a variety of dishes. These *pakoras* are particularly good on a cold rainy day, washed down with a cup of piping hot tea!

$\frac{1}{2}$ lb eggplant
2 cups chickpea flour
1 teaspoon baking powder
salt to taste
$\frac{1}{2}$ teaspoon red chili powder
1 teaspoon sesame seeds
1 teaspoon mango powder
1 teaspoon *garam masala* powder
$1\frac{1}{4}$ cups water (approx)
oil for deep frying

SERVES 6

1  Slice the eggplant into $\frac{1}{4}$ inch slices and put on one side.
2  Sift the flour, baking powder and salt into a large bowl and stir in the remaining ingredients, except for the oil, using the water to mix to a smooth thick batter.
3  Heat the oil in a deep frying-pan or a wok. Drop the eggplant slices into the batter.
4  When the oil is hot, drop about six batter-coated eggplant slices into it at a time, and fry, turning once, until golden on both sides.
5  Remove with a slotted spoon and drain on paper towels.
6  Serve with a freshly made mint or coconut chutney (see page 143 or 141).

## ❧ CHEDDAR CHEESE FRITTERS ❧
### Cheese ke pakoras

$1\frac{2}{3}$ cups self-rising flour
1 teaspoon baking powder
$\frac{1}{4}$ cup grated Cheddar cheese
$\frac{1}{2}$ teaspoon salt
$\frac{1}{2}$ teaspoon red chili powder
1 egg
1 cup milk (approx)
1 cup oil for frying

SERVES 6

1  Sift the flour and baking powder into a large bowl and stir in the cheese, salt and chili powder. Make a well in the center. Beat the egg with the milk and pour into the well. Beat thoroughly to make a thick, smooth batter; add a little more milk if it seems too thick.
2  Heat the oil in a deep frying-pan or wok. When it is hot, drop spoonfuls of batter into it – about six at a time. When they are lightly browned, turn them over and brown the other side.
3  Remove with a slotted spoon and drain on paper towels.
4  Serve, speared on cocktail sticks, with tomato ketchup or a sweet chili sauce.

## ❧ INDIAN CHEESE FRITTERS ❧
### *Paneer pakoras*

*T*his dish is very popular in the North-western part of India and in Punjab. It is delicious served with a cup of tea or, better still, a glass of icy cold beer!

½ lb Indian cheese (see page 28) or
    ricotta cheese
oil for deep frying
FRITTER BATTER
2 cups all-purpose flour or chickpea
    flour
½ teaspoon salt
1 onion
½ teaspoon red chili powder
½ teaspoon baking powder
1 teaspoon *garam masala* powder
1 teaspoon mango powder
    (optional)
a few sprigs of mint, finely chopped
1¼ cups water or milk (approx)
1 egg

SERVES 6

1  Make the batter: sift the flour and salt into a large bowl. Chop the onion very finely and mix it into the flour with the red chili powder, baking powder, *garam masala* and mango powder and the mint.
2  Beat the water or milk with the egg and stir it into the flour mixture to make a thick smooth batter.
3  Heat the oil in a deep frying-pan or wok. Cut the cheese into 1 inch squares and drop them into the batter.
4  When the oil is hot, drop about six of the cheese fritters into it and fry them until they are evenly golden on all sides.
5  Remove with a slotted spoon and drain on paper towels. Keep warm while you fry the remainder.
6  Serve with tomato ketchup.

## ❧ CURRIED FISH-BALL FRITTERS ❧
### *Machhali pakoras*

*S*erve these tasty *pakoras* as cocktail snacks or for a late-night supper. Either way, provide a bowl of mint chutney or tomato ketchup to dip them in. In this recipe, the fish-balls are dipped into a thin batter and then coated with bread crumbs.

1 lb cooked boned fish of any type
    (or use drained and flaked
    canned fish)
2 onions
2 tablespoons curry powder
1 teaspoon salt
1 fresh hot green chili pepper,
    chopped
a few fresh mint leaves, chopped or
    ½ teaspoon dried mint
dried bread crumbs, for coating
oil for frying
FRITTER BATTER
3 tablespoons all-purpose flour
1 egg
¾ cup milk

SERVES 6

1  Make the batter: sift the flour into a bowl and make a well in the center. Beat the egg with the milk and pour into the flour. Gradually beat them together, keeping the batter smooth and free of lumps. If you prefer, mix all the ingredients to a smooth batter in a blender.
2  Mash the fish with a fork to flake it thoroughly. Chop the onions finely and add them to the fish with the curry powder, salt, chili pepper and mint. Mix well, then roll into 24 small balls.
3  Dip the balls into the batter and then roll them in bread crumbs to coat them evenly.
4  Heat the oil in a deep frying-pan or wok and fry the fritters a few at a time, until they are evenly golden. Drain on paper towels.
5  Serve with mint chutney (see page 143) or tomato ketchup.

SHRIMP FRITTERS AND SWEET CHILI SAUCE.

## ❧ SHRIMP FRITTERS ❧
### *Jhinga pakoras*

*S*erve these *pakoras* as an appetizer or as nibbles at a cocktail party.

1 recipe fritter batter (see page 30)
1 egg
½ lb cooked peeled shrimp, thawed
    if frozen or drained well if
    canned
1 cup oil for frying

SERVES 6

1  Make the batter as described. Beat the egg, add it to the batter and beat together well.
2  Stir the shrimp into the batter.
3  Heat the oil in a frying-pan or wok. When it is hot, drop small spoonfuls of the shrimp and batter into it, and fry them until they are golden all over.
4  Remove the fritters with a slotted spoon and drain on paper towels.
5  Serve hot with a sweet chili sauce.

## ❧ SPARERIB FRITTERS ❧
### *Seene ke pakoras*

1 lb pork spareribs or lamb riblets
1 recipe fritter batter (see page 30)
oil for deep frying

SERVES 6

1  Ask the butcher to chop the ribs into quite small pieces. Put into a saucepan and just cover with water. Boil gently until the meat is cooked, drain well and dry on paper towels.
2  Make the batter as described. Heat the oil in a deep frying-pan or wok. When it is hot, quickly dip the ribs into the batter to coat them, then drop them into the oil, a few at a time. Cook until they are evenly golden on all sides.
3  Remove from the oil and drain on paper towels.
4  Serve with tomato ketchup or your favorite chutney.

## ❧ SPICY SEMOLINA FRITTERS ❧
### *Soojee bhajiyas*

3 eggs
1 onion
1 clove garlic
$\frac{1}{2}$ inch piece fresh ginger root
$1\frac{1}{3}$ cups semolina flour
salt to taste
1 teaspoon *garam masala* powder
1 teaspoon red chili powder
$\frac{1}{4}$ cup milk (approx)
oil for deep frying

SERVES 6

1  Beat the eggs together in a large bowl. Finely chop the onion, garlic and ginger and add to the eggs. Gradually beat in the semolina flour, keeping the mixture smooth.
2  Add the salt and remaining spices, then blend in the milk to make a thick batter.
3  Heat the oil in a deep frying-pan or wok. When it is hot, drop spoonfuls of the batter into it – about six at a time. Fry until golden, turning once to cook both sides evenly.
4  Remove with a slotted spoon and drain on paper towels. Keep warm while you cook the remainder.
5  Serve hot with a mint or coriander chutney (see pages 143 or 142) or tomato ketchup.

## ❧ RICE FRITTERS ❧
### *Chawal pakoras*

$1\frac{2}{3}$ cups cold cooked rice
1 teaspoon cumin seeds
2 eggs, beaten
1 teaspoon red chili powder
salt to taste
1 onion
1 fresh hot green chili pepper
1 tomato
$\frac{1}{4}$ cup milk
oil for deep frying

SERVES 6

1  Mix the rice with the cumin seeds, beaten eggs, chili powder and salt.
2  Chop the onion, green chili pepper and tomato finely and stir them into the rice mixture with the milk.
3  Heat the oil in a deep frying-pan or wok. When it is hot, drop six small spoonfuls of the rice mixture into it at a time.
4  Cook until evenly golden, turning once. Remove with a slotted spoon and drain on paper towels.
5  Serve hot with a coconut chutney (see page 141) or a sweet chili sauce.

## SOYBEAN BALLS
### Soya bhajiyas

*T*his is a good recipe for cocktail parties as the small balls can be made in advance and frozen, then reheated in the oven or microwave. Soybeans are extremely nutritious; rich in protein and a good substitute for meat.

$\frac{1}{2}$ lb (about 1 heaping cup) soybeans
6 tablespoons water (approx)
1 onion
1 fresh hot green chili pepper
$\frac{1}{2}$ teaspoon cumin seeds
salt to taste
$\frac{1}{2}$ teaspoon red chili powder
$\frac{1}{4}$ cup soft bread crumbs
$\frac{1}{4}$ cup oil for frying

SERVES 6

1  Pour boiling water over the soybeans to cover them completely. Soak for 4–6 hours; they will swell as they absorb the water.
2  Drain the beans and place in a blender. Add about 6 tablespoons water and blend the beans coarsely.
3  Chop the onion and green chili pepper and add to the beans with the rest of the ingredients, except the oil.
4  Mix everything well together then shape the mixture into small balls.
5  Heat the oil in a frying-pan or wok, fry the soy balls, a few at a time, until golden brown all over. Remove with a slotted spoon and drain on paper towels.
6  Serve with tomato ketchup.

## CURRIED MEATBALLS
### Keema kofte

*S*erve these tasty meatballs as a snack, or as part of a curry meal.

2 lb ground lamb, beef, pork or chicken
1 green pepper
1 clove garlic or 1 teaspoon garlic powder or granules
1 teaspoon red chili powder
1 teaspoon turmeric powder
2 teaspoons coriander powder
1 teaspoon *garam masala* powder
1 teaspoon ground ginger
salt to taste
2 egg yolks
$\frac{1}{4}$ cup lemon juice
oil for deep frying
QUICK CHUTNEY
$\frac{1}{4}$ cup tomato ketchup
2 tablespoons mint sauce

MAKES 40 MEATBALLS

1  Put the ground meat into a large bowl and break it up with a fork.
2  Finely chop the green pepper and crush the garlic, if using fresh. Add these to the meat with all the remaining ingredients, except for the oil. Mix together thoroughly, then shape into 40 balls.
3  Pour about $\frac{1}{4}$ cup oil into a shallow frying-pan and set over a medium heat. Pour sufficient oil for deep frying into another pan and set this over a medium to high heat.
4  Put about 12 balls into the shallow frying-pan and fry them for about 5 minutes, shaking the pan continuously.
5  Remove the balls with a slotted spoon and quickly drop them into the other pan. Cook until well browned, then remove and drain on paper towels.
6  Keep the cooked balls warm while you fry the remainder in the same way.
7  Mix together the tomato ketchup and mint sauce for the chutney and serve with the meatballs.

# GROUND MEAT KABOBS
### Shammi kebabs

*Th*is is Maharaja Bubbles' favorite dish. If he's not entertaining or attending a formal function, he will eat these kabobs every night with the hottest chili sauce you can imagine and if he goes out to relatives or to friends, they always prepare *shammi kebabs* for him. These are really the Indian equivalent of the Western hamburger, but rather more tasty! Make a batch and freeze them, and then reheat them under the broiler, in the microwave or in the oven.

$\frac{3}{4}$ cup water
3 onions
1 lb ground meat – lamb, beef or
    pork
$\frac{1}{4}$ cup dried split peas or lentils
    (*chana dal*)
1 tablespoon finely chopped fresh
    ginger root
1 teaspoon cumin seeds
4 whole cloves
1 teaspoon black peppercorns
1 stick cinnamon
4 whole cardamoms
2 dried hot red chili peppers
2 small fresh hot green chili
    peppers
a few fresh mint leaves
a few fresh coriander (cilantro)
    leaves
$\frac{1}{2}$ cup plain yogurt
salt to taste
1 tablespoon raisins
2 teaspoons sliced almonds
oil for frying
GARNISH
lemon wedges
1 onion, sliced
$\frac{1}{4}$ cup fresh lemon juice
large pinch of salt

MAKES 18 KABOBS

1  Put the water into a large saucepan and bring to a boil.
2  Meanwhile, slice two of the onions and add them to the boiling water together with the ground meat, split peas, ginger, cumin seeds, cloves, peppercorns, cinnamon, cardamoms and red chili peppers. Cook over a medium heat, stirring occasionally, until the water has been absorbed – about 20 minutes. Remove the pan from the heat and set aside to cool.
3  Finely chop the remaining onion, the green chili peppers and the mint and coriander.
4  Put the meat mixture into a food processor with the chopped ingredients and process them together. Alternatively, mix everything together thoroughly with a fork. Add the yogurt and salt and mix again.
5  Form the mixture into 18 balls. Mix the raisins and almonds together and press a tiny amount of this into each ball. Now flatten the balls into cakes, like small hamburgers.
6  Heat 2–3 tablespoons oil in a frying-pan and fry the kabobs a few at a time over a high heat, turning them once, until well browned on both sides. Remove with a spatula and keep warm while you fry the remainder, adding more oil to the pan as necessary.
7  Serve the kabobs hot, garnished with lemon wedges and onion slices which have been soaked in the lemon juice and salt, then drained.

# ❧ INDIAN SPRING ROLLS ❧

*T*his is the Indian version of the popular Chinese spring roll – with a few of my variations. I haven't given it an Indian name as there isn't really a reasonable and sensible translation! Undoubtedly the best way to get a thin, even layer of batter in the pan for these rolls is to use a brand new bath sponge, as described in the recipe. It may sound unorthodox, but give it a try!

**BATTER**
1⅔ cups all-purpose flour
1 teaspoon baking powder
1 cup water (approx)

**MEAT FILLING**
1 tablespoon oil
1 teaspoon cumin seeds
1 onion
1 teaspoon red chili powder
½ teaspoon turmeric powder
2 teaspoons coriander powder
1 teaspoon *garam masala* powder
1 teaspoon ground ginger
salt to taste
1 teaspoon garlic powder or
    granules
½ lb ground meat – lamb, beef or
    pork
oil for deep frying

**SERVES 6**

1  Make the meat filling first: in a heavy-based frying-pan heat the oil and add the cumin seeds. Fry until browned, shaking frequently. Slice the onion finely and add to the pan with all the spices and the salt and garlic. Stir, then add the meat and cook, stirring, until the meat has lost all its pinkness. Leave it over a very low heat, stirring from time to time, while you make the batter.

2  Sift the flour and baking powder into a large bowl and add the water. Mix together with a fork until well combined and the batter is smooth.

3  Heat a non-stick frying-pan over a medium heat. Dip a new round bath sponge into the batter, remove the pan from the heat and press the sponge into it so that there is a thin coating of batter in the pan. Put the pan back on a medium heat. When the batter starts to curl at the sides, peel it off the pan and place it on a clean dish towel.

4  With a rubber spatula or paper towel, remove any bits of batter from the pan, then repeat the cooking process, until all the batter is used up. This amount should make about 18 "wrappers," but reserve a spoonful or two of the batter at the end of cooking. Stack the wrappers on top of one another on the dish towel as they are cooked.

5  Lay one wrapper at a time on a board and place a spoonful of the meat filling at one edge. Fold the sides over this, then roll up the wrapper around the filling, enclosing it completely. Use the remaining batter to seal the end. Make all the rolls in this way.

6  Heat the oil in a pan for deep frying. When it is hot, fry the rolls about six at a time, until they are evenly golden. Drain on paper towels.

7  Serve the rolls hot with the chutney of your choice or with soy sauce.

# ❧ BARBECUED CHICKEN ❧
## *Murgi tikka*

*T*his is really my favorite meat dish. You will find a quick version on page 170.

1 lb boneless chicken breasts
juice of 2 lemons
2 tablespoons oil
2 teaspoons *garam masala* powder
1 teaspoon red chili powder
1 teaspoon turmeric powder
2 teaspoons coriander powder
$\frac{1}{2}$ teaspoon black pepper
2 teaspoons garlic powder or
    granules
2 teaspoons ground ginger
2 teaspoons soy sauce
salt to taste
lemon wedges, to serve

SERVES 6

1 Skin the chicken and cut the flesh into 1 inch cubes. Place in a bowl or dish.
2 Combine all the remaining ingredients, except the lemon wedges and add to the chicken. Mix thoroughly, so that the chicken is coated evenly with the mixture. Cover and leave in a cool place for 2 hours.
3 Preheat the broiler or barbecue. Wipe six metal skewers lightly with oil and thread six to seven chicken pieces onto each one. Broil or barbecue them, turning frequently until they are cooked through, and slightly charred on the outside.
4 Serve with the lemon wedges.

CURRIED MEATBALLS.

# THREE-CORNERED FRIED TURNOVERS
*Aloo samosas*

*Samosas* are known and loved the world over. A filling snack anytime, they are usually eaten in India at coffee or tea-breaks, in fact no tea party would be considered complete without *samosas!* Small bite-size ones can be made to serve at cocktail parties and larger ones for occasions when something more substantial is called for. *Samosas* can be made well in advance of serving and frozen. In this event, they are usually half-fried and then cooled before freezing. Simply fry them in hot oil – straight from frozen – whenever you need them. Or fry them completely before freezing and reheat them from frozen in a microwave oven.

**FILLING**
4 medium-sized potatoes
2 tablespoons oil
1 teaspoon cumin seeds
1 onion
1 teaspoon red chili powder
salt to taste
1 teaspoon *garam masala* powder
1 teaspoon mango powder or
    pomegranate seeds
1 teaspoon dried mint
1 teaspoon coriander seeds

**SAMOSA PASTRY**
3¼ cups self-rising flour
salt to taste
3 tablespoons oil
¾ cup water (approx)
oil for deep frying

**MAKES 32 SAMOSAS**

1 Make the filling first: cook the potatoes in boiling water until tender. Drain and cut into small cubes. Heat the oil in a frying-pan and fry the cumin seeds until browned, shaking the pan frequently. Finely chop the onion and add to the pan. Fry gently until softened, stirring occasionally, then add the potatoes and cook for 2–3 minutes, stirring. Add all the remaining ingredients and cook over a gentle heat for about 5 minutes, stirring frequently. Remove from the heat, cover and put on one side.
2 Make the *samosa* pastry: mix the flour, salt and oil together; the best way to do this is with your fingers. Add the water a little at a time, to make a stiff dough, the consistency of pie pastry.
3 Divide the dough into sixteen pieces and roll out each one to a 4 inch circle. Cut these in half.
4 Lightly dampen the cut edge of one semi-circle with water, lift it up and press the cut edges together. Place a spoonful of the filling into the "shell" then seal the end of the pastry with water, pressing it into a triangular shape. Make all the *samosas* in this way and place them on a plate as you make them. Keep them covered with a clean dish towel.
5 Heat the oil in a wok or deep frying-pan. When it is hot, fry the *samosas*, four at a time, turning them over once. They are ready when they are crisp and golden.
6 Remove them from the oil with a slotted spoon and drain on paper towels. Keep warm.
7 Serve hot with home-made coriander chutney (see page 142) or tomato ketchup.

## SAVORY MEAT TURNOVERS
### *Keema samosas*

*I* have given a slightly different recipe for the pastry here. Try it and the one in the previous recipe and see which you like best.

**FILLING**
1 onion
2 tablespoons oil
1 fresh hot green chili pepper
2 cloves garlic
1 inch piece fresh ginger root
1 teaspoon coriander powder
$\frac{1}{2}$ teaspoon red chili powder
$\frac{1}{2}$ teaspoon turmeric powder
1 lb lean ground meat – lamb or
 beef
salt to taste
a few fresh coriander (cilantro) or
 mint leaves
2 teaspoons raisins (optional)
2 teaspoons lemon juice
1 teaspoon *garam masala* powder
**SAMOSA PASTRY**
2 cups all-purpose flour
$\frac{1}{2}$ teaspoon salt
$\frac{1}{2}$ teaspoon baking powder
2 tablespoons oil or melted *ghee*
$\frac{1}{2}$ cup water (approx)
oil for deep frying

**MAKES 32 SAMOSAS**

1 Make the filling: slice the onion thinly, heat the oil in a heavy-based frying-pan and fry the onion until soft and golden brown. Seed and finely chop the chili pepper, crush the garlic and grate the ginger. Add these to the pan.
2 Put the coriander, chili and turmeric powders in a small bowl and mix to a thick paste with a little water. Add this to the frying-pan and fry for 5 minutes, stirring frequently. Add the meat and salt, stir again, then leave to cook on a very low heat until the moisture is absorbed. Chop the coriander or mint leaves finely and stir into the filling together with the raisins, if using, lemon juice and *garam masala* powder. The filling should be very thick and dry.
3 Make the samosa pastry: sift the flour, salt and baking powder into a large bowl. Make a well in the center and pour in the oil or *ghee*. Mix everything together and add sufficient water to make a stiff dough.
4 Make, fill and cook the samosas as described in steps 3–6 in the previous recipe.

## BARBECUED LIVER
### *Kaleji tikka*

*I* usually make this for Sunday brunch – it is lovely with plain bread.

1 lb lamb liver
salt to taste
2 teaspoons garlic powder or
 granules
1 teaspoon red chili powder
2 tablespoons oil
juice of 2 lemons
**GARNISH**
1 onion
1 tomato
1 fresh hot green chili pepper
lemon wedges

**SERVES 6**

1 Cut the liver into 1 inch pieces, discarding all the stringy bits and tubes. Put into a bowl and add all the remaining ingredients. Mix together thoroughly.
2 Preheat the broiler or a barbecue and wipe six metal skewers lightly with oil.
3 Thread the bits of liver onto the skewers and broil or barbecue them, turning frequently, until they are cooked through.
4 Prepare the garnish by finely slicing the onion, tomato and chili pepper. Sprinkle over the cooked liver and serve immediately with the lemon wedges.

## ⚛ STUFFED LENTIL PASTRIES ⚛
### *Dal kachori*

½ lb (about 1⅓ cups) dried split
   black beans or grams (*urad dal*)
1 teaspoon red chili powder
salt to taste
1 teaspoon peppercorns, coarsely
   crushed
1 teaspoon coriander seeds
3¼ cups self-rising flour
¼ cup oil
¾ cup water (approx)
oil for deep frying

**MAKES 18 PASTRIES**

1 Wash the black beans or grams thoroughly, put in a large bowl, cover with cold water and leave to soak overnight.
2 The next day, drain the *dal* and grind it coarsely in a blender or food processor. Mix with the chili powder, salt, peppercorns and coriander seeds.
3 Mix the flour with the ¼ cup oil, then slowly add the water to make a stiff dough. Knead thoroughly, wrap in foil and put in a cool place for 1 hour.
4 Knead the dough again and divide it into eighteen pieces. Roll into balls. Make a slight depression in the center of each and place a small piece of the bean paste in this. Pull some dough over the paste, then flatten the dough balls.
5 With a rolling pin, roll the balls into circles, 3 inches in diameter.
6 Heat the oil in a frying-pan or wok and fry the pastries a few at a time. Turn them over when the underside is golden brown to cook the other side. Drain on paper towels. Serve hot or cold.

## ⚛ RICE AND LENTIL PANCAKES ⚛
### *Sada dosa*

*Dosas* are Indian pancakes or crêpes and may be made from rice flour, *urad dal* flour or semolina.

⅔ cup dried split black beans or
   grams (*urad dal*)
1⅓ cups rice flour
1 teaspoon baking powder
salt to taste
1¼–2 cups water
1 cup oil for frying

**SERVES 6**

1 Wash the black beans or grams thoroughly, then cover them with cold water and leave to soak overnight.
2 The next day, drain the beans and grind to a paste in a food processor. Put the paste into a large bowl, add the rice flour and mix well. Cover and leave in a cool place for at least 8 hours.
3 Add the baking powder and salt to the mixture, with sufficient water to make a thick batter.
4 Heat 1 tablespoon oil in a heavy-based frying-pan. When it is very hot, pour a large spoonful of the batter into the center of the pan and with a wooden spoon, gently spread the batter in a circular movement until it is 6–8 inches in diameter. Cook for 2–3 minutes, on one side only. Lift out of the pan very carefully so as not to break it and put it onto a clean dish towel. Repeat the cooking process until all the batter is used, adding more oil to the pan as necessary.
5 Serve with *sambhar* (see page 29) and coconut chutney (see page 141).

# POTATO-STUFFED PANCAKES
*Masala dosa*

*T*his is a tasty and more substantial dish using the *dosa* batter. It makes a lovely brunch dish. The *dosas* would usually be a little larger than those shown in the picture below.

1 batch *dosa* batter (see previous recipe)

FILLING
4 potatoes
3 onions
1 fresh hot green chili pepper
1 inch piece fresh ginger root
2 tablespoons oil or melted *ghee*
½ teaspoon mustard seeds
½ teaspoon turmeric powder
a few curry leaves
salt to taste

SERVES 6

1 Make the *dosas* as described in the previous recipe.
2 Cook the potatoes in boiling water with two of the onions until tender. Drain, mash the potatoes and slice the onions.
3 Finely slice the remaining onion, the green chili pepper and the ginger. Heat the oil or *ghee* in a heavy-based pan and add the mustard seeds. As soon as they "pop," add the sliced raw onion, the chili pepper, ginger, turmeric and curry leaves. Cook, stirring, until the onion is golden brown.
4 Add the mashed potatoes and sliced boiled onions and stir to mix well. Add salt to taste. Cook for 1–2 minutes, stirring, then remove from the heat.
5 Place a spoonful of the potato mixture into the center of each *dosa* and fold the pancake over the filling.
6 Serve the *dosas* at once, or heat a little more oil or *ghee* in a large heavy-based frying-pan and cook the filled *dosas* quickly on both sides to crisp them.

POTATO-STUFFED PANCAKES AND CUCUMBER PANCAKES SERVED WITH FRESH CORIANDER CHUTNEY.

## ❧ SEMOLINA PANCAKES ❧
### *Rava dosa*

*Rava* is the Indian word for semolina. These *dosas* are quicker and easier to make than the rice flour ones, although the batter should still be made the previous day.

1⅓ cups semolina flour
1¼ cups water (approx)
2 teaspoons baking soda
2 tablespoons plain yogurt
salt to taste
oil or *ghee* for frying

SERVES 6

1 Soak the semolina in the water for 30 minutes. Add the baking soda, yogurt and salt and beat the mixture well. Then leave it overnight to ferment.
2 The next day, heat a small amount of oil or *ghee* in a heavy-based frying-pan. Drop a large spoonful of batter into the center of the pan and spread it out evenly using a wooden spoon. Cover the pan with a lid and leave for about 1 minute. Remove the pancake from the pan and keep warm while you cook the remainder of the batter in the same way.
3 Serve with *sambhar* (see page 29) or a coconut chutney (see page 141). Or fill the *dosas* with potato curry as described in the recipe for Potato-Stuffed Pancakes on page 43.

## ❧ CUCUMBER PANCAKES ❧
### *Kheera ka cheela*

*T*his type of pancake and the one that follows are different to *dosas*. Preparation of the batter does not need to be started a day in advance.

PANCAKE BATTER
1 cucumber
2 fresh hot green chili peppers
salt to taste
2⅔ cups semolina flour
2 cups water
2 onions
a few fresh coriander (cilantro) or
    mint leaves
oil for frying
CHUTNEY
⅔ cup grated fresh coconut
2 fresh hot green chili peppers
1 tablespoon oil
1 cup fresh coriander (cilantro) or
    mint
a pinch of asafetida
salt to taste
½ cup water
juice of 1 lemon

SERVES 6

1 Grate the cucumber, drain it well, then put it into a large bowl. Chop the chili peppers very finely, or grind them in a pestle and mortar. Add to the cucumber with the salt, semolina and water. Leave in a cool place for 3 hours.
2 Meanwhile make the chutney: put the coconut into a blender or food processor. Chop the chili peppers roughly and fry them lightly in the oil until slightly softened. Add to the coconut with the remaining ingredients. Blend thoroughly, then put the chutney into a screw-top jar and keep in the refrigerator until wanted. It will keep for 3–4 days.
3 Finely chop the onions and coriander or mint leaves for the pancake and add to the cucumber mixture. Mix thoroughly.
4 Heat a little oil in a non-stick frying-pan. When it is very hot drop a large spoonful of batter into the pan and spread it out evenly using a wooden spoon. Cook until the pancake is browned on the underside, then lift it with a slotted spatula and turn it to cook the other side.
5 Keep the pancakes warm while you cook the remainder in the same way. Serve with the chutney.

## ❧ VEGETARIAN PANCAKE ❧
### *Cheela*

*T*hese are good for brunches, or when you aren't going to eat for some time and need something filling – before a journey, perhaps.

1 onion
2 fresh hot green chili peppers
a few fresh coriander (cilantro) or
    mint leaves
a large pinch of red chili powder
$1\frac{3}{4}$ cups rice flour
$\frac{1}{2}$ cup chickpea flour
$1\frac{1}{4}$ cups water (approx)
2 teaspoons melted *ghee* or oil

SERVES 6

**1**  Finely chop the onion, chili peppers and coriander or mint leaves. Mix these with all the remaining ingredients, except for the *ghee* or oil.
**2**  Heat a little *ghee* or oil in a non-stick frying-pan and pour in enough batter to cover the bottom of the pan. Cook for a few minutes, until the underside is lightly browned.
**3**  Flip the pancake over and cook the other side.
**4**  Keep warm while you cook the remainder of the batter in the same way, lightly greasing the pan with *ghee* or oil as necessary.
**5**  Serve hot with tomato ketchup or any kind of chutney.

## ❧ SAVORY RICE PANCAKES ❧
### *Utthapam*

*A* very tasty dish for breakfast or tea-time. I prefer it to the ordinary *dosa* – I find it has more flavor. It can be eaten hot or cold, which makes it good for picnics or school lunches.

$\frac{3}{4}$ cup cold cooked rice
1 cup uncooked long-grain rice
$1\frac{1}{2}$ cups water
$\frac{1}{2}$ lb ($1\frac{1}{3}$ cups) dried split black
    beans or grams (*urad dal*)
salt to taste
2 onions
1 fresh hot green chili pepper
1 inch piece fresh ginger root
$\frac{1}{2}$ cup oil for frying

SERVES 6

**1**  Soak the cooked and raw rice in 1 cup of the water for 2 hours. Soak the black beans or grams in the remaining water for 2 hours. Drain the rice and the *dal*.
**2**  Grind the rice and the *dal* separately to a smooth paste in a blender or food processor, then mix them together to form a thick batter. Cover and leave at room temperature for at least 6 hours to ferment.
**3**  Add some salt to the rice mixture. Finely chop the onions, chili and ginger and mix together.
**4**  Heat 1 tablespoon oil in a non-stick frying-pan and add 2 tablespoons of the batter. Quickly spread it to a circle with the back of a wooden spoon, then sprinkle a little of the onion, chili pepper and ginger onto it. Cook for a few minutes until lightly browned on the underside, then turn it over and cook the other side.
**5**  Remove from the pan and keep warm while you cook the rest of the batter in the same way, adding more oil to the pan as necessary.

ABOVE: HAND-HELD SCALES ARE USED BY A
STREET-VENDOR TO WEIGH OUT HIS TEMPTING
SNACKS – A NEVER CHANGING SIGHT AMONG
THE STREET STALLS.

LEFT: A STREET VENDOR SELLING *PAKORAS*
WHICH HE PREPARES AT HOME AND THEN COOKS
IN THE STREET ON A SMALL PORTABLE STOVE.

## ❧ SAVORY SEMOLINA CEREAL ❧
### *Madrasi upma*

*T*his is another popular snack from South India, generally served for breakfast or as a light meal at night. Vegetables such as peas, sliced potatoes or cauliflower can be added for extra flavor.

1 onion
1 fresh hot green chili pepper
1 teaspoon split yellow chickpeas
   (*chana dal*)
1 teaspoon dried split black beans
   or grams (*urad dal*)
2 tablespoons oil or melted *ghee*
1 teaspoon mustard seeds
1 tablespoon cashew nuts
$1\frac{1}{3}$ cups semolina flour
salt to taste
$1\frac{1}{4}$ cups hot water (approx)

SERVES 6

1  Finely slice the onion and chop the chili pepper. Wash and drain the *dals*.
2  Heat the oil or *ghee* in a frying-pan or wok over a medium heat and add the onion. Cook, stirring, until softened.
3  Add the chili pepper, mustard seeds, cashew nuts and both kinds of *dal*. Cook, stirring, until the *dals* have browned, then add the semolina and salt. Stir thoroughly.
4  Add the hot water and cook, stirring continuously, until the mixture is quite dry.
5  Serve hot with a lemon pickle (see page 145).

## ❧ SEMOLINA STEAMED CAKES ❧
### *Masala rava idlis*

*Idlis* are a type of dumpling, made of a fermented batter and steamed. They are a Southern Indian dish, and although my recipe here is not the real authentic one of the south, it is an easy one to do! Special molded pans are usually used for cooking *idlis*, but an egg-poaching pan does perfectly well.

$2\frac{2}{3}$ cups semolina flour
1 cup water (approx)
$\frac{1}{2}$ cup plain yogurt
salt to taste
$\frac{1}{2}$ teaspoon baking powder
1 fresh hot green chili pepper
1 onion

SERVES 6

1  Soak the semolina overnight in the water. The next day, stir in the yogurt, salt and baking powder.
2  Finely chop the chili pepper and onion and stir them into the batter, mixing everything together thoroughly. If the batter seems too thick – it should be of a thick pouring consistency – add more water.
3  Lightly grease an egg-poacher or *idli* molded pan and pour a little batter into each cup. Cover with a lid and steam the *idlis* over boiling water for about 10 minutes – until springy to the touch.
4  Carefully unmold the *idlis* and keep warm while you cook the others in the same way.
5  Serve with coconut chutney (see page 141) or *sambhar* (see page 29).

## ❧ FRIED CHICKPEAS ❧
### *Tale chane*

*F*ried chickpeas are popular fare of street vendors and are generally available at all street corners in Jaipur. Making your own, however, is a good idea for hygienic reasons, if nothing else! They are spicy, hot and delicious, but do not eat too many at a time; they are inclined to make you flatulent! This and the next few recipes are for snack-type nibbles that you would serve with drinks or eat to overcome between-meal hunger-pangs. Very tasty but very fattening!

½ lb (about 1 heaping cup) dried chickpeas
oil for deep frying
salt to taste
1 teaspoon red chili powder
1 teaspoon *chaat masala* (see page 29)
1 teaspoon mango powder

1 Soak the chickpeas overnight in cold water. The next day, drain them and dry on a clean dish towel.
2 Heat the oil in a deep frying-pan or wok and fry the chickpeas a few at a time, until they pop open. Keep stirring them gently until they do this, then remove them and drain on paper towels.
3 When all the chickpeas have been fried, rub off the excess oil with paper towels. Put in a large bowl and add the salt, chili powder, *chaat masala* and mango powder. Mix well, then cool completely and store in an airtight jar.

## ❧ FRIED MUNG BEAN DAL ❧
### *Tali moong dal*

*O*ne of my husband's favorite snacks. When he's at home, he'll always have some at five o'clock in the afternoon so I have to make sure there is enough for him. Children will like this, too, as it is not spicy. It will keep for at least a month.

2 cups split yellow mung beans (*moong dal*)
oil for deep frying
salt to taste

1 Soak the mung beans overnight in cold water. The next day, drain them and dry thoroughly on a clean dish towel.
2 Heat the oil in a deep frying-pan or wok, and fry spoonfuls of the mung beans at a time until they are deep golden. Remove and drain on paper towels while you cook the remainder.
3 Put the cooked *dal* into a large bowl and add salt. Cool completely and store in an airtight container. Try them with a glass of Pimms or a pink gin!

## ❧ HOT FRIED DAL ❧
### *Jaipuri sanganeri dal*

*T*his is a specialty of a small village called Sanganer, not far from Jaipur. Like *sundal mundal* (see page 50), it is sold in paper cones, but this time at the Sanganer Railway Station. When I was a kid, it was always a special treat to buy it from the railway carriage while on our way to Delhi, and it was very cheap, so we could afford to buy it with our own pocket money! It is available at all grocery shops in the Jaipur markets.

2 cups split yellow chickpeas
  (*chana dal*)
oil for deep frying
salt to taste
2 teaspoons red chili powder

1  Soak the chickpeas overnight in cold water. The next day, drain them and pat dry on paper towels.
2  Heat the oil in a deep frying-pan or wok and fry the chickpeas, a spoonful or so at a time. When they turn a deep golden, remove and drain on paper towels. Keep doing this until all the chickpeas have been fried. Rub off any excess oil with paper towels.
3  Mix the salt and chili powder with the chickpeas in a large bowl. Leave to cool completely, then store in an airtight container. The mixture will keep for up to one month.

## ❧ ROASTED PEANUTS ❧
### *Bhuni mungphali*

*R*oasted peanuts were a great favorite of mine. When I was at school in Jaipur, every Friday night was a social night for the boarders. No boys were allowed, however, so we girls all danced together. As seniors, we were allowed to wear our saris and we were taught all the ballroom dances, together with the barn dances and the Scottish reels. We felt very grown up! It was on these occasions that we were served with cups of coffee and these roasted peanuts, and I could never figure out how they were made. Twenty-five years later, my Chinese neighbor in Nigeria, Roslind, taught me how to make them!

2 lb salt
1 lb raw shelled peanuts

1  Wash the peanuts thoroughly in water several times.
2  Put the salt in a deep frying-pan or wok and heat it over a medium heat. Add all the peanuts, stirring them into the salt. Keep stirring all the time and after about 15–20 minutes, you will hear them starting to "pop." Keep stirring – the salt will turn black, or dark gray, but keep stirring for another 10–15 minutes until the skins of the peanuts come off easily.
3  Tip the salt and peanuts into a colander and shake over a bowl, so that the salt escapes through the holes of the colander. You can use the salt again to roast peanuts. Cool the peanuts and keep them in a screw-top jar. Or eat them when they are hot – they are lovely!

## CHICKPEAS WITH MANGO AND COCONUT
### *Sundal mundal*

*I* had this dish on the Marina Beach in Madras, and it brings back nostalgic memories of Madras where I once lived for about two years. The little vendors on the beach would sell *sundal mundal* in small paper cones – my kids loved it. We would sit beside an old Greek shipwreck, and wriggle our feet in the silvery sand in the moonlight – relishing this dish!

½ lb (about 1 heaping cup) dried chickpeas
½ teaspoon turmeric powder
salt to taste
1 fresh hot green chili pepper
2 tablespoons oil
1 teaspoon mustard seeds
a few curry leaves
2 tablespoons shredded fresh or dried coconut
1 tablespoon chopped green mango

1 Soak the chickpeas overnight in cold water. Drain them and hold the sieve or colander under cold running water for a few seconds. Place the chickpeas in a heavy saucepan with the turmeric and salt and enough water to cover them. Simmer until tender, then drain. Or cook the chickpeas in a pressure cooker for speed.

2 Finely chop the green chili pepper. Heat the oil in a saucepan and add the chili pepper, with the mustard seeds and curry leaves. Add the chickpeas and cook for a few minutes, stirring thoroughly.

3 Remove from the heat and stir in the shredded coconut and mango. Serve – on a plate or in a paper cone, whichever you prefer!

## SALTY FRIED CRACKERS
### *Nimki*

*S*alty fried crackers such as these are lovely with a cold glass of lemonade or beer, although in India, we always serve them with tea. They will keep for at least two weeks in an airtight screw-top jar. I always make them on Friday afternoon to last through the following week.

3¼ cups self-rising flour
salt to taste
3 tablespoons oil
1 teaspoon red chili powder
1 teaspoon sesame seeds or cumin seeds
¾ cup water (approx)
oil for deep frying

1 Sift the flour and salt together. Add the oil, chili powder and sesame or cumin seeds and mix everything together with your fingers. Add the water gradually, kneading the mixture into a pliable dough.

2 Divide the dough in two and roll each piece out thinly. Cut into little diamond shapes.

3 Heat oil in a deep frying-pan or wok. When it is hot, drop a few crackers at a time into the pan. Quickly turn them over, then remove with a slotted spoon and drain on paper towels.

4 Let the crackers cool completely, then store in an airtight container. They are lovely mixed with roasted peanuts or cashews.

SPICY SNACK MIX (LEFT) AND CHICKPEAS WITH MANGO AND COCONUT (RIGHT).

## ❧ POPPADUM SPRING ROLLS ❧

*A* sort of a cross between a *samosa* and a spring roll, this is a wonderful snack to make for
unexpected visitors or to serve as a cocktail nibble. The rolls are folded exactly like a spring roll and
then deep-fried. It is important to use lentil *poppadums*, not those made from rice.

12 raw lentil *poppadums*
1 cup water
1 cup oil
FILLING
4 cooked potatoes
1 small onion
1 teaspoon cumin powder
salt to taste
½ teaspoon red chili powder
1 teaspoon mango powder or
   lemon juice
a few fresh coriander (cilantro) or
   mint leaves, chopped (optional)

SERVES 6

1  Make the filling: cut the potatoes into tiny cubes and finely
chop the onion. Mix with the remaining filling ingredients.
2  Soak each *poppadum* in the water for a few seconds until
softened, then place on a board. Divide the filling between
them, placing a spoonful in the center and spreading it
roughly.
3  Fold the lower part of the *poppadums* up over the filling,
then fold in both sides. Roll tightly from the bottom end and
press the ends firmly to seal the rolls.
4  Heat the oil in a deep pan or wok. Deep fry the *poppadum*
rolls, turning them once. Cook until crispy and brown all over.
Drain on paper towels.
5  Serve the rolls hot with tomato ketchup or a chutney.

## SPICY SNACK MIX
### *Bombay chiwra mix*

*T*his is a variation of the lovely spicy "Bombay Mix," now widely available in health food shops. It can be made in lots of different ways, with all sorts of ingredients.

oil for deep frying
2 cups cornflakes
⅓ cup Uncle Ben's rice or 4 cups
    puffed rice
1 tablespoon raisins
1 tablespoon fresh or dried coconut
1 tablespoon cashew nuts
2 tablespoons roasted peanuts
1 fresh hot green chili pepper
salt to taste
1 tablespoon sugar
1 teaspoon red chili powder
1 teaspoon dried lemon powder
1 teaspoon mustard seeds
a few curry leaves

1  Heat oil in a deep frying-pan or wok. Add the cornflakes and fry for a few seconds, then remove and drain on paper towels.
2  Add the rice to the oil and cook until it fluffs up. If using rice cereal, fry it in the hot oil for a few seconds. Remove and drain on paper towels.
3  Add the raisins and coconut to the oil and fry until crisp. Remove and drain on paper towels.
4  Add the cashews and peanuts, fry for a few seconds, then remove and drain them, too.
5  Slice the green chili pepper, fry it quickly in the hot oil, then remove and drain.
6  Mix all the fried ingredients together in a large bowl and add the salt, sugar and chili pepper and lemon powders. Mix together well.
7  Heat about 1 tablespoon oil from the frying-pan in a separate shallow frying-pan and add the mustard seeds and curry leaves. As soon as the mustard seeds "pop," remove from the oil and add to the other ingredients. Mix well, then cool. Store the mixture in an airtight container – it will keep very well for at least one month.

## YOGURT TOAST
### *Dahi toast*

*I* learnt this from my friend, Madhu Malhotra. It is very quick to make, but very tasty, too – great for cocktail parties, but serve with lots of paper napkins as it is quite greasy to handle.

4 slices bread
1 fresh hot green chili pepper
¼ cup plain yogurt
1 teaspoon mustard seeds
salt to taste
1 cup oil for frying

MAKES 16 SQUARES

1  Cut each slice of bread into four squares.
2  Finely chop the chili pepper and mix with the yogurt, mustard seeds and salt.
3  Heat the oil in a frying-pan or wok. Spread the yogurt mixture over each bread square and place four of them at a time into the hot oil.
4  Fry until the bread is golden (there is no need to turn it over). Remove with a slotted spoon and serve hot.

## ❧ CURRIED TOAST ❧
### *Curry masala toast*

Curried toast makes a good dish for a quick breakfast – paricularly if you have the prospect of a long day ahead! It is very similar to a French toast but it is savory instead of sweet. Good for packed lunches, too; it is tastier than a sandwich.

6 slices bread
2 eggs
½ cup milk
1 small onion
1 fresh hot green chili pepper
   (optional)
salt to taste
½ teaspoon red chili powder
½ teaspoon dried mint leaves
½ cup oil (approx) for frying

SERVES 6

1 Cut off the crusts from the bread and put the slices on one side.
2 Beat the eggs with the milk in a shallow bowl. Finely chop the onion and the chili pepper, if using, and add to the eggs with all the remaining ingredients, except the bread and oil.
3 Heat 1 tablespoon oil in a non-stick frying-pan. Dip a slice of bread into the egg mixture, then quickly put it into the pan. Fry until golden, then turn it over to fry the other side, adding more oil if necessary.
4 Put the bread onto a serving dish and keep warm while you fry the remainder in the same way.

NOTE A great way to serve these toasts is to sandwich two slices together with tomato ketchup in the middle. Cut them in half before eating.

## ❧ AMERICAN TOAST ❧

This was a favorite dish of my childhood, although I do not know how it got its name. I learnt to make it from a dear family doctor, known to the whole of Jaipur as "Aunty." She was British but married a Goanese doctor and lived in Jaipur, where she brought all of us into the world. She died a few years ago, but is fondly remembered by all those who knew her. Make the toasts in an electric sandwich maker if you have one.

8 slices bread
1 onion
1 fresh hot green chili pepper
   (optional)
½ cup grated Cheddar cheese
⅔ cup tomato ketchup
salt to taste
½ teaspoon red chili powder
½ teaspoon mustard powder
½ cup oil for frying

SERVES 4

1 Cut off the crusts from the bread and put the slices on one side.
2 Finely chop the onion and green chili pepper, if using. Mix these with the cheese, tomato ketchup, salt and the red chili and mustard powders.
3 Spread the tomato ketchup mixture on one side of four of the slices of bread. Top with the remaining slices.
4 Heat 1 tablespoon oil in a non-stick frying-pan and fry the sandwiches one at a time. When the underside of the bread is golden brown, turn the sandwiches over, adding more oil to the pan if necessary. Press down on the sandwiches with a spatula to make them stick together. Keep warm while you cook the remainder of the sandwiches in the same way.
5 Cut the sandwiches into fingers for serving.

CLOCKWISE FROM LEFT: POTATO SOUP, SOUTH INDIAN TOMATO SOUP AND CORN SOUP.

## CORN SOUP
### Makka ka shorva

*This* is my Indian version of the better-known Chinese-style soup. It's very tasty and nutritious.
Omit the curry powder for a milder version – children generally prefer it.

16 oz can whole kernel corn
2 tablespoons butter
2 teaspoons flour
1 cup milk
2 cups light stock or water
salt to taste
1 teaspoon curry powder
2 teaspoons cornstarch
4 teaspoons water
2 egg whites
soy sauce, to serve

SERVES 6

1  Drain the corn and reduce to a purée in a blender or food processor.
2  Melt the butter in a saucepan and sprinkle in the flour. Cook for 1 minute, stirring, then gradually stir in the milk. Bring to simmering point, lower the heat and simmer for 5 minutes, stirring frequently.
3  Add the stock or water, corn purée, salt and curry powder. Stir continuously and bring to a boil.
4  Mix the cornstarch with the water and stir it into the soup. Cook for a minute or two, then stir in the egg whites.
5  Pour the soup into individual serving bowls and add a dash of soy sauce to each one.

## ALMOND SOUP
*Badaam ka shorva*

*A* special-occasion soup – good for dinner parties or elegant lunches.
Serve it hot or icy cold.

1⅔ cups almonds
1 tablespoon butter
2 teaspoons all-purpose flour
1 cup milk
1 teaspoon sugar
salt to taste
dash of pepper
2½ cups hot water
½ cup cream
2 teaspoons sliced almonds, for
   garnish

SERVES 6

1  Put the almonds in a bowl, cover with cold water and soak overnight.
2  The next day, drain the almonds and peel them, then grind them to a paste in a nut mill, coffee grinder or food processor.
3  Melt the butter in a saucepan and sprinkle in the flour. Cook for 1 minute, stirring, then gradually stir in the milk. Add the sugar and some salt and pepper. Bring to a boil, lower the heat and simmer for 5 minutes, stirring occasionally.
4  Add the almond paste and the hot water and simmer for 10–15 minutes more, until the soup has thickened.
5  While the soup is simmering, toast the sliced almonds for garnish.
6  Fold the cream into the soup and sprinkle with the toasted almonds just before serving.

## VEGETABLE SOUP
*Sabzi ka shorva*

*V*egetable soup can be made from any seasonal vegetables, and is nutritious and healthy – as well as tasty. My servant – Bahadur – makes it for us for lunch every day when we are in India.

2 onions
1 inch piece fresh ginger root
2 cloves garlic
3 potatoes
3 large tomatoes
¼-lb piece winter squash (optional)
2 tablespoons oil
½ teaspoon peppercorns
2 whole cloves
2½ cups water or light stock
salt to taste
½ teaspoon sugar
½ teaspoon black pepper
1 teaspoon lemon juice
1 scallion, for garnish

SERVES 6

1  Finely chop the onions and ginger and crush the garlic. Peel the potatoes and cut into cubes; skin and chop the tomatoes. Peel the squash, if using, discard the seeds and chop the flesh into small cubes.
2  Heat the oil in a heavy-based saucepan. Add the peppercorns and cloves. Stir for a few seconds, then add the onions and cook over a medium heat until softened.
3  Add the garlic and ginger, then the potatoes, tomatoes and squash. Cook, stirring, for 5 minutes.
4  Add the water and seasonings. Bring the soup to a boil, then lower the heat and simmer for about 30 minutes until all the vegetables are tender.
5  Reduce to a purée in a blender, then rub the soup through a sieve.
6  Stir the lemon juice into the soup and reheat before serving. Serve garnished with the scallion, finely chopped.

## ❧ CARROT SOUP ☙
*Gajjar shorva*

*M*ake this colorful soup when carrots are cheap and plentiful and put a batch in the freezer.

4 large carrots
1 onion
1 clove garlic
1 tablespoon oil
salt to taste
½ teaspoon freshly ground black
    pepper
1 teaspoon sugar
1 cup water
1½ cups milk
6 tablespoons plain yogurt
chopped parsley, for garnish

SERVES 6

1  Peel and slice the carrots and cook in boiling water until tender. Drain and reduce to a purée in a blender or food processor.
2  Finely chop the onion and garlic. Heat the oil in a saucepan and sauté the onion and garlic until softened.
3  Add the carrot purée to the pan with salt, pepper and sugar. Stir in the water and milk, bring to a boil, then lower the heat and simmer for 10 minutes.
4  Pour the soup into individual serving bowls and add a spoonful of yogurt and a sprinkling of parsley to each one.

## ❧ POTATO SOUP ☙
*Aloo ka shorva*

*I* devised this tasty soup in Nigeria, where one has to be particularly imaginative owing to the shortage of a great variety of groceries.

1 onion
2 cloves garlic
4 potatoes
2 tablespoons oil
salt to taste
1 teaspoon curry powder
2½ cups water or light stock
1 cup milk
1 teaspoon dried mint leaves
1 extra potato, grated and deep
    fried, for garnish

SERVES 6

1  Finely chop the onion and garlic. Peel the potatoes and cut into small cubes.
2  Heat the oil in a heavy-based saucepan and fry the onion and garlic until softened. Add the potatoes, salt, curry powder and water or stock. Bring to a boil, then lower the heat and simmer for 20 minutes, until the potatoes are cooked.
3  Add the milk and mint and simmer for 5 minutes more. Then remove from the heat, cool slightly and reduce to a purée in a blender.
4  Reheat the soup before serving. Sprinkle with the fried grated potato and serve very hot.

# CHICKPEA FLOUR SOUP
*Khaata*

*C*hickpea flour soup is usually eaten with plain boiled rice, but it can also be served on its **own as** a soup. It generally has *pakoras* in it, but if you like you can omit these and add lots of cho**pped** scallion or spinach instead.

**PAKORAS**
1¼ cups chickpea flour
½ cup water (approx)
salt to taste
1 teaspoon red chili powder
1 teaspoon baking powder
1 teaspoon cumin seeds
1 onion
1 cup oil for frying
**KARHI**
1 cup chickpea flour
1 cup plain yogurt
2½ cups water
salt to taste
1 teaspoon sugar
1 teaspoon red chili powder
**SEASONING OR BAGHAR**
2 tablespoons oil
1 teaspoon mustard seeds
1 teaspoon cumin seeds
a few curry leaves
2 cloves garlic

**SERVES** 6

1  Mix the first six ingredients for the *pakoras* together in **a** large bowl. Finely chop the onion and add this. Stir to com**bine** the ingredients evenly.
2  Heat the oil in a frying-pan or wok and drop in about six spoonfuls of the batter at a time. Fry until golden brown on both sides, turning once. Drain on paper towels and put on one side.
3  Make the *karhi*: mix the chickpea flour with the yogurt, water, salt, sugar and chili powder. Beat the ingredients together until smooth and lump-free. Pour into a saucepan **and** heat over medium heat, stirring all the time. Bring to a boil, then lower the heat and simmer for about 30 minutes, stirring frequently, to keep a thick creamy consistency. Remove from the heat and add the *pakoras*.
4  Heat the oil for the *baghar* in a small frying-pan. Add the mustard and cumin seeds and the curry leaves. Crush the garlic and add this too. Fry for about 1 minute, then add to the *karhi*. Mix well.
5  Spoon the soup into individual serving bowls.

# SOUTH INDIAN TOMATO SOUP
*Tamatar rassam*

*Rassam* is the Southern Indian version of tomato soup. It is extremely popular there and is often eaten with rice. It is nice and spicy.

5 large tomatoes
1 teaspoon mustard seeds
1 teaspoon cumin seeds
½ teaspoon black peppercorns
1 tablespoon oil
a few curry leaves
2½ cups water
a few coriander (cilantro) leaves
salt to taste

**SERVES** 6

1  Blanch the tomatoes quickly in boiling water and peel off their skins. Mash the flesh with a fork and put on one side.
2  Crush the mustard and cumin seeds together with the black peppercorns. Heat the oil in a saucepan and add these spices together with the curry leaves. Add the tomatoes and stir everything together. Cook for 1–2 minutes, then add the **water**.
3  Add the coriander leaves and salt to taste. Bring to a boil, then lower the heat and simmer for 15 minutes. Serve hot.

# MAIN DISHES

*I*ncluded in this section are main dishes for meat, poultry and game, fish and eggs. A simple Indian meal would include one such dish served with a rice dish, a *dal* dish, probably an accompanying vegetable dish, a yogurt salad or *raita* and some bread or *roti.* In addition it would be usual to serve a chutney of some sort and perhaps some *poppadums.* As the meal gets more elaborate or more people are being served, so there will be more main course dishes – perhaps a meat and a fish dish, or quite possibly more than one of each.

Meat is known as mutton in India, and it is usually lamb or goat. In nearly all curries you could substitute beef or pork. Mutton forms part of the daily fare in the Northern parts of India, especially among the Rajputs and Punjabis and all Muslims and Christians. Mutton is a very versatile meat – and can be cooked in all sorts of ways as the recipes on the following pages show. Apart from the many different types of curry, it can also be barbecued, roasted Indian-style, made into kabobs or mixed with rice in pilaus.

The most popular poultry in India is chicken, known as *murgi* (feminine) or *murga* (male). It's more expensive than mutton, so tends to be regarded as party or special festive occasion fare. Because of its "luxury" nature, in days gone by it was mostly only served at the Royal dining table, but today nearly everyone in India enjoys chicken as part of their weekly menu. Undoubtedly the most popular chicken dish in India is *tandoori,* and of all Indian dishes, this is the one that is best known throughout the world.

Game is popular in many parts of India – a legacy from the times when the only way to obtain meat was by hunting. *Shikaar* means hunting in India, and it has always been a favorite sport of the Maharajas. In many parts of Northern India,

Rajasthan in particular, hunting is still a sport enjoyed by many – my husband for one! However; modern-day restrictions and preservation regulations have made *shikaar* meat more of a rarity, and therefore a luxury. There are many kinds of *shikaar* meats; deer or venison – *hiran,* rabbit – *khargosh,* partridge – *teetar,* wild geese or duck – *batakh* and wild boar – *soor,* are just a few.

Unlike its domesticated counterparts, wild game meat can often be tough, so it is common to use a meat tenderizer when cooking it. An old Indian method for tenderizing meat is to add a slice of green papaya to the dish while it is cooking. Try this, but remember to remove the papaya before serving.

Fish – *maachi* or *machhali* – is popular in coastal towns, particularly in Bengal and along the southern coastal areas of Bombay, Kerala and Madras. In Bengal, a fish dish will nearly always form part of the daily meal. All sorts of fish, including such shellfish as crabs, shrimp and lobsters, are turned into delicious curries, often with coconut and yogurt forming an important part of the dish. Fried fish is another favorite. It would be impossible to tell you about all the different fish that are caught in India's coastal waters; simply substitute your favorite fish in the fish recipes in this chapter.

At the end of the chapter there are a few main course recipes using eggs. Eggs do not form as important a part of Indian daily fare as they do in the west, although the menfolk will often have an omelette for breakfast – in anticipation of having no lunch! Many vegetarians will include eggs in their diet – indeed a new "breed" of vegetarians who do eat eggs are beginning to be called "eggitarians!" As in other traditions of cooking, Indian ladies look to eggs as a great standby for meals for unexpected visitors.

A CLASSIC WAY TO SERVE A COMPLETE MEAL IS TO USE A *THAALI*, WHICH CONSISTS OF A SILVER TRAY AND MATCHING BOWLS. THE *THAALI* ALLOWS YOU TO DIP INTO A SELECTION OF SMALL DISHES. THE CHOICE HERE INCLUDES CHICKEN IN SPICY SAUCE, PLAIN YOGURT, POTATO AND SPINACH CURRY, *POORIS* AND BOILED RICE. THE MEAL IS USUALLY SERVED WITH ICED WATER.

## MOST POPULAR MEAT CURRY
*Rogan josh*

*A* very popular dish – all restaurants will have their own version of this recipe. It tastes good with hot *chappatis* or saffron rice (see page 126 or 177).

2 lb lean boneless meat – lamb, beef or pork
2 teaspoons *garam masala* powder
2 teaspoons red chili powder
½ cup oil
6 onions
4 bay leaves
1 teaspoon turmeric powder
3 tablespoons coriander powder
2½ cups hot water
8 cloves garlic
2 inch piece fresh ginger root
salt to taste
4 tomatoes
4 cardamoms
chopped coriander (cilantro), for garnish

**SERVES 6**

1  Cut the meat into small cubes, then mix with the *garam masala* and chili powders.
2  Heat the oil in a large, heavy-based pan and fry the meat until browned on all sides. Remove the meat with a slotted spoon and put to one side.
3  Grate the onions, then reheat the oil and add the bay leaves and grated onions, together with the turmeric and coriander powders and ½ cup of the water. Crush the garlic and grate the ginger and add them, too. Cook gently, stirring from time to time, until the onions are soft.
4  Return the meat to the pan with the remaining water and salt to taste. Cover and simmer the meat gently for 20–25 minutes.
5  Add the tomatoes and cook for about 15 minutes more, until the meat is tender.
6  Crush the cardamoms and add them to the meat. Stir well, then serve sprinkled with chopped coriander.

## INDIAN GOULASH
*Hindustaani gosht goulash*

*T*his is an Indian version of goulash – my mother often used to make it when we had friends to a meal. It is always a popular dish.

12 onions
12 cloves garlic
2 inch piece fresh ginger root
2 lb boneless chicken or veal
1 small fresh hot red chili pepper
6 tablespoons oil
4 large tomatoes or ¼ cup tomato paste
1 cup tomato juice
1 cup hot water
salt to taste
2 teaspoons prepared mustard
¼ cup cream

**SERVES 8**

1  Finely chop the onions, garlic and ginger. Cut the meat into bite-sized cubes. Chop the red chili pepper very finely or grind in a pestle and mortar.
2  Heat the oil in a heavy-based saucepan and fry the onions until lightly browned. Add the garlic, ginger and meat. Turn up the heat and cook, stirring, until the meat is well browned.
3  Add the chili pepper, tomatoes or tomato paste and tomato juice. Stir, then add the water. Lower the heat and simmer very gently for about 45 minutes, until the meat is tender. Add salt to taste.
4  Mix together the mustard and cream and stir into the meat just before serving.

## ❧ MUTTON OR LAMB CURRY ❧
*Gosht ka saalan*

*H*ere is my basic recipe for this common curry. It forms the basis of so many meals, it is important to learn how to make it to your taste. This curry, or a slight variation, is made daily in my kitchen.

6 onions
¼ cup oil
2 teaspoons whole *garam masala* (see page 29)
1½ cups water
1 inch piece fresh ginger root
6 cloves garlic
2 teaspoons turmeric powder
2 teaspoons red chili powder
4 teaspoons coriander powder
2 tablespoons tomato paste or 2 tomatoes
2 lb lean boneless lamb, beef or pork
salt to taste
2 teaspoons *garam masala* powder
2 tablespoons lemon juice
chopped mint or coriander (cilantro), for garnish

**SERVES 6**

1 Grate the onions. Heat the oil in a large, heavy-based pan and add the whole *garam masala*. Add the onions and cook over a medium-to-high heat, stirring, until well browned.
2 Add ½ cup of the water, lower the heat and let the onions stew in this, until a thick mixture is formed. This is important, as it forms the thick base of the curry.
3 Grate the ginger and crush the garlic and add to the onions. Stir well, then stir in the turmeric, chili and coriander powders. Add the tomato paste, or chop the tomatoes, if using fresh, and add them. Cook over a medium heat until the sauce is bubbling, and the oil separates out. This is how you judge when the spices are cooked.
4 Cut the meat into cubes. Add to the mixture in the pan and stew gently, covered, for 20–30 minutes, until the liquid has evaporated.
5 Add the remaining water and salt and simmer until the meat is tender. Leave the curry covered until ready to serve.
6 Mix the *garam masala* powder with the lemon juice and stir into the curry. Sprinkle with the mint or coriander and serve.

## ❧ WHOLE MASALA CURRY ❧
*Sabat masal ka gosht*

2 lb boneless lamb, beef or pork
½ lb onions
¼ cup melted *ghee* or oil
4 fresh hot red chili peppers
1 teaspoon whole coriander seeds
4 whole cardamoms
1 inch cinnamon stick
6 whole cloves
½ teaspoon peppercorns
salt to taste
8 cloves garlic
1 cup plain yogurt
1 cup hot water
½ cup milk

**SERVES 6**

1 Cut the meat into bite-sized cubes, discarding all fat. Finely chop or grate the onions.
2 Mix all the ingredients, except the milk, together in a large heavy-based saucepan with a tight lid and cook over a medium heat for about 45 minutes–1 hour, stirring occasionally, until the meat is tender.
3 When ready to serve, stir in the milk.

NOTE If you prefer, cook the curry in a pressure cooker – it will take about 15 minutes.

# CURRY FROM KASHMIR
## *Kashmiri keema curry*

8 onions
11 cloves garlic
2 inch piece fresh ginger root
½ cup oil or melted *ghee*
1 teaspoon whole *garam masala*
   (see page 29)
1 teaspoon cumin seeds
2 teaspoons whole coriander seeds
2 tablespoons poppy seeds
12 blanched almonds
12 shelled pistachio nuts
a small piece of shelled fresh
   coconut
2 lb ground lean lamb, beef or pork
salt to taste
2½ cups plain yogurt
6 fresh hot red chili peppers
4 tomatoes
1 teaspoon cardamom powder
pinch of saffron
1 teaspoon *kewra* or rosewater
   essence
2 teaspoons chopped mint

SERVES 6

1  Finely slice four of the onions, and mince the remainder in a food processor. Crush three of the garlic cloves and finely slice the remainder. Peel the ginger and grind it in a pestle and mortar or grate it finely.

2  Heat the oil or *ghee* in a large-based saucepan and add the sliced and minced onions, the crushed and sliced garlic, the ginger, whole *garam masala* and the cumin and coriander seeds. Stir well, then cook over medium heat for 10 minutes.

3  Meanwhile, grind the poppy seeds in a pestle and mortar and slice the almonds, pistachios and coconut. Add these to the pan and cook for 1–2 minutes, stirring.

4  Add the meat and salt and cook over medium-to-high heat, stirring, for about 15 minutes, until the meat is well browned.

5  Stir in the yogurt, lower the heat a little and cook for 5–10 minutes more.

6  Add the whole red chili peppers and cook until tender, stirring the mixture from time to time to prevent it sticking.

7  Chop the tomatoes and stir them into the curry together with the cardamom powder, saffron, *kewra* or rosewater essence and mint.

8  Serve this curry with hot buttered *chappatis*, sliced bread or boiled rice.

QUEEN'S CURRY (LEFT) AND CAULIFLOWER MEAT CURRY (RIGHT).

## CURRIED MEAT WITH PEAS
### Keema matar

4 onions
¼ cup oil
1 teaspoon whole *garam masala*
   (see page 29)
½ cup water
1 inch piece fresh ginger root
4 cloves garlic
4 tomatoes or 2 tablespoons tomato
   paste
1 teaspoon red chili powder
½ teaspoon turmeric powder
2 teaspoons coriander powder
salt to taste
2 lb ground lamb, beef or pork
¾ cup shelled fresh or frozen peas
2 teaspoons *garam masala* powder
1 tablespoon lemon juice
chopped mint, for garnish

SERVES 6

1 Finely chop the onions. Heat the oil in a heavy-based saucepan and add the whole *garam masala*, then the onions. Cook over a medium-to-high heat to brown, then add the water, lower the heat and let the onions simmer for 5 minutes.
2 Peel and grind the ginger in a pestle and mortar or grate it finely and add to the onions with the whole garlic cloves. Chop the tomatoes, if using fresh, and add them or the tomato paste to the pan. Stir well to mix. Add the red chili, turmeric and coriander powders and cook for about 5 minutes, stirring occasionally.
3 Season to taste with salt, then cook until the oil floats to the top of the spice mixture. Add the ground meat and stir in thoroughly. Simmer for about 20 minutes, stirring occasionally.
4 Add the peas and *garam masala* powder and simmer until the peas are cooked. Stir in the lemon juice. Keep covered until ready to serve, then garnish with the mint.
5 Serve with boiled rice or *roti*.

## CAULIFLOWER MEAT CURRY
### Gobhi ka gosht

2 lb boneless lamb
4 onions
3 tablespoons oil
1 inch piece fresh ginger root
salt to taste
1 teaspoon turmeric powder
2 teaspoons red chili powder
1 tablespoon coriander powder
¼ cup water
6 cloves garlic
2 cups meat stock
1 cauliflower, cut into florets
1 cup hot water
1 teaspoon *garam masala* powder
2 teaspoons lemon juice
GARNISH
2 onions
2 tablespoons oil
chopped coriander (cilantro)

SERVES 6

1 Cut the meat into bite-sized cubes and put in a heavy-based pan. Cover with water, then simmer gently for 30 minutes.
2 Meanwhile, mince the onions in a food processor. Heat the oil in a separate heavy-based pan and fry the onions over a high heat for about 5 minutes, until browned.
3 Grind the ginger in a pestle and mortar, or grate it finely and add to the onions with salt to taste.
4 Mix the turmeric, red chili and coriander powders with the water and stir into the pan. Crush the garlic and add it too, stirring everything together well. Cook for 5 minutes or until the oil separates out.
5 Add the meat with its cooking liquid. Cover and cook for 15 minutes, adding the meat stock gradually when the mixture looks dry.
6 Add the cauliflower florets together with the hot water and cook for about 25 minutes more.
7 When the meat is tender, add the *garam masala* powder and lemon juice.
8 Finely slice the onions for the garnish and fry them in the oil until browned and crisp. Sprinkle over the curry together with the chopped coriander.

## ❧ KING'S CURRY ❧
### Shahi korma

*K*ing's curry is so called for no other reason than it is indeed a curry fit for a king! It is a popular one for entertaining.

4 onions
8 cloves garlic
$\frac{1}{4}$ cup oil
2 inch piece fresh ginger root
2 teaspoons red chili powder
2 teaspoons coriander powder
2 lb lean boneless lamb, beef or
     pork
2 cups hot water
2 cups milk
12 whole blanched almonds
1 tablespoon poppy seeds
8 green cardamoms
salt to taste
$\frac{1}{4}$ cup *khoa* or cooked thickened
     milk mixture (see page 28)

**SERVES 6**

1 Mince the onions and garlic together in a food processor. Heat the oil in a heavy-based saucepan and fry the onion and garlic until softened.
2 Peel the ginger and grind it in a pestle and mortar, or grate it finely. Add to the pan with the chili and coriander powders.
3 Cut the meat into bite-sized cubes and add to the pan. Cook for about 15 minutes, stirring, over a medium heat until the mixture is quite dry.
4 Add the hot water and simmer over a very low heat for about 20 minutes, or until all the water is absorbed and the meat is tender.
5 Add the milk and almonds. Grind the poppy seeds and cardamoms in a pestle and mortar and add them, too, together with the salt and *khoa*. Mix everything together well and simmer very slowly for 10 minutes.
6 Serve with hot *chappatis* or fried rice.

## ❧ QUEEN'S CURRY ❧
### Mumtaz curry

*T*ry this simple variation to an ordinary mutton or lamb curry. Just make the mutton or lamb curry recipe on page 61 to your taste and serve it topped with these spicy scrambled eggs. Serve the curry quickly when the scrambled eggs are ready.

4 eggs
2 onions
1 teaspoon red chili powder
salt to taste
1 teaspoon oil

**SERVES 6**

1 Beat the eggs together in a large bowl. Finely chop the onions and stir them into the eggs with the chili powder and salt to taste.
2 Heat the oil in a small non-stick saucepan. Add the egg mixture and stir over a low heat until lightly scrambled.
3 Spoon the eggs over the curry and serve.

## ❦ SPICED MEATBALLS ❦
*Kofte*

*M*ake this dish in advance and freeze it. Serve it with other dishes at a curry party.

1 lb ground lamb, beef or pork
$\frac{1}{2}$ cup water
2 medium-size and 1 small onion
2 tablespoons oil
salt to taste
$\frac{1}{2}$ teaspoon black pepper
1 teaspoon red chili powder
1 egg
small bunch of coriander (cilantro)
    leaves
oil for deep frying

**SERVES 6**

1  Put the ground meat into a heavy-based saucepan with the water. Cook over medium heat, stirring frequently, until the water has evaporated. Remove from the heat.
2  Finely chop the two medium-size onions. Heat the oil in a heavy-based frying-pan or wok and brown the chopped onions. Add the meat, salt, pepper and chili powder and mix well. Then remove from the heat and leave to cool.
3  Beat the egg lightly and add to the ground meat mixture. Roll into small balls.
4  Chop the remaining onion very finely. Chop the coriander and mix with the onion. Push a little of this mixture into the center of each *kofta* and re-form the meat around it.
5  Heat the oil for deep frying and fry the balls until they are evenly browned. Drain on paper towels and serve with a *raita* (see pages 134–137), *chappatis* and chutneys.

## ❦ MEATBALL CURRY ❦
*Kofta curry*

*A*nother recipe using the spiced meatball mixture above; here it is served in a delicious curry sauce.

1 portion spiced meatball recipe
    (see above)
**CURRY SAUCE**
4 onions
6 cloves garlic
2 inch piece fresh ginger root
4 tomatoes
1 cup plain yogurt
salt to taste
1 teaspoon turmeric powder
2 teaspoons red chili powder
4 teaspoons coriander powder
1 cup hot water
**GARNISH**
1 onion
1 tablespoon oil
$\frac{1}{4}$ cup plain yogurt
chopped coriander (cilantro)

**SERVES 6**

1  Make the sauce: mince the onions, garlic and ginger together in a food processor. Chop the tomatoes. Place all these in a heavy-based saucepan with all the remaining ingredients and simmer gently until the sauce has thickened.
2  Meanwhile make the *kofte* following the recipe above.
3  Add them to the sauce and simmer everything together for a few minutes. Transfer to a serving dish.
4  Chop the onion for garnish and fry in the oil. Stir the extra yogurt into the sauce, then sprinkle with the onions and chopped coriander.

## ❧ POTATO MEAT CURRY ❧
### *Aloo gosht*

6 onions
$\frac{1}{4}$ cup oil
6 cloves garlic
1 teaspoon ground ginger
1 teaspoon turmeric powder
2 teaspoons red chili powder
1 tablespoon coriander powder
$\frac{1}{4}$ cup water
2 tomatoes or 2 tablespoons tomato paste
2 lb lean boneless lamb
6 potatoes
$\frac{1}{2}$ cup hot water
salt to taste
1 teaspoon *garam masala* powder
GARNISH
2 fresh hot green chili peppers
a few lemon wedges
chopped mint

SERVES 6

1  Mince the onions in a food processor. Heat the oil in a heavy-based saucepan and brown the onions lightly in it.
2  Grind the garlic with the ginger and add to the onions.
3  Mix the turmeric, red chili and coriander powders with the water to make a paste and stir this into the onions in the pan. Cook gently for 10 minutes, until the mixture is bubbling and the oil separates out.
4  Chop the tomatoes, if using fresh, and add to the pan. Or add the tomato paste. Cut the meat into bite-sized pieces and add this too. Cook for about 15 minutes.
5  Halve or quarter the potatoes if large and add to the pan. Cover and cook gently for about 15 minutes or until the potatoes are tender. Carefully remove them and keep them warm.
6  Add the hot water to the pan with salt to taste and cook for 15 minutes more, or until the meat is tender. Return the potatoes to the pan with the *garam masala* powder.
7  Chop the chili peppers for garnish and serve the curry with these and the lemon wedges, and sprinkled with chopped mint.

## ❧ POTATO AND MEAT CURRY ❧
### *Dumpukhat*

*T*his is a slight variation on the above recipe – a nice easy one to make and good to do when you have visitors.

$\frac{1}{2}$ lb potatoes
4 onions
6 cloves garlic
1 teaspoon turmeric powder
2 teaspoons red chili powder
4 teaspoons coriander powder
1 teaspoon *garam masala* powder
$\frac{1}{4}$ cup water
oil for greasing
salt to taste
1 cup plain yogurt
2 lb lean boneless lamb, beef or pork
6 tablespoons butter or *ghee*
1 cup hot water

SERVES 6

1  Cut the potatoes in half. Mince the onions with the garlic in a food processor. Mix the turmeric, red chili, coriander and *garam masala* powders to a paste with the water.
2  Grease a heavy-based saucepan with oil and place the potatoes in a single layer in it. Mix the onions and garlic with the spice paste and stir in the salt and yogurt. Cut the meat into small bite-sized pieces and stir them into the onion and yogurt mixture, then spoon this evenly over the potatoes.
3  Melt the butter or *ghee* and pour over the ingredients. Cover tightly with a lid and cook over a very low heat for about 30 minutes. Add the water and cook for about 30 minutes more, until the meat is tender.
4  Serve with boiled rice.

# AFGHANISTAN CURRY
### Afghani korma

*T*he late Maharaja's cook – Ahmed Ali – used to cook this curry for palace dinners.

2 lb lean boneless lamb, beef or
  pork
2 cups water
2 lb onions
2 inch piece fresh ginger root
2 whole garlic bulbs
½ cup oil or melted *ghee*
2 bay leaves
salt to taste
8 dried hot red chili peppers
2 cups plain yogurt
1 cup hot water
juice of 1 lemon
a few drops of *kewra* or rosewater
  essence

SERVES 6

1  Cut the meat into bite-sized pieces and put into a heavy-based saucepan with the water. Bring to a boil, then lower the heat and simmer for about 30 minutes.
2  Meanwhile, finely slice ½ pound of the onions and mince the remainder in a food processor with the ginger. Crush all the garlic cloves.
3  Heat the oil or *ghee* in a heavy-based pan and fry the sliced onions until brown. Add the minced onions, ginger, garlic, bay leaves and salt, then cook, stirring occasionally for about 15 minutes, until the mixture is well browned.
4  Add the boiled meat with its juices and cook over a high heat for about 5 minutes, stirring.
5  Crumble the dried chili peppers and add to the mixture with the yogurt. Cook for a few minutes, stirring, then add the hot water. Simmer very gently for about 15 minutes. Add the lemon juice and simmer for about 5 minutes more.
6  Add the *kewra* or rosewater essence just before serving.

MEATBALL CURRY (LEFT) AND POTATO MEAT CURRY (RIGHT).

## ❦ BEER MEAT CURRY ❦
*Beer ka gosht*

*T*he beer acts as a tenderizer in this recipe – ever a popular one with men!

8 onions
2 cloves garlic
1 inch piece fresh ginger root
6 tablespoons oil
2 whole cloves
1 teaspoon turmeric powder
1 tablespoon red chili powder
2 tablespoons coriander powder
$\frac{1}{4}$ cup water
2 lb boneless lamb, pork or beef
1 cup plain yogurt
1 cup beer
salt to taste
2 teaspoons *garam masala* powder
2 teaspoons chopped fresh mint

**SERVES 6**

1 Mince six of the onions with the garlic and ginger in a food processor.
2 Heat the oil in a heavy-based pan and add the minced onion mixture with the cloves. Fry until the onions have softened.
3 Mix the turmeric, red chili and coriander powders with the water. Add to the mixture in the frying-pan.
4 Cut the meat into bite-sized pieces and add to the pan with the yogurt. Simmer gently for about 20 minutes, then add the beer and salt to taste. Simmer for about 15 minutes more, but stir frequently to prevent sticking. Add more water if the mixture looks too dry.
5 When the meat is tender, stir in the remaining onions, finely chopped, the *garam masala* powder and the chopped mint. Keep covered until ready to serve.

## ❦ OKRA MEAT CURRY ❦
*Bhindi ka gosht*

*I* often cook this curry on Sundays when I am serving a big curry lunch. You can buy okra in many supermarkets.

$\frac{1}{2}$ lb fresh or frozen okra
6 onions
1 inch piece fresh ginger root
6 cloves garlic
$\frac{1}{2}$ cup oil
1 teaspoon whole *garam masala*
　(see page 29)
1 teaspoon turmeric powder
2 teaspoons red chili powder
1 tablespoon coriander powder
$\frac{1}{4}$ cup water
2 lb boneless lamb, beef or pork
1 cup hot water
salt to taste
1 cup plain yogurt
1 teaspoon *garam masala* powder

**SERVES 6**

1 Chop the okra roughly. Mince the onions, ginger and garlic together in a food processor.
2 Heat the oil in a heavy-based pan and fry the okra until lightly browned. Remove with a slotted spoon and put on one side.
3 Add the whole *garam masala* to the pan together with the minced onion mixture and fry for 5 minutes.
4 Mix the turmeric, red chili and coriander powders with the water. Add to the pan, stir well and cook for 5 minutes.
5 Cut the meat into bite-sized cubes and add to the pan with the hot water. Simmer gently for about 25 minutes, or until the water has been absorbed.
6 Add the salt, yogurt and fried okra. Simmer very gently for another 20–30 minutes, or until the meat is tender. Stir frequently to prevent the mixture sticking.
7 Stir in the *garam masala* powder and remove from the heat.
8 Serve with hot buttered *chappatis* or warmed, buttered pita bread (available at most supermarkets).

## ❧ BRAIN CURRY ❧
*Bheja curry*

*T*his recipe for brains is a rather more substantial dish than the one that follows. Overcome any prejudice you may have against brains and give these two recipes a try – they are very tasty.

4 onions
6 cloves garlic
5 tablespoons oil
½ teaspoon turmeric powder
1 teaspoon red chili powder
2 teaspoons coriander powder
¼ cup water
⅔ cup plain yogurt
1 teaspoon *garam masala* powder
salt to taste
3 lamb brains
2 tomatoes

SERVES 6

1  Mince half the onions and all the garlic together in a food processor. Heat half the oil in a heavy-based pan and fry this mixture until lightly browned.
2  Mix the turmeric, red chili and coriander powders with the water and add to the pan with the yogurt, *garam masala* powder and salt. Cook for 10 minutes, then remove the pan from the heat and put on one side.
3  Wash the brains and cut into small pieces. Slice the remaining onions. Heat the rest of the oil in a frying-pan and add the brains and onion. Slice the tomatoes and add them too. Cook everything together gently for about 10 minutes, stirring from time to time.
4  Mix the curry mixture with the brains and serve at once with plain boiled rice.

## ❧ CURRIED BRAINS ❧
*Masala bheja*

*T*his is another of my husband's favorite dishes; he likes it for Sunday brunch. When cooked, it looks rather like scrambled egg.

3 lamb brains
½ cup water
salt to taste
½ teaspoon red chili powder
2 teaspoons chopped coriander
  (cilantro) or mint
2 fresh hot green chili peppers
1 teaspoon coriander powder
1 teaspoon turmeric powder
2 onions
2 tablespoons oil
1 inch piece fresh ginger root
6 cloves garlic

SERVES 6

1  Put the brains into a medium-sized saucepan with the water, salt, red chili powder and chopped coriander or mint. Finely chop the green chili peppers and add them with the coriander and turmeric powders. Mix everything together, bring to a boil, then lower the heat and simmer for 10 minutes.
2  Meanwhile, chop the onions and fry them in the oil in a separate pan, until golden brown. Grind the ginger and garlic together in a pestle and mortar or chop very finely and add to the onion. Cook for another 5 minutes. Stir the brains, together with the spices and liquid, into the onions and simmer gently for about 10 minutes more.
3  Serve with hot *chappatis* or warmed pita bread.

# CHICKEN IN SPICY SAUCE
*Murgi masala*

1 whole chicken, weighing 3 lb or
   1½ lb boneless chicken breasts
2 tablespoons chili sauce
½ cup tomato ketchup
2 tablespoons sweet soy sauce
1 tablespoon *garam masala*
   powder
salt to taste
1 inch piece fresh ginger root
2 cloves garlic
juice of 1 lemon

SERVES 4–6

1 Cut the chicken meat from the carcass, if using a whole chicken, then cut the meat into small bite-sized pieces. Put in a shallow dish.

2 Mix together the chili sauce, tomato ketchup, sweet soy sauce, *garam masala* powder and salt. Crush the ginger in a pestle and mortar or grate it finely. Crush the garlic. Add these to the mixture and mix thoroughly.

3 Pour the spicy mixture over the chicken. Mix well to coat the chicken evenly, then marinate for at least 3 hours.

4 Place a frying-pan or wok over a very low heat and add the chicken and sauce. Cook, stirring from time to time, until the chicken is cooked and the sauce has thickened.

5 Transfer the chicken to a casserole dish and place in an oven heated to 350° for 10–15 minutes.

6 Serve with the lemon juice squeezed over the chicken.

NOTE  If you use ordinary soy sauce, add 1 teaspoon sugar to the marinade.

TANDOORI CHICKEN (LEFT) AND CHICKEN IN SPICY SAUCE (RIGHT) WITH *NAAN*.

## CUMIN CHICKEN CURRY
### *Jeera murga*

*T*his recipe is a particular specialty of mine. It is very tasty – serve it with hot buttered *chappatis*.

6 boneless chicken breasts, skinned
2 onions
¼ cup oil
6 cloves garlic
1 inch piece fresh ginger root
2 teaspoons cumin powder
½ teaspoon black pepper
salt to taste
1 teaspoon *garam masala* powder
1 tablespoon lemon juice
½ cup hot water (see recipe)

SERVES 6

1  Cut the chicken into small cubes and grate the onions.
2  Heat the oil in a heavy-based pan and sauté the onions until soft and lightly golden. Add the chicken and cook, stirring, for 5–10 minutes, until the chicken has lost all its pinkness.
3  Crush the garlic and grate the ginger; add to the pan with all the remaining ingredients except the water. Cover and cook over a medium heat for about 10 minutes.
4  Uncover the pan and stir the mixture well. If the chicken is not yet tender and mixture looks a little dry, add the hot water, a little at a time, and stir continuously.
5  Cover the pan and leave on a very low heat until you are ready to serve the curry.

## TANDOORI CHICKEN
### *Tandoori murga*

*T*his is the most popular Indian chicken dish of all. It is best eaten with *naan*.

1 chicken, weighing 3 lb
1 cup plain yogurt
1 tablespoon *tandoori masala* (see note below)
1 teaspoon salt
1 teaspoon *garam masala* powder
GARNISH
raw onion rings
1 tablespoon lemon juice
lemon wedges

SERVES 4

1  Cut the chicken into four pieces, cutting out and discarding the backbone. Make gashes all over the flesh with a sharp knife.
2  Lightly whisk the yogurt, then whisk in the *tandoori masala*, salt and *garam masala* powder. Place the chicken in a shallow dish and pour the yogurt mixture over it. Turn the chicken to coat it evenly with the marinade. Leave in a cool place for at least 4 hours, or overnight.
3  Either broil the chicken, about 2–3 inches from the source of heat, grill over a barbecue or cook in an oven heated to 375° for about 45 minutes.
4  Soak the onion rings for the garnish in the lemon juice while the chicken is cooking. Then drain them and sprinkle over the cooked chicken. Serve accompanied by the lemon wedges.

NOTE You can buy *tandoori masala* in specialist Indian shops and some grocers, or you can make your own by mixing together the following:
1 teaspoon red chili powder
1 teaspoon cumin powder
1 teaspoon coriander powder
a few drops of red food coloring

## 🌿 CHICKEN BALLS 🌿
### *Murgi kebab*

*S*erve these spicy meatballs as part of a curry meal or at a buffet or cocktail party. Spear them on cocktail sticks and serve with a dip (see recipe).

**CHICKEN BALLS**
2 lb boneless chicken breasts
2 large onions
1 fresh hot green chili pepper
1 tablespoon *garam masala*
    powder
juice of 1 lemon
1 tablespoon bottled sweet-and-
    sour sauce (Chinese)
1 egg
1 tablespoon chopped mint or
    coriander (cilantro)
1 tablespoon soy sauce
1 teaspoon salt
oil for deep frying
**CHUTNEY**
$\frac{1}{4}$ cup bottled sweet-and-sour sauce
2 teaspoons soy sauce
$\frac{1}{2}$ teaspoon garlic powder
1 teaspoon chili sauce
salt to taste

**MAKES 18–20**

1  Grind the chicken in a meat grinder or food processor and finely chop the onions and chili pepper.
2  Mix all the ingredients, except the oil, for the chicken balls, combining thoroughly and pressing together with your hands. Form into walnut-size balls.
3  Heat the oil for deep frying and fry the balls a few at a time, until evenly browned. Remove with a slotted spoon and drain on paper towels. Keep warm while you fry the remainder.
4  Make the chutney by mixing all the ingredients together thoroughly. Serve as a dip.

## 🌿 CURRIED CHICKEN LIVERS 🌿
### *Murgi kalegi*

*T*his was the traditional Sunday brunch dish at my boarding school in Jaipur.
Very healthy and nutritious!

$\frac{1}{2}$ lb chicken livers
4 onions
4 cloves garlic or 1 teaspoon garlic
    powder or granules
2 tablespoons oil
$\frac{1}{2}$ teaspoon whole *garam masala*
    (see page 29)
1 teaspoon *garam masala* powder
$\frac{1}{2}$ teaspoon black pepper
$\frac{1}{2}$ teaspoon turmeric powder
salt to taste
juice of 1 lemon

**SERVES 6**

1  Wash the chicken livers and cut in small pieces, discarding any stringy bits. Finely slice the onions and crush the garlic, if using cloves.
2  Heat the oil in a heavy-based frying-pan and add the whole *garam masala*. Add the onions and fry for about 5 minutes over medium heat.
3  Add the chicken livers and cook for a few minutes, stirring. Add all the remaining ingredients, except the lemon juice. Cover and simmer for about 10 minutes, until the moisture has been absorbed.
4  Sprinkle with the lemon juice and serve in a ring of mashed potato, if liked.

## ❧ FRIED CHICKEN I ❧
### *Tali murgi I*

*S*erve this as part of a curry meal or as a light lunchtime dish.

1½ lb boneless chicken breasts
2 onions
1 inch piece fresh ginger root or 2
    teaspoons ground ginger
2 teaspoons garlic granules or
    powder or 12 cloves garlic
2 teaspoons *garam masala* powder
1 teaspoon turmeric powder
1 teaspoon red chili powder
2 teaspoons coriander powder
1 teaspoon salt
oil for deep frying
**GARNISH**
1 onion
2 teaspoons lemon juice
salt
slices of lemon

**SERVES 6**

1 Cut the chicken into bite-sized pieces and prick these with a fork. Grate the onions and fresh ginger, if using, and crush the garlic cloves, if using.
2 Mix the onions, ginger and garlic with the *garam masala*, turmeric, red chili and coriander powders and add the salt.
3 Rub this spicy mixture into the chicken and leave to marinate for 1 hour.
4 Heat the oil for deep frying and fry the chicken pieces a few at a time until they are browned. Drain on paper towels and keep warm while you fry the remainder.
5 Slice the onion for the garnish finely and soak in the lemon juice mixed with a little salt. Drain and scatter over the cooked chicken. Serve with the lemon slices.

## ❧ FRIED CHICKEN II ❧
### *Tali murgi II*

*C*hildren (and grown-ups) love these tasty "finger-licking" drumsticks. They are ideal for eating with the fingers – but provide lots of paper napkins!

12 chicken drumsticks
4 onions
2 fresh hot green chili peppers
1 inch piece fresh ginger root
⅔ cup plain yogurt
salt to taste
oil for deep frying
2 teaspoons lemon juice
chopped coriander (cilantro), for
    garnish

**SERVES 6**

1 Make two or three slashes with a sharp knife into the flesh of the chicken drumsticks. Finely chop the onions and green chili peppers. Grind the ginger in a pestle and mortar or grate it finely.
2 Mix the onions, chili peppers, ginger, yogurt and salt together and rub into the chicken. Leave to marinate for 2 hours.
3 Heat the oil for deep frying and fry two or three drumsticks at a time, until they are cooked through and evenly browned. Remove with tongs and keep warm while you fry the remainder.
4 Serve sprinkled with lemon juice and chopped coriander.

# ❧ WHOLE STUFFED CHICKEN ❧
## *Murg-mussallam*

*T*his wonderful dish has been handed down from the Mogul era. It is extremely rich – most suitable for a dinner party. Serve on a bed of saffron rice (see page 177).

1 chicken, weighing about 3½ lb
6 onions
12 cloves garlic
1 inch piece fresh ginger root
½ cup oil or melted *ghee*
1 teaspoon turmeric powder
2 teaspoons red chili powder
4 teaspoons coriander powder
¼ cup water
2 hard-boiled eggs
salt to taste
1 teaspoon cumin seeds
2 teaspoons *garam masala* powder
½ cup hot water
GARNISH
2 onions
2 tablespoons oil

SERVES 4–6

1 Wash the chicken and pat it dry inside and outside with paper towels. Cook in a steamer for 1 hour.
2 Meanwhile, mince the onions in a food processor with the garlic. Finely chop the ginger.
3 Heat half the oil or *ghee* in a large frying-pan and fry the onions, garlic and ginger. Mix the turmeric, red chili and coriander powders together with the water and pour over the onions. Stir well and cook for about 5 minutes. Remove from the heat and add the whole hard-boiled eggs and salt to the mixture.
4 Stuff the chicken with this mixture and stitch the opening together with a needle and thread to hold the stuffing in place. Leave any leftover stuffing on one side.
5 Heat the remainder of the oil or *ghee* in a large clean heavy-based pan. Add the cumin and *garam masala* powder, and cook for 2–3 minutes, stirring all the time. Add any leftover stuffing together with the chicken and spoon the spices over the chicken until it is well coated.
6 Cover the pan with a lid and cook over a low heat for about 15 minutes, adding splashes of hot water to the pan if the spices begin to stick to the bottom.
7 Finely slice the onions for the garnish and fry them in the oil in a separate pan until crisp. Scatter over the chicken.

ABOVE: MANJU ENTERTAINING AT HOME. SHE IS SEATED IN FRONT OF A MAGNIFICENT CURRY MEAL WHICH SHE HAS PREPARED FOR HER GUESTS.

LEFT: MANJU, AT THE CITY PALACE, PERFORMING THE HAND-WASHING RITUAL THAT TAKES PLACE AT THE END OF A MEAL.

## ❧ STUFFED CURRIED PARTRIDGE ❧
### *Sabat titar*

*S*erve this special dish on an important occasion – such as a small family gathering.

3 partridges
1 portion *samosa* meat filling recipe
  (see page 41) using $\frac{1}{2}$ lb ground
  meat
1 tomato
1 onion
1 green chili pepper
$\frac{1}{4}$ cup vinegar
12 blanched almonds
1 cup oil for frying

SERVES 6

1 Cook the partridges in a steamer for 30 minutes.
2 Meanwhile make the spicy ground meat mixture following the recipe on page 41.
3 Finely chop the tomato, onion and green chili pepper, then mix these with the ground meat mixture, together with the vinegar. Slice the almonds and add these, too.
4 Stuff the partridges with this mixture and stitch the back openings with a needle and thread to hold the stuffing in place.
5 Heat the oil in a wok or heavy-based, large, deep pan and fry the partridges over a medium heat until browned.
6 Remove the partridges from the pan and cut each one in half for serving.

## ❧ CURRIED FRIED PARTRIDGE ❧
### *Tala titar*

*N*ot an economical dish, but certainly a very impressive one, so serve it when you want to make an impression. It goes very well with icy cold beer, incidentally.

3 partridges
1 onion
6 cloves garlic
1 inch piece fresh ginger root
2 cups chickpea flour
$\frac{1}{4}$ cup water
salt to taste
1 teaspoon cumin seeds
2 teaspoons *garam masala* powder
1 teaspoon mango powder
$\frac{1}{2}$ teaspoon black pepper
$\frac{1}{2}$ teaspoon red chili powder
1 teaspoon coriander powder
$\frac{1}{2}$ teaspoon baking powder
oil for deep frying

SERVES 6

1 Cut the partridges into quarters and place in a shallow dish.
2 Mince the onion, garlic and ginger in a food processor and mix with all the remaining ingredients except the oil.
3 Pour this mixture over the partridge pieces, turning them to coat evenly. Leave for 10 minutes.
4 Heat the oil for deep frying. Lift the partridge pieces with tongs from the onion mixture and fry them, two or three at a time, in the hot oil. Drain on paper towels and keep warm while you fry the remainder.

# VENISON PATTIES
## Hiran ke kebab

*My* daughter, Shivina, loves these and would eat them every day, given the chance!
She was lucky when my husband used to go hunting in Jaipur with friends, for he would usually
bring home a large deer. This would be duly butchered and frozen, and we would eat it every day
for the next two weeks or so!

2 lb boneless venison
2 cups water
2 onions
6 cloves garlic
2 tablespoons roasted poppy seeds
   (see page 28)
12 blanched almonds
2 dried hot red chili peppers
1 teaspoon cumin seeds
1 inch piece fresh ginger root
2 teaspoons coriander seeds
salt to taste
1 cup chickpea flour
$\frac{1}{2}$ cup oil for frying
**FILLING**
2 onions
2 fresh hot green chili peppers
1 inch piece fresh ginger root
small bunch fresh coriander
   (cilantro) or mint, chopped
**GARNISH**
1 onion
juice of 1 lemon

**SERVES 6**

1 Cut the venison into bite-sized cubes and place in a heavy-based saucepan with the water. Bring to a boil, then lower the heat and simmer gently until all the moisture has evaporated. Grind the cooked meat in a food processor and put on one side.

2 Mince the onions, garlic, roasted poppy seeds, almonds, red chili peppers, cumin, ginger and coriander seeds together in a food processor, until pulped and well mixed. Add this mixture to the meat with the salt and flour, mixing everything together well with your hands. The texture of the mixture should be that of a soft dough (see note below).

3 Make the filling: finely chop the onions, chili peppers and ginger. Mix these with the chopped coriander or mint.

4 Take a small amount of the venison mixture in one hand and mold it into a sort of cup shape. Place a small amount of the filling into the center indentation, then mold the venison mixture around the filling. Flatten the meat between the palms of your hands into a small patty shape. Repeat this process until you have used all the venison mixture and the filling.

5 Heat a heavy-based frying-pan over medium-to-high heat and add 1 teaspoon oil. Fry three or four patties in this, cooking them until they are well browned on one side. Turn them carefully so as not to break them and fry the other side. Remove with a slotted spatula and drain on paper towels. Keep warm until all the patties are cooked.

6 Garnish with the onion, finely sliced into rings, and sprinkle with lemon juice. Serve with tomato ketchup.

NOTE If the venison seems too moist or watery after grinding it, add two boiled, mashed potatoes to it; this will make it firmer and easier to handle.

## GOOSE OR DUCK CURRY
### Batakh curry

1 goose or large duck
8 onions
½ cup oil
1 tablespoon whole *garam masala*
   (see page 29)
1¼ cups cold water
12 cloves garlic
¼ cup hot water
1 teaspoon turmeric powder
2 teaspoons red chili powder
4 tablespoons coriander powder
1 inch piece fresh ginger root
2 teaspoons salt
1 cup plain yogurt
¼ cup lemon juice
½ cup orange juice
chopped coriander (cilantro) or
   mint, for garnish

SERVES 4–6

1 Wash the goose or duck and prick it all over with a fork. Dry on paper towels, then stuff it with four whole peeled onions. Stitch up the opening with a needle and thread.
2 Heat the oil in a large, heavy-based pan and add the whole *garam masala*. Place the bird in the oil and brown on all sides. Add the cold water to the pan, lower the heat and cook, covered, for 45 minutes, or until tender, turning frequently. When cooked, remove the bird. Cut the thread, remove the onions and discard them. Put the bird on a carving board and keep warm.
3 While the bird is cooking, mince the remaining onions with the garlic in a food processor. Add to the pan in which the bird was cooked and fry for 5 minutes. Add the hot water, and then the turmeric, red chili and coriander powders. Simmer for 5 minutes.
4 Grind the ginger in a pestle and mortar or grate it finely and add it to the pan with the salt and yogurt. Cook for 5 minutes, stirring, then lower the heat and cook, covered, for a further 10 minutes.
5 Stir the lemon and orange juices into the mixture and heat gently. Cut up the bird and place in a serving dish. Pour the sauce over the bird and sprinkle with the chopped coriander or mint.

## INDIAN-PORTUGUESE PORK CURRY
### Vindaloo

*T*his is included with the game recipes as it would traditionally have been made of wild boar.

2 lb boneless pork
12 cloves garlic
2 teaspoons cumin seeds
2 teaspoons coriander seeds
2 tablespoons mustard seeds
2 inch piece fresh ginger root
2 cups vinegar
½ cup hot water
12 fresh hot red chili peppers
1 onion
2 tablespoons oil
1 teaspoon turmeric powder
salt to taste

SERVES 6

1 Cut the pork into bite-sized cubes. Grind the garlic, cumin, coriander and mustard seeds and the ginger to a fine paste in a food processor with half the vinegar and the hot water.
2 Rub the pork with this spicy paste and leave, tightly covered, in a cool place for 24 hours.
3 Heat a heavy-based frying-pan over a medium heat and roast the chili peppers until browned on all sides. Grind them to a paste with the remaining vinegar in a food processor.
4 Chop the onion. Heat the oil in a large, heavy-based frying-pan and fry the onion until browned.
5 Add the turmeric powder, chili paste and the pork with its marinade. Cook over a low heat until the meat is tender, about 45 minutes. Add salt to taste.

# RABBIT MEAT CURRY
## *Khargosh mokul*

1 rabbit
6 onions
$\frac{3}{4}$ cup oil or melted *ghee*
12 cloves garlic
1 inch piece fresh ginger root
2 teaspoons cumin powder
2 teaspoons red chili powder
1 teaspoon turmeric powder
2 teaspoons coriander powder
$\frac{1}{4}$ cup water
1 tablespoon poppy seeds
2 tablespoons finely grated fresh
   coconut
2 cups plain yogurt
salt to taste
1 teaspoon *garam masala* powder
pinch of saffron powder
1 tablespoon warmed milk
1 teaspoon rosewater
a pinch of grated nutmeg
GARNISH
2 onions
3 tablespoons oil
1 fresh hot green chili pepper

SERVES 6

1  Put the rabbit in a saucepan large enough to contain it comfortably, cover with water and bring to a boil. Lower the heat and simmer for about $1\frac{1}{2}$ hours, or until the rabbit is very tender. Leave to cool, then remove the meat from the bones and shred it with your fingers.

2  Finely chop the onions. Heat the oil or *ghee* in a large, heavy-based pan and brown the onions. Crush the garlic and grind the ginger in a pestle and mortar or grate it finely. Add to the onions with the cumin and cook for 1–2 minutes.

3  Add the red chili, turmeric and coriander powders and cook them, stirring, until the oil or *ghee* separates out.

4  Add the water. Grind the poppy seeds in a spice or coffee grinder and add them with the coconut. Stir, then add the yogurt and simmer until the oil or *ghee* separates out again.

5  Add the salt and shredded rabbit to the mixture, cover and simmer until everything is well combined.

6  Add the *garam masala* powder, together with the saffron mixed with the milk, the rosewater and a pinch of nutmeg.

7  Slice the onions finely for the garnish and fry them in the oil until they are brown and crisp. Finely chop the chili pepper. Sprinkle the curry with the onions and chili pepper just before serving.

STUFFED CURRIED PARTRIDGE.

## ❧ FISH CURRY ❧
*Machhli ki curry*

**BATTER**
¼ cup yellow mustard seeds
1 teaspoon turmeric powder
1 teaspoon black peppercorns
6 cloves garlic
4 fresh hot red chili peppers
1 teaspoon whole coriander seeds
salt to taste
½ cup water
1 cup chickpea flour or whole
    wheat flour
1 lb white fish fillet, such as cod or
    haddock
corn oil for deep frying

**CURRY SAUCE**
2 tablespoons oil
½ teaspoon fenugreek seeds
2 cloves garlic
a pinch of asafetida
2 tablespoons mango powder
¼ cup chickpea flour
salt to taste
1 cup plain yogurt

**SERVES 6**

1  Make the batter: grind the first seven ingredients to a paste with the water in a blender or food processor. Beat in the flour, keeping the batter smooth and lump free.
2  Cut the fish into 2 inch cubes and drop into the batter.
3  Heat the oil for deep frying and when it is hot, drop the pieces of fish into it, a few at a time. Fry until golden, then remove and drain on paper towels. Keep warm.
4  Make the curry sauce: heat the oil in a heavy-based pan and add the fenugreek seeds. Crush the garlic into the oil and add the asafetida and mango powder. Add any batter left over from the fish, then stir in the flour, salt and yogurt. Simmer very gently for about 5 minutes, or until beginning to thicken. Add the fish pieces, simmer for a minute or two longer, then serve immediately with boiled rice.

**NOTE**  You could serve the fish without the curry sauce if you prefer, with chutney or tomato ketchup.

## ❧ FISH COOKED ON SKEWERS ❧
*Seekh ki machhali*

*C*ook these on a barbecue for the best results.

1 lb white fish fillet
6 cloves garlic
salt to taste
1 tablespoon *garam masala*
    powder
2 teaspoons coriander powder
⅔ cup plain yogurt
2 tablespoons melted *ghee*

**GARNISH**
1 onion
2 tablespoons vinegar
½ teaspoon salt
2 fresh hot green chili peppers
1 lemon

**SERVES 6**

1  Cut the fish into bite-sized pieces and put on one side.
2  Crush the garlic and mix with the salt, *garam masala* and coriander powders and the yogurt.
3  Dip the fish pieces into this mixture and thread them onto six skewers.
4  Place on a barbecue or under a broiler, pour a little *ghee* over the fish and cook, turning, until the fish is lightly charred.
5  While the fish is cooking, prepare the garnish: slice the onion finely and soak in the vinegar with salt added. Finely slice the green chili peppers. Serve the fish sprinkled with the chilies and drained onions, accompanied by lemon wedges.

## MASHED CURRIED FISH
*Machhali bhurta*

*Y*ou can use this as a very tasty crêpe filling. Or mix it into rice to form a sort of kedgeree.

1 lb white fish, such as cod or
    haddock
3 onions
1 fresh hot green chili pepper
2 tablespoons oil
1 teaspoon cumin seeds
½ teaspoon turmeric powder
1 teaspoon red chili powder
2 teaspoons coriander powder
⅔ cup plain yogurt
salt to taste
1 teaspoon *garam masala* powder
2 teaspoons lemon juice
chopped coriander (cilantro) or
    mint

**SERVES 6**

1  Cook the fish either by poaching or steaming, or wrapping in foil and cooking in an oven heated to 350°. Cook it until it flakes easily, then mash it removing and discarding all skin and bones.
2  Finely chop the onions and green chili pepper. Heat the oil in a heavy-based frying-pan and add the cumin seeds, onion and green chili. Cook over medium heat for about 5 minutes, then add the turmeric, red chili and coriander powders with the yogurt. Cook for 5 minutes.
3  Add the salt and fish, and cook, stirring gently, until the fish is brown and crisp and the moisture has been absorbed.
4  Add the *garam masala* powder, lemon juice and chopped coriander or mint.
5  Serve with rice pancakes – *dosas* (see page 42) or *chappatis.*

## FRIED FISH FROM HYDERABAD
*Hyderabadi tali machhali*

*T*his is a spicy fried fish recipe from Hyderabad. Serve it as part of a curry meal.

1½ lb white fish fillet
1 tablespoon cumin seeds
1 teaspoon poppy seeds
1 tablespoon fenugreek seeds
1 tablespoon sesame seeds
2 onions
6 cloves garlic
1 teaspoon turmeric powder
1 teaspoon red chili powder
2 teaspoons coriander powder
salt to taste
oil for deep frying

**SERVES 6**

1  Cut the fish into six equal pieces and place in a large bowl.
2  Heat a heavy-based pan or iron griddle and separately roast the cumin seeds, poppy seeds, fenugreek seeds and sesame seeds. Chop the onions finely and roast them, too, then grind each roasted ingredient separately in a spice or coffee grinder.
3  Mix the ground ingredients together. Crush the garlic and add to the mixture with the turmeric, red chili and coriander powders. Add some salt, then tip this mixture over the fish and mix together thoroughly. Cover and leave in a cool place for 3 hours.
4  Heat the oil for deep frying and fry the pieces of fish one or two at a time until brown. Drain on paper towels and keep warm while you fry the remainder.
5  Serve at once with homemade coriander or mint chutney (see pages 142 and 143).

Whole Fish stuffed with Chutney (top) and Fish cooked on Skewers (bottom).

## FISH CURRY FROM HYDERABAD
*Hyderabadi machhali*

½ fresh coconut
2 onions
1 tablespoon fenugreek seeds
2 tablespoons sesame seeds
1 tablespoon cumin seeds
1 lb white fish fillet, such as cod or
    haddock
6 tablespoons oil
salt to taste
1 teaspoon freshly ground black
    pepper
2 teaspoons coriander powder
2 teaspoons ground ginger
2 teaspoons red chili powder
1 teaspoon turmeric powder
6 cloves garlic
½ cup tamarind water (see page 29)

SERVES 6

1 Grate the coconut flesh and chop the onions. Heat a heavy-based pan or iron griddle and "roast" the fenugreek seeds, then the sesame seeds, then the cumin seeds, and finally the coconut and onion, keeping each ingredient separate. Cook, stirring, until browned in each case, then grind each roasted ingredient separately in a spice or coffee grinder.
2 Cut the fish into 2 inch pieces. Heat the oil in a heavy-based pan and add the fish. Cover the pan with a lid and cook the fish gently for 10 minutes, so that it cooks in its own steam.
3 Remove the lid and turn the fish over, then add all the ground spices together with the salt, pepper and remaining spices. Crush the garlic and add it, too.
4 Add the tamarind water and cook for 10–15 minutes more until the fish is tender.
5 Serve with boiled rice, *poppadums* and a hot chutney.

## WHOLE FISH STUFFED WITH CHUTNEY
*Saabut machhali chatni ki*

*I*f you like, wrap the stuffed fish in foil and cook it on a barbecue.

1 flounder, weighing about 1lb
oil for frying
**CHUTNEY**
¾ cup chopped coriander (cilantro)
    or mint
salt to taste
2 fresh hot green chili peppers
1 tablespoon tamarind
4 cloves garlic
**MARINADE**
1 teaspoon red chili powder
salt to taste
⅔ cup plain yogurt
1 tablespoon *garam masala*
    powder
4 cloves garlic

SERVES 4

1 Clean the fish leaving it whole, or ask the fish merchant to do this for you.
2 Make the chutney by grinding all the ingredients together in a food processor.
3 Ease the fillets away from the backbone of the fish, leaving them attached at the sides, to form "pockets." Stuff with the chutney mixture and place in a shallow dish.
4 Prepare the marinade: mix together the first four ingredients. Crush the garlic and add this. Pour over the fish and turn to coat both sides. Leave in a cool place to marinate for 1 hour.
5 Heat the oil in a large deep frying-pan and fry the fish until golden on both sides. Serve on a bed of saffron rice (see page 177).

## ❧ BENGAL ROASTED FISH ❧
*Bengali bhuni machhali*

1½ lb white fish fillet, such as cod or
   haddock
½ lb onions
6 tablespoons oil
2 teaspoons whole *garam masala*
   (see page 29)
5 fresh hot green chili peppers
1 inch piece fresh ginger root
1 cup plain yogurt
salt to taste
1 teaspoon sugar
GARNISH
2 onions
2 tablespoons oil
chopped coriander (cilantro) or
   mint
lemon wedges

SERVES 6

1  Cut the fish into six pieces. Finely chop the onions.
2  Heat the oil in a large frying-pan and fry the onions with the whole *garam masala* for about 5 minutes.
3  Finely chop the chili peppers and ginger and add to the pan with the yogurt and salt. Cook gently for about 5 minutes, or until the mixture has thickened.
4  Add the fish pieces to the pan and cook for about 10 minutes, or until tender, turning once. Stir in the sugar.
5  Slice the onions for garnish finely and fry them in the oil until brown and crisp. Sprinkle over the fish with the coriander or mint and serve with the lemon wedges.

## ❧ FRIED FISH IN BATTER ❧
*Tali machhali*

1 lb white fish fillet, such as cod or
   haddock
1 teaspoon *garam masala* powder
½ teaspoon red chili powder
salt to taste
6 cloves garlic
⅔ cup plain yogurt
1 cup chickpea flour
oil for deep frying

SERVES 6

1  Cut the fish into bite-sized pieces and put on one side.
2  Mix the spices and salt together. Crush the garlic and add to the spices with the yogurt, mixing well.
3  Drop the fish into the spicy yogurt mixture, turning it to coat evenly. Cover and leave in a cool place for 1 hour.
4  Put the flour in a shallow dish. Remove the fish from the marinade and roll each piece in the flour.
5  Heat the oil for deep frying and drop four or five fish pieces into it at a time. When browned, remove with a slotted spoon and drain on paper towels. Keep warm while you fry the remainder.
6  Serve hot with any spicy chutney.

VARIATION Try this slight variation on the above recipe: mix together the spices, crushed garlic, salt and yogurt and beat in the flour to make a smooth batter. Add 1 teaspoon carom seeds and 2 teaspoons mango powder. Dip the pieces of fish into this batter to coat them evenly, then deep fry them in the hot oil.

## STUFFED POMFRET FISH
### Bharva machhali

*T*his party dish comes from Bombay, where pomfret is a popular and common fish.
Substitute porgy or flounder.

1 porgy or flounder, weighing about
   1 lb
4 onions
2 fresh hot green chili peppers
2 scallions
2 tomatoes
2 tablespoons oil
1 teaspoon red chili powder
1 teaspoon cumin powder
chopped coriander (cilantro) or
   mint
salt to taste
oil for deep frying
1 teaspoon turmeric powder
1 tablespoon lemon juice, to serve

SERVES 4

1  Clean the fish leaving it whole, or ask the fish merchant to
do this for you.
2  Finely chop the onions, green chili peppers, scallions and
tomatoes.
3  Heat the oil in a heavy-based pan and brown the onions.
Add the chili peppers, scallions and tomatoes with the chili and
cumin powders, coriander or mint and salt to taste. Cook for a
few minutes, stirring frequently.
4  Ease the fillets away from the backbone of the fish, leaving
them attached at the sides, to form "pockets." Fill these with
the fried stuffing.
5  Heat the oil for deep frying in a pan large enough to take the
fish. Add the turmeric to the oil, then fry the fish, turning once,
to brown both sides.
6  Serve sprinkled with lemon juice, together with some saffron
rice (see page 177) or hot buttered *chappatis.*

## STUFFED EGGS
### Bharwa ande

*I*n this dish, the eggs are curried after they have been stuffed. It tastes good with boiled rice.

2 tablespoons dried shredded
   coconut
2 tablespoons water
6 hard-boiled eggs
1 teaspoon curry powder (see page
   29)
½ teaspoon *garam masala* powder
1 onion
2 tablespoons butter
2 tablespoons tomato paste
salt to taste
½ cup hot water
a few fresh mint leaves, for garnish

SERVES 6

1  Soak the coconut in the 2 tablespoons water.
2  Cut the eggs in half, remove the yolks and mash them with
the curry and *garam masala* powders.
3  Drain the coconut and add to the yolk mixture. Now stuff
this mixture back into the halved egg whites.
4  Chop the onion. Melt the butter in a frying-pan and sauté the
onion for about 5 minutes. Stir in the tomato paste, salt and
hot water and simmer for about 5 minutes.
5  Add the eggs to the sauce and simmer very gently until the
sauce thickens.
6  Transfer to a serving dish and garnish with the mint.

# ❧ Madras Egg Curry ❧
## *Madrasi ande ki kari*

*A* hot curry which tastes best served with boiled rice. Serve a *raita* and *poppadums* with it, too.

2 cloves garlic
1 onion
2 tablespoons oil
½ cup water
1 tablespoon hot curry powder (use
 a commercial one)
1 tablespoon tomato paste
6 hard-boiled eggs
salt to taste
1 tablespoon lemon juice
½ cup coconut milk (see page 28)
1 tablespoon dried shredded
 coconut

SERVES 6

1 Finely slice the garlic and onion. Heat the oil in a frying-pan or wok and cook the garlic and onion for about 5 minutes, stirring frequently.
2 Add the water and simmer for 5 minutes more, then stir in the curry powder and tomato paste and simmer for a further 5 minutes.
3 Cut the eggs in half and add them to the mixture with some salt, the lemon juice and coconut milk. Simmer gently for 10–15 minutes, until the sauce is thick.
4 Serve the curry on a flat dish surrounded by a ring of boiled rice. Sprinkle with the shredded coconut just before serving.

THE BANQUET-STYLE MEALS SERVED TODAY AT THE RAMBAGH PALACE ARE SIMILAR IN SPLENDOR TO THE FEASTS HELD THERE DURING THE HEYDAY OF THE MAHARAJAS. HERE MANJU'S DAUGHTERS, SHIVINA AND RUPINA, SAMPLE THE DELICACIES ON OFFER.

# EGG AND POTATO CURRY
## *Ande ke aloo*

*S*erve this dish for a light lunch.

4 potatoes
1 onion
2 cloves garlic
1 fresh hot green chili pepper
3 tablespoons oil
1 teaspoon cumin seeds
½ cup water
1 teaspoon turmeric powder
1 teaspoon ground ginger
2 tablespoons coriander powder
salt to taste
6 eggs
dash of paprika

SERVES 6

1 Cook the potatoes in their skins in boiling water until just tender. Peel them and cut into thick slices. Put on one side.
2 Finely slice the onion, garlic and green chili pepper. Heat the oil in a frying-pan or wok and add the cumin seeds, then the onion, garlic and green chili pepper. Cook, stirring, for about 5 minutes, then add the water with the rest of the spices, the salt and potatoes. Mix well and simmer for a minute or two.
3 Break the eggs over the mixture in the pan and sprinkle with paprika. Leave on the heat until the eggs are cooked, but do not stir the dish during cooking. Serve at once.

## ❧ EGGS IN DAL ❧
### *Ande ki dal*

½ lb (1⅓ cups) split yellow mung
    beans (*moong dal*)
½ lb pigeon peas (*toor dal*)
3 cups water (approx)
1 teaspoon turmeric powder
salt to taste
5 onions
1 fresh hot green chili pepper
2 tablespoons oil
1 teaspoon cumin seeds
small bunch coriander (cilantro)
    leaves, chopped
4 eggs

SERVES 6

1  Wash the beans and peas and put them in a saucepan with the water, turmeric and salt. Simmer gently until they are tender – this will take 30–45 minutes or 15 minutes in a pressure cooker.
2  Slice two of the onions and finely chop the chili pepper. Heat the oil in a large pan and add the cumin seeds and the onion. Cook, stirring, for a minute or two, then add the green chili pepper and chopped coriander. Finely chop the remaining onions and add them too.
3  Add the cooked *dal* to this mixture and let it all simmer for about 10 minutes.
4  Beat the eggs and gradually add to the *dal*, stirring all the time. Simmer on a low heat for 5 minutes more, then serve.

## ❧ PARSI OMELETTE ❧
### *Parsee aamlate*

4 onions
6 tablespoons oil
6 eggs plus 6 egg yolks
1 green pepper
6 cloves garlic
small bunch coriander (cilantro)
    leaves, chopped
1 tablespoon sugar
½ cup tamarind water (see page 29)
salt to taste

SERVES 6

1  Chop the onions. Heat the oil in a large frying-pan and add the onions. Cook, stirring occasionally, for about 10 minutes over medium heat, until soft.
2  Meanwhile, break the 6 eggs into a bowl, add the egg yolks and beat them together. Finely chop the green pepper and garlic and add to the eggs with all the remaining ingredients.
3  Pour the egg mixture onto the onion and simmer gently until the underneath of the egg is set.
4  Hold the pan under the broiler to cook the top of the eggs. As soon as they have set, slide the omelette onto a flat dish, cut into six wedges and serve with tomato ketchup and hot buttered toast.

## ❧ SPICY SCRAMBLED EGGS ❧
### *Ande ki bhurji*

2 onions
2 tablespoons butter
6 eggs
1 fresh hot green chili pepper,
    chopped or 1 teaspoon red chili
    powder
salt to taste
1 tablespoon chopped coriander
    (cilantro)

SERVES 6

1  Slice the onions and fry them in the butter until soft.
2  Beat the eggs and finely chop the chili pepper, if using. Then mix the eggs and chili pepper or chili powder together with some salt and the coriander.
3  Add the egg mixture to the onions and cook, stirring now and again, until the eggs are just set. Serve at once.

## ⁕ SPICED EGG CURRY ⁕
*Hyderabadi dum ke ande*

*T*his is a dish from Hyderabad – my husband's town. Hyderabadis love their food and both men and women like to cook. Their dishes are somewhat exotic, with a rich flavor.

2 tablespoons poppy seeds
4 onions
4 cloves garlic
1 inch piece fresh ginger root
12 blanched almonds
6 tablespoons oil
1 teaspoon turmeric powder
1 teaspoon red chili powder
salt to taste
1½ cups plain yogurt
6 eggs
a few coriander (cilantro) leaves,
    for garnish

SERVES 6

1  Roast the poppy seeds in a dry frying-pan over medium heat for a few minutes.
2  Chop the onions, garlic and ginger. Peel and slice the almonds.
3  Heat the oil in a frying-pan and add the onions, garlic, ginger, almonds and poppy seeds. Cook, stirring, until the onions are soft and golden.
4  Remove the mixture from the pan with a slotted spoon, draining it well, then grind it to a paste in a food processor.
5  Heat the oil remaining in the pan again and return the paste to it with turmeric and chili powders and salt. Stir, then add the yogurt and let the mixture simmer gently for 10 minutes.
6  Break the eggs one-by-one into the bubbling gravy, cover the pan, reduce the heat and simmer for about 5 minutes.
7  Carefully transfer the curry to an ovenproof casserole and bake it in an oven heated to 350° for about 20 minutes. Serve garnished with the coriander.

## ⁕ COCONUT EGG CURRY ⁕
*Nariyal ande ka saalan*

*T*his dish is cooked with a delicious coconut curry sauce. Serve it with rice.

2 cloves garlic
1 onion
2 tablespoons oil
1 teaspoon whole *garam masala*
    (see page 29)
½ cup water
1 teaspoon turmeric powder
1 teaspoon cumin powder
1 teaspoon red chili powder
1 teaspoon ground ginger
2 cups coconut milk (see page 28)
6 hard-boiled eggs
salt to taste
1 tablespoon lemon juice
a few coriander (cilantro) leaves,
    for garnish

SERVES 6

1  Crush the garlic and chop the onion. Heat the oil in a frying-pan or wok and add the *garam masala*, then the garlic and onion.
2  Fry for about 5 minutes, stirring, then add the water and let the mixture simmer for 5 minutes more.
3  Add all the spices and simmer for another 5 minutes, then add the coconut milk and cook over medium heat until the sauce thickens.
4  Cut the eggs in half and add them to the sauce with the salt and lemon juice. Cover the pan and let the mixture simmer very gently for 5–10 minutes more.
5  Transfer to a serving dish and garnish with the coriander.

# VEGETABLE DISHES

Vegetables are an essential part of the daily diet in Indian cuisine and they are prepared with all sorts of different spices to give a rich variety of tastes. Yogurt and coconut milk are often added to vegetable dishes to vary the flavor still further. Even non-vegetarians will often eat a meal excluding meat and fish and comprising only vegetable curries, served, of course, with the usual accompaniments of a rice dish or bread, *dal, raita* and chutney and pickles. Try serving such a vegetarian feast sometimes, choosing two or three different vegetable curries from this chapter and perhaps one of the pancake recipes from Chapter One.

All vegetables used in India are fresh – frozen vegetables are never considered, even for convenience, although I do use some when I am in Britain. Thus we use only those vegetables in season. In the winter this means cauliflower, carrots and peas in particular, while in the summer there are potatoes, onions, beans and tomatoes to add to the repertoire. Some vegetables are in season throughout the year – all the leafy vegetables such as spinach, for example, and also okra and eggplant.

Fresh vegetables should be included in the meals every day – they help to promote a healthy skin and a good digestion.

## WHOLE SPICE VEGETABLE CURRY
### Sabut masale ki tarkaari

*T*his is a very colorful vegetable curry and makes a good accompaniment to a curry meal. It is a popular dish in Rajasthan.

4 potatoes
1 small cauliflower
1¼ cups green peas (use frozen ones)
2 cloves garlic
1 onion
1 inch piece fresh ginger root
¼ cup oil
1 teaspoon cumin seeds
½ cup hot water
1 teaspoon turmeric powder
2 teaspoons coriander seeds
1 teaspoon *garam masala* powder
salt to taste
4 teaspoons lemon juice
2 dried hot red chili peppers
1 teaspoon roasted cumin seed powder (see page 28), to garnish

SERVES 6

1 Peel the potatoes and cut into cubes. Soak in cold water for about 30 minutes. Divide the cauliflower into florets and soak these in warm salted water. Soak the peas in hot water.
2 Finely slice the garlic, onion and ginger, then heat the oil in a frying-pan or wok and add these three ingredients together with the cumin seeds.
3 Drain the potatoes, cauliflower and peas and add to the frying-pan with the hot water. Stir, then add the spices, salt and lemon juice. Crush the chili peppers and add them too.
4 Cover the pan and cook very gently for 15–20 minutes, stirring occasionally to prevent the vegetables burning. Keep simmering until the vegetables are tender, crisp and dry.
5 Transfer to a serving dish and sprinkle with the roasted cumin seed powder.

W**HOLE** S**PICE** V**EGETABLE** C**URRY WITH** *CHAPPATIS.*

## ❧ RAILWAY STATION POTATO CURRY ❧
### *Station waale aloo*

*T*his dish is so-called because you will always find it being cooked and sold at railway stations!
It is usually eaten with hot *pooris* and it is very easy to make as all the ingredients are just
mixed together and cooked.

3 tablespoons oil
1 teaspoon cumin seeds
1 lb potatoes
1 teaspoon turmeric powder
1 teaspoon red chili powder
2 teaspoons coriander powder
1 teaspoon mango powder
1 teaspoon *garam masala* powder
salt to taste
2 tomatoes
2 cups water (approx)

SERVES 6

1  Heat the oil in a heavy-based pan over medium heat. Add the
cumin seeds.
2  Peel the potatoes and cut into small cubes. Add to the pan
with all the spices and salt to taste. Chop the tomatoes and add
these, with water to cover.
3  Cook until the potatoes are tender and most of the liquid
has been absorbed, stirring from time to time to prevent the
mixture sticking. Serve hot.

## ❧ PICKLED POTATO CURRY ❧
### *Aachaari aloo*

*A* favorite dish from Rajasthan, this is usually served at special parties. Serve it with *pooris* – the dish
itself is quite dry.

1 large onion
6 large potatoes
$\frac{1}{4}$ cup oil
1 teaspoon nigella seeds
1 teaspoon cumin seeds
1 teaspoon anise seeds
6 cloves garlic
1 teaspoon red chili powder
1 teaspoon turmeric powder
salt to taste
3 dried hot red chili peppers
2 fresh hot green chili peppers
1 teaspoon mango powder or 1
    tablespoon lemon juice

SERVES 6

1  Finely slice the onion and cut the potatoes into cubes.
2  Heat the oil in a frying-pan or wok and add all the seeds.
Stir, then add the onion and cook, stirring, for about 5 minutes.
3  Add the potatoes and continue cooking for 10–15 minutes
more, stirring frequently.
4  Add the whole cloves of garlic with the chili and turmeric
powders and the salt. Crumble in the red chili peppers.
Finely slice the green chili peppers and add them with the
mango powder or lemon juice. Continue cooking over low-to-
medium heat, stirring frequently until the potatoes are tender.

NOTE  The potatoes should be quite crisp in the finished dish –
not soft and mushy. If the mixture becomes too dry during
cooking so that the potatoes begin to stick to the pan, add
some hot water, but keep stirring all the time.

# POTATO AND YOGURT CURRY
### Dahi ke aloo

*P*otato and yogurt curry has a somewhat sour flavor and tastes best if it is served with a rice pullao or fried rice.

1 lb potatoes
2 tablespoons oil
1 teaspoon cumin seeds
2 onions
2 cloves garlic
1 inch piece fresh ginger root
a pinch of asafetida
1 cup plain yogurt
1 teaspoon turmeric powder
1 teaspoon red chili powder
2 teaspoons coriander powder
1 teaspoon *garam masala* powder
salt to taste
1 cup water
chopped coriander (cilantro), for
   garnish

SERVES 6

1  Cook the potatoes in boiling water until just tender, drain and cut into small cubes.
2  Heat the oil in a heavy-based pan and add the cumin seeds. Finely chop the onions, garlic and ginger and add to the pan with the asafetida. Fry, stirring, for 5 minutes.
3  Add the yogurt, all the remaining spices and salt. Stir well, then add the potatoes and mix everything together thoroughly.
4  Add the water and simmer gently for about 10 minutes, stirring from time to time.
5  Serve garnished with the chopped coriander.

# CURRIED MASHED POTATOES
### Aloo bharta

*A*loo bharta is so quick and easy to make. You can use it as a filling for many dishes such as *aloo parantha, aloo bonda,* stuffed cabbage leaves, stuffed peppers, stuffed tomatoes and so on. On its own, serve it with rice, *dal* and coriander chutney (see page 142), a *raita* and *poppadums.* If you are really in a hurry use instant mashed potatoes instead of boiling the potatoes.

1 lb potatoes
2 tablespoons oil
1 teaspoon cumin seeds
1 fresh hot green chili pepper
1 onion
1 teaspoon red chili powder
1 teaspoon *garam masala* powder
salt to taste
1 teaspoon bottled mango pickle
   (optional)
1 teaspoon mango powder
1 teaspoon lemon juice
coriander (cilantro) leaves, for
   garnish

SERVES 6

1  Cook the potatoes in boiling water until tender. Drain and mash them.
2  Heat the oil in a heavy-based frying-pan and add the cumin seeds, then the potatoes. Stir together.
3  Finely chop the green chili pepper and onion and add to the pan with all the other ingredients. Stir well to mix, then cover and cook gently for about 5 minutes, stirring from time to time.
4  Serve garnished with coriander leaves.

# POTATO AND SPINACH CURRY
### *Aloo paalak*

¾ lb potatoes
3 tablespoons oil
1 teaspoon cumin seeds
a pinch of asafetida
2 onions
2 cloves garlic
2 tomatoes
1 teaspoon turmeric powder
1 teaspoon red chili powder
1 teaspoon coriander powder
salt to taste
10-oz package frozen, chopped
    spinach, thawed and well drained
1 inch piece fresh ginger root
1 teaspoon *garam masala* powder
1 tablespoon lemon juice

**SERVES 6**

**1** Cook the potatoes in boiling water until just tender. Drain and cut into small cubes.

**2** Heat the oil in a frying-pan or wok over medium heat and add the cumin seeds and asafetida. Finely slice the onions and garlic and add them to the pan. Cook for about 5 minutes, stirring occasionally.

**3** Chop the tomatoes and add them to the pan with the turmeric, chili and coriander powders. Add salt to taste, stir, then cook for 5 more minutes.

**4** Add the potatoes and spinach and mix well. Grind the ginger in a pestle and mortar or grate it finely and add it to the pan with the *garam masala* powder and lemon juice. Serve hot.

**P**OTATO AND **S**PINACH **C**URRY (LEFT) AND **C**URRIED **P**OTATOES, **O**KRA AND **G**REEN **P**EPPERS (RIGHT)

## ❧ GUJRATI POTATO CURRY ❧
### *Gujrati aloo*

*P*eople from Gujrat like to add sugar to their curries. Also, many Gujrati Jains do not eat onion or garlic, so this vegetable dish contains neither. It is particularly good with *pooris*.

1 tablespoon tamarind
½ cup hot water
1 tablespoon brown sugar
1 lb potatoes
¼ cup oil
1 teaspoon mustard seeds
1 teaspoon turmeric powder
1 teaspoon red chili powder
2 teaspoons coriander powder
salt to taste
1 fresh hot green chili pepper
2 tablespoons dried shredded
   coconut

**SERVES 6**

1  Soak the tamarind in the hot water for 1 hour. Then squeeze the pulp and strain the liquid through a fine sieve. Add the brown sugar to the tamarind water and put on one side.
2  Cut the potatoes into cubes. Heat the oil in a frying-pan or wok and add the mustard seeds and potatoes. Fry for 5 minutes, stirring.
3  Add all the remaining spices and some salt. Stir to mix, then cover and cook over a gentle heat for 10–15 minutes, stirring frequently.
4  Slice the green chili pepper finely and add with the tamarind water and coconut. Cover and cook until the potatoes are tender.

## ❧ WHITE POTATO CURRY ❧
### *Safed aloo ki tarkaari*

*T*his is one of the dishes that is always prepared in the Royal Palace of Jaipur on *sharad poonam* day in October. All the dishes are white in color so as to resemble the moonlight. My granny used to tell me how in her day the ladies would look at the reflection of the full moon in a deep silver dish filled with water and then they would drink the water. This was supposed to lengthen the life of the King. Try this curry with a rice pullao.

6 potatoes
10 cloves garlic
4 onions
1 inch piece fresh ginger root
2 tablespoons poppy seeds
¼ cup melted *ghee*
1 teaspoon whole *garam masala*
   (see page 29)
3 bay leaves
2 teaspoons coriander seeds
salt to taste
4 dried hot red chili peppers
1 cup plain yogurt
1 cup hot water
1 cup milk

**SERVES 6**

1  Cut the potatoes into chunks. Mince the garlic, onions and ginger together in a food processor.
2  Roast the poppy seeds in a small, dry frying-pan over a medium heat. Grind them in a spice or coffee grinder.
3  Heat the *ghee* in a heavy-based pan. Add the whole *garam masala* and the bay leaves. Fry for 1–2 minutes, stirring, then add all the other ingredients, except for the milk.
4  Stir everything together thoroughly, and cook over a low heat for 20–25 minutes, until the potatoes are just tender.
5  Add the milk and simmer for 5 minutes more.

## ❧ POTATO CURRY FOR FASTING ❧
*ShivRatri ke aloo*

*I* always prepare this curry on *Shivratri* day – that is Lord Shiva's birthday, which is a day of fasting. Only one meal may be eaten and it must not contain sea salt or any kind of cereal. Consequently we make *pooris* out of water chestnut flour on fasting days, to serve with this curry.

½ lb potatoes
3 fresh hot green chili peppers
3 tablespoons melted *ghee*
1 cup plain yogurt
1 teaspoon powdered rock salt

SERVES 6

1 Cook the potatoes in boiling water until tender. Drain and cut into cubes.
2 Grind the chili peppers in a pestle and mortar or coffee grinder. Heat the *ghee* in a frying-pan or wok and add the green chilies. Cook for a few minutes, stirring.
3 Stir in the yogurt, potatoes and rock salt. Simmer over a low heat until most of the moisture has been absorbed. Serve the curry hot.

NOTE You can substitute ordinary salt for rock salt if you are not fasting!

## ❧ CURRIED POTATOES, OKRA AND GREEN PEPPERS ❧
*Sindhi sabzi*

*I* got this recipe from my friend, Janaki, who lives in Jakarta, after she had served it at a ladies' lunch one day. The vegetables are crisply fried – no water is added during cooking. To make it look attractive and to ensure evenness of cooking, cut the vegetables into uniform-length strips.

2 onions
4 cloves garlic
3 potatoes
4 small green peppers
1 inch piece fresh ginger root
6 oz okra
5 tablespoons oil
1 teaspoon cumin seeds
1 teaspoon sesame seeds
1 teaspoon turmeric powder
1 teaspoon red chili powder
2 teaspoons coriander powder
salt to taste
2 teaspoons *garam masala* powder
2 tablespoons lemon juice
2 teaspoons roasted cumin seed
    powder (see page 28)

SERVES 6

1 Slice the onions and garlic. Peel the potatoes and slice into sticks. Slice the peppers into sticks and slice the ginger finely. Wash the okra and leave them whole.
2 Heat the oil in a heavy-based frying-pan or wok. Add the cumin and sesame seeds. When they "pop," add the onions and garlic and fry, stirring, over medium heat for about 5 minutes.
3 Add the potatoes, green peppers, okra and ginger, and fry over low heat for 15–20 minutes. Keep the pan covered, but stir occasionally to prevent the vegetables sticking.
4 Add the turmeric, red chili and coriander powders together with the salt. Stir well, then fry for 10 minutes more, stirring frequently.
5 When the vegetables are all tender, add the *garam masala* powder and lemon juice.
6 Serve the vegetable curry sprinkled with the roasted cumin seed powder.

## ❧ CURRIED MASHED EGGPLANT ❧
### *Baigan ka bharta*

*T*his is a popular dish in Rajasthan and Punjab, where it is usually eaten with hot buttered *chappatis*. Yogurt can be added to the base mixture to turn it into a *raita* or a party dip.

4 large eggplants
2 cloves garlic
1 inch piece fresh ginger root
2 onions
2 tomatoes
1 fresh hot green chili pepper
2 tablespoons oil
1 teaspoon cumin seeds
2 teaspoons coriander powder
1 teaspoon red chili powder
1 teaspoon *garam masala* powder
1 teaspoon mango powder
salt to taste
2 teaspoons lemon juice
chopped coriander (cilantro) or
   mint, for garnish

SERVES 6

1 Pierce each eggplant on a fork and rotate over a gas flame until the skin starts to shrivel. Peel off the skins and put the flesh into a bowl. Alternatively, put the eggplants into a saucepan, cover with cold water, bring to a boil and simmer for a few minutes. Drain and peel off the skins. Mash the eggplant flesh with a fork.
2 Finely slice the garlic and ginger and finely chop the onions, tomatoes and green chili pepper.
3 Heat the oil in a frying-pan or wok and add the cumin seeds, garlic and ginger. Cook for 1–2 minutes, stirring, then add the onions and tomatoes. Cook for 5 minutes over medium heat, stirring, then add the green chili pepper and all the spices. Add some salt, and let the mixture simmer gently for 5 minutes.
4 Add the mashed egplant. Mix well and heat through.
5 Add the lemon juice, transfer to a serving dish and garnish with the chopped coriander or mint.

## ❧ STUFFED OKRA ❧
### *Bharwa bhindi*

*F*resh okra can be bought in many supermarkets as well as Indian grocery shops. This tasty curry is good with hot *chappatis*.

¾ lb okra
1 teaspoon turmeric powder
1 teaspoon red chili powder
1 tablespoon coriander powder
1 teaspoon mango powder
1 teaspoon *garam masala* powder
salt to taste
3 tablespoons oil
2 tomatoes

SERVES 6

1 Wash the okra and wipe dry on paper towels. Cut off the tops and bottoms from the okra, then slit them along their lengths, without cutting all the way through.
2 Mix all the spices and salt together and sprinkle this mixture into the insides of the okra.
3 Heat the oil in a frying-pan or wok and add the okra. Chop the tomatoes finely and add to the pan. Cover and cook gently for 20–30 minutes until the okra are tender. Serve at once.

## CURRIED EGGPLANT
### Baghare baigan

*T*his is a specialty of Hyderabad, and it tastes good with *Biryani* and a *raita* (see pages 134–137). It has a nutty sweet and sour taste.

2 tablespoons dried shredded
    coconut
½ cup water
6 small eggplants
5 tablespoons oil
2 onions
1 tablespoon coriander seeds
3 dried hot red chili peppers
4 cloves garlic
½ cup tamarind water (see page 29)
1 teaspoon turmeric powder
salt to taste
1 tablespoon brown sugar
2 tablespoons roasted sesame seeds
1 tablespoon melted *ghee*
1 teaspoon mustard seeds
1 fresh hot green chili pepper

SERVES 6

1  Put the coconut in a bowl and add water. Leave to soak.
2  Cut the eggplants into quarters lengthwise, but do not separate them from the stalk. Heat 3 tablespoons oil in a frying-pan or wok and fry the eggplants on a low heat, turning them frequently. Leave them to cook gently.
3  Chop the onions and cook them in the remainder of the oil in another pan with the coriander seeds and red chili peppers. When the onions are browned, remove from the pan with a slotted spoon and put into a blender or food processor with the drained soaked coconut and garlic. Reduce to a purée.
4  Stir the tamarind water and turmeric powder into the purée, then tip into a saucepan and bring to a boil, stirring. Add the salt and sugar. Grind the roasted sesame seeds and add them, too. Lower the heat and cook, covered, for 5–10 minutes, until the sauce is thick.
5  Heat the *ghee* in a small pan and add the mustard seeds. Fry for 1 minute. Finely slice the green chili pepper and add to the pan. Cook for 1 minute more, stirring.
6  Put the eggplants into a serving dish, pour the sauce over them and then pour the mustard seed *baghar* over the top. Serve at once.

## DRY GREEN BEAN CURRY
### Sookhe beans

*T*his is a popular dish in South India where it is eaten with rice and *sambhar* (see page 29). It has a bland rather than very spicy taste, and may be eaten hot or cold.

½ lb green beans
2 fresh hot green chili peppers
2 tablespoons oil
1 teaspoon mustard seeds
½ teaspoon split yellow chickpeas
    (*chana dal*)
a few curry leaves
8 cloves garlic
salt to taste
½ cup water
2 tablespoons dried shredded
    coconut

SERVES 6

1  Cut the beans into small pieces. Wash them, drain well and put on one side. Slice the chili peppers.
2  Heat the oil in a frying-pan or wok and add the mustard seeds, split yellow chickpeas and curry leaves. Cook for 1 minute, then add the beans and chili peppers together with all the remaining ingredients (leave the garlic whole), except the coconut.
3  Cook, covered, stirring from time to time and adding more water if necessary, to prevent the beans burning or sticking. When the beans are tender, transfer to a serving dish and sprinkle with the coconut.

## ❧ CURRIED CABBAGE ❧
### *Masala bundgobhi*

*E*ven those who do not like cabbage will like this dish. Serve it with rice, *dal* or *chappatis*.

1 medium-sized cabbage
3 onions
6 cloves garlic
1 inch piece fresh ginger root
4 tomatoes
5 tablespoons oil
1 teaspoon mustard seeds
1 teaspoon turmeric powder
1 teaspoon red chili powder
2 teaspoons coriander powder
2 teaspoons *garam masala* powder
1 teaspoon mango powder
salt to taste
1 tablespoon raisins – use more raisins
handful of potato chips

SERVES 6

**1** Shred the cabbage finely and wash it in warm, salted water. Drain. Finely slice the onions, garlic and ginger and chop the tomatoes.
**2** Heat the oil in a frying-pan or wok and add the mustard seeds, then the onions, garlic and ginger. Cook over a low heat for about 10 minutes, stirring frequently.
**3** Add the chopped tomatoes and all the spices together with the salt. Simmer for 5 minutes more, then add the cabbage and mix well.
**4** Cover the pan and cook gently for 15–20 minutes. Add the raisins and stir. Increase the heat if necessary and cook until all the liquid evaporates.
**5** Turn into a serving dish. Crush the potato chips roughly and sprinkle them on top.

THE MYSTICAL ELEMENT IS AN IMPORTANT ASPECT OF INDIAN LIFE – THE MASK HANGING FROM THIS FRUIT AND VEGETABLE STALL IS INTENDED TO WARD OFF EVIL SPIRITS.

## SPICY CAULIFLOWER CURRY
*Gobi masala*

*S*erve this at lunchtime with *pooris*.

1 large cauliflower
1 teaspoon coriander seeds
2 tablespoons oil
1 teaspoon mustard seeds
1 tablespoon chickpea flour
salt to taste
½ cup tamarind water (see page 29)
1 teaspoon red chili powder
1 teaspoon turmeric powder
1 cup coconut milk (see page 28)
½ cup hot water (approx – see recipe)
coriander (cilantro) leaves, for garnish

**SERVES 6**

**1** Cut the cauliflower into florets. Coarsely crush the coriander seeds in a pestle and mortar, or with the back of a wooden spoon.
**2** Heat the oil in a frying-pan or wok and add the mustard seeds. Mix all the other ingredients, except the water, together and add to the pan. Cover and cook on a very low heat until the cauliflower is tender, adding the water to the pan if the mixture becomes too dry.
**3** Serve garnished with the coriander leaves.

## CURRIED VEGETABLE PIE
*Sabzi ki pie*

*H*ere is my version of a vegetable pie – good for lunch with warmed bread rolls.

2 onions
6 oz green beans
4 carrots
1 tomato
1 tablespoon oil
1 teaspoon cumin seeds
1¼ cups frozen peas, thawed
1 teaspoon red chili powder
½ teaspoon turmeric powder
salt to taste
½ cup water
2 tablespoons butter
3 tablespoons all-purpose flour
1 cup milk
1 tablespoon grated Cheddar cheese
chopped coriander (cilantro), for garnish

**SERVES 6**

**1** Chop the onions, green beans, carrots and tomato.
**2** Heat the oil in a frying-pan or wok and add the cumin seeds and onions. Fry, stirring, until the onions are beginning to brown.
**3** Add the beans, carrots, tomato and peas together with the red chili and turmeric powders and salt to taste. Stir together, then add the water. Cook over gentle heat, stirring occasionally, until the vegetables are tender and the moisture has been absorbed.
**4** While the curry is cooking, make a white sauce: melt the butter in a saucepan and stir in the flour. Add the milk gradually, stirring all the time to keep the sauce smooth. When it has thickened, add salt to taste and remove from the heat.
**5** Grease a shallow round baking dish and spoon the vegetable curry into it. Pour the white sauce evenly over the vegetables, then sprinkle with the grated cheese.
**6** Bake in an oven heated to 350° for 10–20 minutes, until the cheese is melted and bubbling. Sprinkle with the chopped coriander.

## SPICY MIXED VEGETABLE CURRY
*Pau bhaji*

*Pau bhaji* is a popular Bombay "roadside" snack, sold mainly in the evenings at small sidewalk stalls. Around midnight the poor and elite rub shoulders by these stalls waiting to get a portion of *pau bhaji* served on toasted buns or bread rolls. Traditionally the dish is cooked on a large iron griddle over hot charcoal, but it can be cooked in a frying-pan or wok.

$1\frac{1}{3}$ cups cubed potatoes
1 cup diced green beans
1 cup diced carrots
$\frac{3}{4}$ cup frozen peas or whole kernel corn
2 onions
4 tomatoes
6 cloves garlic
5 tablespoons melted *ghee*
1 teaspoon turmeric powder
1 teaspoon red chili powder
1 teaspoon *garam masala* powder
salt to taste
6 bread rolls and butter, to serve

SERVES 6

1  Cook the potatoes, beans and carrots with the peas or corn in boiling water until tender. Drain well.
2  Chop the onions and tomatoes and crush the garlic. Heat the *ghee* in a frying-pan or wok and cook the onions and garlic for 5 minutes, stirring. Add the mixed cooked vegetables, then stir and "mash" them together with the back of a wooden spoon.
3  Add the tomatoes and spices together with some salt. Keep stirring until the vegetables and spices are well blended.
4  Heat the rolls, spread them lightly with butter and serve with a portion of this dish.

NOTE  You could use a package of frozen mixed vegetables instead of fresh for convenience.

## CURRIED MOCK FISH COCOYAM
*Arvi ki machi*

*Cocoyam* or *arvi* is a somewhat sticky-textured root vegetable, from the yam and sweet potato family. It can generally be bought in Indian grocery shops, but if it is not available, use potatoes instead. Fried *arvi* tastes like fried fish – hence the name of the dish. Try it with rice, *dal* and coriander chutney (see page 142).

1 lb *arvis*
2 teaspoons turmeric powder
2 teaspoons red chili powder
4 teaspoons coriander powder
1 teaspoon mango powder
salt to taste
$\frac{1}{4}$ cup oil
1 teaspoon carom seeds
2 tablespoons lemon juice
1 fresh hot green chili pepper
coriander (cilantro) leaves

SERVES 6

1  Peel the *arvis* and cook them in boiling water until tender. Drain and cool, then press each one flat between your palms. Take care not to let them break; they should remain whole.
2  Mix the spices and salt together and sprinkle evenly over the *arvis*, rubbing the mixture gently into the vegetables.
3  Heat the oil in a frying-pan or wok and add the carom seeds. Add the spiced *arvis* to the pan, but take care as they will splatter. Cook them, turning, until they are crisp on the outside.
4  Place on a serving dish and sprinkle with lemon juice. Chop the green chili pepper finely and garnish the dish with this and the coriander leaves.

**C**LOCKWISE FROM TOP: SPICY MACARONI AND PEAS, RED KIDNEY BEAN CURRY AND MUSHROOM CURRY SERVED ON TOAST.

## ❦ RED KIDNEY BEAN CURRY ❦
### Raajma

*T*his is a very popular, thick curry eaten mainly in Punjab with boiled rice.

1 lb (2¼ cups) dried red kidney
    beans (*raajma*)
5 cups water
salt
2 onions
4 cloves garlic
1 inch piece fresh ginger root
¼ cup oil
1 teaspoon cumin seeds
½ teaspoon mustard seeds
½ teaspoon nigella seeds
1 fresh hot green chili pepper
1 teaspoon turmeric powder
1 teaspoon red chili powder
2 teaspoons coriander powder
2 teaspoons *garam masala* powder
3 tablespoons plain yogurt
6 tomatoes
1 cup hot water (approx)
a few coriander (cilantro) leaves, for
    garnish

**SERVES 6**

1 Soak the kidney beans in cold water to cover overnight. The next day, drain them and put in a large saucepan with the 5 cups water and 1 teaspoon salt. Bring to a boil, then simmer until the beans are tender. Drain and put on one side.
2 Finely chop the onions and slice the garlic and ginger. Heat the oil in a frying-pan or wok and add the cumin, mustard and nigella seeds. Add the onions, garlic and ginger and stir everything together.
3 Cook for a few minutes, then finely chop the green chili pepper and add with the remaining spices. Mix well and stir in salt to taste and the yogurt. Chop the tomatoes and add these too.
4 Let the mixture simmer gently for about 10 minutes, adding a little hot water if it seems too thick or is sticking to the pan. Simmer for 5 minutes more.
5 Add the kidney beans and let them heat through, then spoon the mixture into a serving dish and garnish with the coriander leaves.

## ❦ CURRIED CARROTS AND PEAS ❦
### Gajjar aur matar ki sabzi

*A* tasty colorful dish – good with rice, *dal* and *raita*. You can use a can of carrots rather than fresh if you prefer.

½ lb carrots
1 onion
2 cloves garlic
2 tablespoons oil
1 teaspoon cumin seeds
1¼ cups frozen, fresh shelled or
    canned peas
1 teaspoon turmeric powder
1 teaspoon red chili powder
1 teaspoon coriander powder
1 teaspoon *garam masala* powder
salt to taste
1 tablespoon lemon juice
1 cup hot water
1 teaspoon dried mint

**SERVES 6**

1 Slice the carrots, onion and garlic.
2 Heat the oil in a frying-pan or wok and add the cumin seeds with the onion and garlic. Cook, stirring for about 5 minutes, or until the onion has softened.
3 Add the carrots and peas together with all the spices, salt and lemon juice. Pour the hot water into the pan, stir, then cover and simmer very gently until the vegetables are tender and the water has been absorbed.
4 Serve hot with the dried mint sprinkled on top.

# CHICKPEA AND POTATO CURRY
## Kabli chane

*T*his is a hot, dry tangy curry which goes well with *bhaturas*, *pooris* or pita bread.

1 lb (2¼ cups) chickpeas
5 cups water
1 teaspoon baking soda
salt
6 large tomatoes, chopped
3 onions
4 cloves garlic
1 inch piece fresh ginger root
¼ cup oil
1 teaspoon cumin seeds
1 teaspoon red chili powder
1 teaspoon turmeric powder
2 teaspoons coriander powder
1 teaspoon *garam masala* powder
1 tablespoon mango powder
**GARNISH**
4 potatoes
1 onion
1 tomato
2 fresh hot green chili peppers
lemon wedges
2 teaspoons roasted cumin seed
    powder (see page 28)
small bunch coriander (cilantro),
    chopped

**SERVES 6**

1 Soak the chickpeas overnight in cold water to cover. Drain them and put into a saucepan with the 5 cups water, soda and 1 teaspoon salt. Bring to a boil, then simmer gently until the chickpeas are tender. Drain and put on one side. Chop the tomatoes and put on one side.
2 Grate the onions, and crush the garlic and ginger together in a pestle and mortar (or mince them all together in a food processor).
3 Heat the oil in a frying-pan or wok and add the cumin seeds, together with the onions, garlic and ginger. Cook gently for about 10 minutes, then add all the spices and some salt.
4 Add the tomatoes to the pan, stir everything together and simmer for about 10 minutes.
5 Meanwhile, prepare the garnish: boil the potatoes and cut into cubes. Thinly slice the onion and tomato and cut the chili peppers into quarters lengthwise.
6 Add the chickpeas to the curry and let them heat through. Spoon the mixture into a flat dish and surround with the onion and tomato slices. Put the chili peppers and lemon wedges down the center and the cubed potatoes on either side on top of the curry. Sprinkle with the cumin powder and chopped coriander.

# MUSHROOM CURRY
## Khumbi or Cgucchi ki sabzi

*M*ushroom curry is quick to make and the curry adds flavor to the mushrooms. Try it with rice or bread, or on a slice of toast. In India, mushrooms are seasonal and may be black or white in color; however, button mushrooms are the best sort to use for this curry.

½ lb mushrooms
2 onions
6 cloves garlic
3 tablespoons oil
1 teaspoon turmeric powder
1 teaspoon red chili powder
salt to taste
2 tomatoes

**SERVES 6**

1 Wash the mushrooms under cold running water. Dry on paper towels and slice. Chop the onions and garlic.
2 Heat the oil and fry the onions gently until they are soft. Add the garlic, turmeric and chili powders and some salt. Stir everything together and cook for a minute or two.
3 Chop the tomatoes and add them to the pan with the mushrooms. Stir, then cook on a very low heat until the mushrooms are tender. Serve at once.

## ❧ CLUSTER BEAN CURRY ❧
### *Shahi guar ki phali*

*C*luster beans are very popular in Rajasthan and are usually eaten with *chappatis* and red chili chutney. They are available elsewhere, fresh or dried, in Indian grocery stores. If you can't get them, use green beans instead.

3 tablespoons oil
1 teaspoon cumin seeds
5 cloves garlic
2 onions
1 cup plain yogurt
1 teaspoon turmeric powder
1 teaspoon red chili powder
2 teaspoons coriander powder
2 teaspoons *garam masala* powder
1 teaspoon mango powder
1 lb cluster beans
salt to taste
1 inch piece fresh ginger root
1 cup hot water
½ cup heavy cream

SERVES 6

1  Heat the oil in a frying-pan or wok and add the cumin seeds. Crush two of the cloves of garlic and slice the onions. Add both of these to the pan. Cook, stirring, over medium heat for about 5 minutes until the onions are soft.
2  Mix the yogurt with all the spices and tip into the pan. Stir everything together and simmer gently for about 10 minutes.
3  Chop the cluster beans, and add them with the salt and the remaining cloves of garlic, crushed. Finely chop the ginger and add this with the hot water. Simmer gently, covered, until the beans are tender, adding more water if necessary.
4  Stir the cream into the curry and transfer to a serving dish.

## ❧ SPICY MACARONI AND PEAS ❧
### *Masala macaroni aur matar*

*T*his brings back memories of school for me, for it was one of the traditional tea-time dishes.

1 lb macaroni
½ lb (1⅔ cups) frozen peas
4 onions
1 clove garlic or 1 teaspoon garlic
    purée
1 inch piece fresh ginger root
3 tablespoons oil
1 teaspoon cumin seeds
⅔ cup plain yogurt
1 teaspoon turmeric powder
1 teaspoon red chili powder
1 teaspoon *garam masala* powder
salt to taste
2 teaspoons lemon juice
1 fresh hot green chili pepper
chopped mint or coriander
    (cilantro), for garnish

SERVES 6

1  Cook the macaroni in boiling water until tender. Drain well. Cook the peas as instructed on the package and drain. Put these ingredients on one side.
2  Slice the onions, crush the garlic, if using fresh, and grind the ginger in a pestle and mortar or grate it finely. Heat the oil in a frying-pan or wok and add the cumin seeds, onions, garlic and ginger. Cook, stirring, over medium heat until the onions are beginning to brown.
3  Add the yogurt and all the spices. Let the mixture simmer gently for 3 minutes, then add the macaroni and peas. Add salt to taste and cook gently for 5 minutes, stirring occasionally.
4  Add the lemon juice. Chop the chili pepper and add this, then transfer the mixture to a serving dish and sprinkle with the chopped mint or coriander.

# BEAN AND LENTIL DISHES

Beans and lentils form an important part of Indian cuisine, particularly for those people who are strict vegetarians. Being rich in protein, they are often referred to as "the poor man's meat" and they certainly help to bulk out a meal. Many bean and lentil dishes are referred to as *dals* although, strictly speaking, it is the various split peas or lentils that are called by this name.

Many, many different types of beans and *dals* are used in India and they can be cooked in many different ways – curried, made into various snacks or sweets, even ground into flour and used to make *roti*. In many instances a *tarka* or *baghar* (see page 28) is added to a cooked *dal* dish before serving.

Many of the different types of bean and *dal* are now widely sold in supermarkets and grocery stores, but some you will have to seek out in specialist Indian shops. It's worth experimenting – they can add great variety to a meal.

Store *dals* in a glass jar in a cool place. Mixing them with cooking oil – 1 tablespoon oil to 2 pounds *dals* – helps to keep them fresh. Always pick over beans and *dals* before cooking to remove small stones or pieces of grit, etc. Then wash them well under cold running water. Some types need to be soaked before cooking to help soften them. If a recipe calls for a *dal* to be ground, soak it overnight in cold water to soften and then grind to a paste in a food processor or blender with some water – $\frac{1}{2}$ cup water to 1 pound *dal* is the correct proportion.

It is not always possible to give wholly accurate cooking times for the different types of bean and *dal* as this will often vary according to how fresh they are. Most take quite some time to cook, and a pressure cooker can greatly speed up the process. If cooking them on a stove in an ordinary pan, keep an eye on them to make sure there is sufficient water, otherwise they will stick to the pan and begin to burn. As always in Indian cooking, it is the various spices that are added to the beans and *dals* that will give each dish its flavor and in many instances it makes them easier to digest.

CHANA DAL – *split yellow chickpeas*
This is probably the most versatile and widely used of all the *dals*. It can be used in all the ways mentioned above, and also is sometimes incorporated into *baghars* (seasonings) and chutneys. *Besan* or gram flour can also be made from *chana dal*.

KAALA CHANA – *black grams or black chickpeas*
These are cousins of *kabli chana* or chickpeas (see below). They are a little smaller and a blackish-brown color and they must be soaked before cooking. Very popular in the cuisine of Rajasthan and Maharastra, they go particularly well with *pooris*.

KABLI CHANA – *chickpeas or garbanzos*
Chickpeas can be bought dried or in cans – and you will find them in most supermarkets. They are used extensively in the cuisines of India, the Middle East and South America. In India, they are usually curried in some way; in Middle Eastern countries, they are more frequently puréed to make the well-known dip, Hummus.

LOBIA – *blackeye peas or cowpeas*
The various kinds of these beans are used extensively in the cuisines of India, South America and Africa. Although they are a rich source of protein, they induce flatulence and should not be eaten on a daily basis!

BLACKEYE PEA DAL (LEFT) AND PINK LENTIL DAL (RIGHT) SERVED WITH PLAIN YOGURT AND *POPPADOMS.*

MAAH KI DAL – *whole black beans*

This is a great favorite in Punjab where it is usually cooked into a thick mixture with lots of ginger and curry flavorings and then served with lots of butter poured on top! It is eaten with hot buttered *chappatis*.

MALKA MASOOR DAL – *pink lentils*

Of all the *dals*, these are probably the easiest to find in grocery stores. They are also the quickest to cook. Be particularly vigilant in checking them over for small pieces of dirt and grit.

MATAR DAL – *split peas*

These are also widely available in supermarkets and grocery stores and are good for soups and curries. They need to be soaked for at least 1 hour before cooking.

MOONG DAL – *split yellow mung beans*

This *dal* is produced by splitting and removing the dark green covering of the mung bean. The yellow inside splits easily in two. Because it is easy to digest, it is often used in making a sort of soft kedgeree for invalids or babies.

MOWTH DAL – *red mung beans*

This is a red version of the mung bean. Sometimes these beans are allowed to sprout, or they are used as a *dal* or they can be ground into a flour. High in protein, they are popular particularly in Rajasthan and Gujrat.

RAAJMA – *red kidney beans*

Another *dal* that is widely available, red kidney beans are very popular in the cuisines of Punjab and Rajasthan, where they are made into a thick curry with lots of onions, tomatoes, garlic and ginger. Served with boiled rice, this makes a highly nutritious meal as the beans are rich in protein.

SABAT MASOOR – *black lentils*

These lentils are good for soups or curries.

SABUT MOONG DAL – *mung beans*

The commonly used beansprout comes from mung beans, but try using them as a *dal*, too. They taste good curried with rice dishes.

TOOR DAL – *pigeon peas*

Lemon, tamarind or raw green mangoes are usually put with this *dal* to complement the flavor. It is similar in appearance to yellow split peas.

URAD DAL – *split black beans or grams*

This *dal* is the result of splitting the whole *maah ki dal*. It cooks to a thick consistency.

# SOUR DAL
### Khatti dal

2 cups pigeon peas (*toor dal*)
1 quart water (approx)
salt to taste
½ cup tamarind water (see page 29)
1 teaspoon turmeric powder
2 teaspoons coriander powder
**BAGHAR**
1 tablespoon *ghee* or butter
1 teaspoon mustard seeds
2 cloves garlic
a few curry leaves
2–3 dried hot red chili peppers

SERVES 6

1 Wash the *dal* and put into a saucepan with the water, salt, tamarind water and spices. Bring to a boil, then lower the heat and cook until tender – 30–45 minutes, or 15 minutes in a pressure cooker. Transfer to a serving dish.

2 Heat the *ghee* or butter for the *baghar* and add the mustard seeds. Slice the garlic and add to the pan with the curry leaves and crumbled chili peppers. Cook for 1 minute shaking the pan, then pour over the *dal*, and serve, immediately without stirring.

NOTE Try serving this somewhat sour-tasting *dal* with Gujrati Potato Curry (see page 95), some *poppadums* and a *raita* for a filling vegetarian meal.

## ❦ PIGEON PEA DAL ❦
### Arhar ki dal

*A* popular lunchtime dish; serve it with boiled rice, mango chutney, *poppadums* and a vegetable curry for a complete meal. Note that this *dal* takes longer to cook than some of the others.

2 cups pigeon peas (*toor dal*)
1 quart water (approx)
salt to taste
1 teaspoon turmeric powder
1 teaspoon red chili powder
2 teaspoons coriander powder
1 small piece of green mango or
   3 or 4 pieces of dried mango
**BAGHAR**
1 tablespoon *ghee* or butter
1 teaspoon cumin seeds
2 cloves garlic
2 dried hot red chili peppers
chopped coriander (cilantro), for
   garnish

**SERVES 6**

1 Wash the *dal* carefully and put into a saucepan with the water, salt and spices. Finely chop the green mango, if using, and add this, or the dried mango. Bring to a boil, then lower the heat and simmer until tender – about 45 minutes–1 hour, or 20 minutes in a pressure cooker. Transfer to a serving dish.
2 Heat the *ghee* or butter for the *baghar* in a small frying-pan and add the cumin seeds. Slice the garlic and add to the pan with the crumbled chili peppers. Cook for 1 minute, then pour over the *dal*. Serve without stirring, garnished with the chopped coriander.

## ❦ SPICY DAL ❦
### Dal masaledar

$\frac{2}{3}$ cup pigeon peas (*toor dal*)
$\frac{2}{3}$ cup split yellow chickpeas (*chana dal*)
$\frac{2}{3}$ cup split yellow mung beans (*moong dal*)
$\frac{2}{3}$ cup pink lentils (*malka masoor dal*)
1 quart water
4 tablespoons *ghee* or butter
1 teaspoon whole *garam masala*
   (see page 29)
2 onions
8 cloves garlic
1 inch piece fresh ginger root
4 tomatoes
1 teaspoon turmeric powder
1 teaspoon red chili powder
2 teaspoons coriander powder
salt to taste
1 cup plain yogurt
2 teaspoons *garam masala* powder
chopped coriander (cilantro), for
   garnish

**SERVES 6–8**

1 Wash all the *dals* and put them in a large saucepan with the water. Bring to a boil, then lower the heat and simmer until tender – about 45 minutes, or 20 minutes if using a pressure cooker.
2 Heat the *ghee* or butter in a large frying-pan and add the whole *garam masala*. Chop the onions, garlic and ginger and add to the pan. Cook, stirring, until the onions are soft and golden.
3 Chop the tomatoes and add to the pan with the spices and salt. Simmer until the tomatoes are very soft.
4 Beat the yogurt and add it to the pan with the *garam masala* powder. Cook for 5 minutes more.
5 Spoon the cooked *dals* into the frying-pan, stir everything together and cook gently for 10–15 minutes more.
6 Serve sprinkled with chopped coriander.

# ❧ DRY MUNG BEAN DAL ❧
*Dry mogar dal*

1¾ cups dried mung beans (*sabut moong dal*)
2 onions
6 cloves garlic
1 inch piece fresh ginger root
2 tablespoons *ghee* or butter
1 teaspoon cumin seeds
¼ cup hot water
1 teaspoon turmeric powder
1 teaspoon red chili powder
2 teaspoons coriander powder
salt to taste
2 cups water (approx)
2 tablespoons lemon juice
1 fresh hot green chili pepper
1 teaspoon roasted cumin seed powder (see page 28)
chopped coriander (cilantro), for garnish

SERVES 6

1  Wash the mung beans, put in a bowl and cover with cold water. Leave to soak for 3 hours.

2  Chop the onions and finely slice the garlic and ginger. Heat the *ghee* or butter in a frying-pan and add the cumin seeds. When they "pop," add the onions, garlic and ginger. Cook, stirring, for 3–5 minutes.

3  Add the hot water, turmeric, red chili and coriander powders and salt and simmer for 5 minutes.

4  Drain the beans and add to the pan with the 2 cups water. Bring to a boil, then lower the heat and simmer until tender – 30–45 minutes, adding more water if the mixture looks too dry. Put in a serving dish and stir in the lemon juice.

5  Finely chop the green chili pepper and sprinkle it over the cooked *dal* together with the cumin seed powder and chopped coriander. Serve at once.

DRY MUNG BEAN DAL (LEFT) AND BLACK LENTIL DAL (RIGHT).

## ❧ THE QUEEN'S FAVORITE DAL ❧
### Dal Maharani

*Dal Maharani* is mostly served in restaurants, but try making it at home – it is quite delicious.
It tastes wonderful with *tandoori roti* (see page 128), together with yogurt chutney (see page 182)
or a *raita* of your choice.

$\frac{5}{6}$ cup split black beans or grams
  (*urad dal*)
$\frac{5}{6}$ cup split yellow or green mung
  beans (*moong dal*)
1 quart water (approx)
1 teaspoon ground ginger
salt to taste
1 teaspoon red chili powder
2 teaspoons coriander powder
1 teaspoon *garam masala* powder
1 tablespoon lemon juice
$\frac{1}{2}$ cup light cream
BAGHAR
1 onion
1 tablespoon oil
1 tablespoon butter
1 teaspoon cumin seeds
2 cloves garlic
GARNISH
coriander (cilantro) sprigs
lemon wedges

SERVES 6

1  Wash the *dals* together and put in a pan with the water. Add the ginger, salt and spices. Bring to a boil, then lower the heat and simmer until tender – 30–45 minutes, or 15 minutes in a pressure cooker. Add the lemon juice and transfer to a warmed serving dish.
2  Stir the cream into the cooked *dal*.
3  While the *dals* are cooking, finely slice the onion for the *baghar* and fry in the oil over a high heat until dark brown.
4  Heat the butter in a separate small frying-pan and add the cumin seeds. Crush the garlic into the pan and cook for 1–2 minutes, stirring, then pour this over the *dal*. Sprinkle with the fried onions and garnish with the coriander sprigs and lemon wedges just before serving.

## ❧ SPINACH DAL ❧
### Paalak ki dal

2 cups split yellow mung beans
  (*moong dal*)
$\frac{1}{2}$ lb fresh bulk spinach or 1 large
  can spinach, drained
1 quart water (approx)
salt to taste
1 teaspoon turmeric powder
2 teaspoons coriander powder
4 dried hot red chili peppers
1 teaspoon mango powder
1 teaspoon *garam masala* powder
1 inch piece fresh ginger root
BAGHAR
1 tablespoon *ghee* or butter
1 teaspoon mustard seeds
2 cloves garlic

SERVES 6

1  Wash the *dal*. If using fresh spinach, wash it and tear the leaves roughly. Chop the canned spinach.
2  Place spinach in a large pan with the *dal*, water, salt and all the spices. Finely slice the ginger and add this. Bring to the boil, then lower the heat and simmer until the *dal* is cooked – 30–45 minutes, or 15 minutes in a pressure cooker. Transfer to a serving dish.
3  Heat the *ghee* or butter for the *baghar* and add the mustard seeds. Finely slice the garlic and add to the pan. Fry until the garlic is brown and crispy, then pour over the cooked *dal*.

# RICE AND CEREAL DISHES

Rice is the staple food of Eastern and Southern India. It is called *chaawal* when it is raw and *bhaat* when cooked. It can be cooked in many different ways – boiled or steamed, curried, cooked in coconut milk or turned into biryanis or pilafs. Recipes for the latter dishes are included in this chapter, although they are really meals in themselves rather than accompaniments to curries.

You will find many different kinds of rice on sale in most grocery stores and supermarkets. The best type to use as an accompaniment to curry is Basmati. Wash it well before use to remove excess starch, and soak in cold water for 1 hour. This helps to keep the grains separate and fluffy when the rice is cooked.

Cooking rice so that it does not go mushy is very simple. Measure the rice before washing it, then put it in a saucepan with twice its volume of water and some salt – about 1 teaspoon to 2 cups rice. Stir once and cook over a low heat until nearly all the water has been absorbed. Turn off the heat and leave the rice in the covered pan on the stove until ready to serve.

## ROYAL RICE PILAF
### Zarda pullao

2 cups Basmati, long-grain or Patna rice
1 lb meat with bone – chicken pieces or lamb or pork chops
4 onions
4 cloves garlic
$7\frac{1}{2}$ cups water
$\frac{1}{4}$ cup oil
4 large black cardamoms
$\frac{1}{4}$ cup whole *garam masala* (see page 29)
4 teaspoons anise seed
2 teaspoons whole coriander seeds
salt to taste
GARNISH
2 onions
1 tablespoon oil

SERVES 6

1 Wash the rice under cold running water and leave to soak in cold water for about 1 hour. Drain well.
2 Put the meat into a heavy-based saucepan. Slice the onions and add half of them to the pan with the garlic cloves and 3 cups water. Bring to a boil, then simmer for about 30 minutes. Drain.
3 In another large saucepan, heat the oil and add the cardamoms and remaining onions. Cook for 5 minutes. Add the boiled meat and cook for about 10 minutes more, stirring.
4 In a separate pan, bring the remaining $4\frac{1}{2}$ cups water to a boil and add the whole *garam masala*, anise seed and coriander. Simmer for 20 minutes, covered, then drain, reserving the water.
5 Add the strained spicy water to the pan with the meat, together with the rice and salt. Cook for about 25 minutes until the liquid has been absorbed and the rice is tender.
6 Keep the pan covered until ready to serve. Prepare the garnish by slicing the onions finely and frying them in the oil until brown and crisp. Sprinkle on top of the pilaf and serve.

CLOCKWISE FROM TOP LEFT: CHICKEN RICE, TOMATO RICE AND SPICY COCONUT RICE.

## ❧ PLAIN FRIED RICE ❧
### *Chaawal ka sada pullao*

*T*his is a simple dish, but just a little bit more special than plain boiled rice. Serve it with a vegetable curry, a *raita* and *poppadums*, together with some chutney or pickle.

2 cups Basmati or long-grain rice
¼ cup oil or melted *ghee*
1 teaspoon whole *garam masala*
   (see page 29)
2 bay leaves
1 onion
1 quart water
salt to taste
GARNISH
1 onion
1 tablespoon cashew nuts
1 tablespoon oil

SERVES 6

1 Wash the rice under cold running water and soak in cold water for about 1 hour. Drain well.
2 Heat the oil or *ghee* in a heavy-based pan and add the *garam masala* and bay leaves. Cook for 1 minute.
3 Finely slice the onion and add to the oil. Cook, stirring, for a few minutes, then add the rice and stir. Add the water to the pan together with some salt. Cover and simmer on a very gentle heat until all the water has been absorbed and the rice is tender.
4 Leave the rice covered until ready to serve.
5 Just before serving, finely slice the onion for garnish and fry this and the cashew nuts in the oil over a high heat until crisp.
6 Turn the rice out onto a flat serving dish and sprinkle with the onion and cashew nuts.

## ❧ MUSHROOM PILAF ❧
### *Gucchi pullao*

*M*ushroom pilaf is a great favorite with my children. I love cooking it when we are in England as it is always possible to buy lovely fresh mushrooms. Try serving it with a chicken curry, a *raita* and some fried *poppadums*.

2 cups Basmati rice
1 onion
5 fresh button mushrooms
3 tablespoons oil
1 teaspoon cumin seeds
½ teaspoon cloves and peppercorns,
   mixed
2 bay leaves
1 teaspoon turmeric powder
½ teaspoon red chili powder
1 teaspoon coriander powder
1 quart water
salt to taste

SERVES 6

1 Wash the rice under cold running water and soak in cold water for about 1 hour. Drain well.
2 Finely slice the onion and mushrooms. Put on one side.
3 Heat the oil in a deep saucepan and add the cumin seeds, cloves and peppercorns and the bay leaves. Stir, then add the sliced onion and fry, stirring, until the onion is golden.
4 Add the remaining spices and the drained rice. Cook, stirring, for 5 minutes, then add the mushrooms.
5 Add the water with some salt and stir thoroughly. Cook, covered, over a low-to-medium heat until the water has been absorbed and the rice is just tender. Keep covered until ready to serve.

## SPINACH PILAF
### Paalak pullao

*I* concocted this recipe out of dire necessity, when returning to England from Nigeria. I found my larder almost bare except for some cans of spinach. Having always told my children about the "goodness" of spinach, they were happy to eat this dish and liked it so much it has now become a regular weekly feature in our house!

2 cups Basmati rice
1 quart water
1 onion
1 clove garlic
1 inch piece fresh ginger root
¼ cup oil
1 teaspoon cumin seeds
½ teaspoon cloves and peppercorns, mixed
1 teaspoon turmeric powder
½ teaspoon red chili powder
1 teaspoon coriander powder
1 teaspoon *garam masala* powder
salt to taste
1 large can spinach
1 tablespoon lemon juice

SERVES 6

1 Wash the rice under cold running water and soak in cold water for about 1 hour. Drain well. Put into a saucepan with the water and cook gently, covered, until the water has been absorbed and the rice is tender.
2 Meanwhile, finely slice the onion and chop the garlic and ginger.
3 Heat the oil in a frying-pan or wok and add the cumin seeds and the cloves and peppercorns. Stir in the onion and cook until lightly browned.
4 Add the garlic and ginger and stir-fry for 1 minute, then add all the spices with some salt to taste.
5 Drain the spinach and add to the pan with the lemon juice. Cook, stirring, for 2–3 minutes.
6 Gradually stir the cooked rice into the spinach mixture using a large fork so that the rice does not break up or become lumpy. When it has all been mixed in, cover and keep warm.
7 Serve the rice with a *raita*, a fish or potato curry and some *poppadums* for a complete meal.

## POTATO PILAF
### Aloo ka pullao

2 cups Basmati or long-grain rice
6 tablespoons oil or melted *ghee*
2 bay leaves
1 teaspoon whole *garam masala* (see page 29)
1 tablespoon raisins
2 onions
3 potatoes
1 cup plain yogurt
salt to taste
1 quart water

SERVES 6

1 Wash the rice under cold running water and soak in cold water for about 1 hour. Drain well.
2 Heat the oil or *ghee* in a heavy-based pan and add the bay leaves, *garam masala* and raisins. Stir over a gentle heat for 1 minute.
3 Finely slice the onions and add them to the pan. Cook for 5 minutes, stirring.
4 Cut the potatoes into bite-sized pieces and add to the pan. Cook, stirring, for another 5 minutes. Add the drained rice, yogurt, salt and water.
5 Let the mixture simmer, covered, until the liquid has been absorbed and the rice and potatoes are tender. Keep the pan covered until ready to serve.

ABOVE: COLORFUL GARLANDS OF FRESH FLOWERS ARE TRADITIONAL DECORATIONS AT FESTIVAL TIME. THEY ARE ALSO PRESENTED AS OFFERINGS AT THE TEMPLES.

RIGHT: ONE OF THE MANY SACRED COWS THAT WANDER THE STREETS WITH IMPUNITY SAMPLES A GARLAND OF MARIGOLDS!

## ❧ VEGETABLE PILAF ❧
*Sabzi ka pullao*

2 cups Basmati rice
½ cup oil or melted *ghee*
1 cup finely diced potatoes
1 cup finely diced carrots
1½ cups small cauliflower florets
1 cup chopped green beans
¾ cup peas, fresh or frozen
2 bay leaves
1 teaspoon whole *garam masala*
   (see page 29)
2 onions
1 inch piece fresh ginger root
2 fresh hot green chili peppers
salt to taste
4½ cups water
**GARNISH**
1 onion
1 tablespoon oil

**SERVES** 6

1 Wash the rice under cold running water and leave to soak in cold water for about 1 hour. Drain well.
2 Heat the oil or *ghee* in a heavy-based pan and add all the vegetables. Fry over a low heat for 10–15 minutes, stirring. Remove from the pan with a slotted spoon and set aside.
3 Add the bay leaves and *garam masala* to the oil. Finely slice the onions, ginger and chili peppers and add them to pan with the salt and drained rice. Cook, stirring, for 5 minutes.
4 Add all the vegetables and the water. Cook, covered, over a low heat until all the water has been absorbed and the rice and vegetables are just tender. Keep covered until ready to serve.
5 Just before serving, finely slice the onion for garnish and fry in the oil until crisp. Sprinkle over the rice.

## ❧ CURRIED VEGETABLE AND RICE PILAF ❧
*Navrattan pullao*

2 cups Basmati rice
5 tablespoons oil or melted *ghee*
1 teaspoon whole *garam masala*
   (see page 29)
2 bay leaves
2 onions
1 cup finely diced carrots
1⅓ cups mushrooms
1 cup small cauliflower florets
⅔ cup cubed potatoes
¾ cup peas, fresh or frozen
1 teaspoon red chili powder
salt to taste
1 tablespoon raisins
4½ cups water
**GARNISH**
about 20 cashew nuts
1 tablespoon oil
chopped coriander (cilantro)

**SERVES** 6

1 Wash the rice under cold running water, and soak it in cold water for 1 hour. Drain well.
2 Heat the oil or *ghee* in a heavy-based pan and add the *garam masala* and bay leaves. Stir for 1 minute.
3 Finely slice the onions and add them to the pan. Cook for about 5 minutes, stirring.
4 When the onions are lightly browned, add all the vegetables and cook, stirring, for 5 minutes. Add the chili powder, salt, raisins and drained rice. Stir together, then add the water.
5 Cook over a very gentle heat, covered, until the water has been absorbed and the rice and vegetables are just tender. They should not be mushy.
6 Fry the cashew nuts in the oil until crisp and sprinkle these on top of the rice, together with the coriander, just before serving.

## ❧ PEPPER RICE ❧
### *Kaali mirch ke chaawal*

*A* rich dish from the south of India. Serve it with *sambhar* (see page 29), plain yogurt and *poppadums* for a filling meal.

2 cups long-grain Patna rice
3 tablespoons oil
1 teaspoon mustard seeds
a few curry leaves
1 teaspoon split yellow chickpeas
   (*chana dal*)
1 teaspoon ground black pepper
salt to taste
about 20 cashew nuts

**SERVES 6**

1 Wash the rice under cold running water and leave to soak in cold water for about 1 hour. Drain well.
2 Cook the rice as described on page 114 and put on one side.
3 Heat 2 tablespoons oil in a frying-pan and add the mustard seeds, curry leaves and split yellow chickpeas. When the chickpeas are browned, remove from the heat. Season the mixture with pepper and salt and pour over the cooked rice. Mix together with a fork until well blended.
4 Fry the cashew nuts in the remaining oil until browned. Sprinkle over the rice and serve at once.

## ❧ CORN OR MILLET PILAF ❧
### *Bajra ka soyata*

*T*his looks and tastes like American "grits," except it is spicier, and is eaten the same way – that is with hot melted butter poured on top. It is good for lunches and dinners on a cold day. Try it with yogurt, *raita*, *poppadums* and chutney. Use cornmeal if you cannot get millet.

1 lb (2⅔ cups) millet
6 onions
12 cloves garlic
½ cup oil
2 teaspoons turmeric powder
1 tablespoon red chili powder
2 tablespoons coriander powder
1 tablespoon mango powder
1 lb lamb chops
3 cups water
salt to taste
3½ cups buttermilk
1 tablespoon *garam masala*
   powder
**GARNISH**
1 onion
1 tablespoon oil
chopped coriander (cilantro)

**SERVES 6**

1 Soak the millet in cold water overnight. The next morning, drain it and grind it coarsely in a coffee grinder.
2 Mince the onions and garlic in a food processor. Heat the oil in a heavy-based pan and fry the onions and garlic for about 5 minutes. Add the turmeric, chili, coriander and mango powders. Stir to mix everything together well.
3 Add the lamb together with 1 cup water and cook for 25 minutes.
4 Add the salt, ground millet and the remaining water. Cover and cook over a low-to-medium heat for 25 minutes more, stirring frequently.
5 Add the buttermilk and continue simmering, covered, until the meat and millet are cooked. Add the *garam masala* and remove from the heat.
6 Prepare the garnish by slicing the onion and frying it in the oil until brown and crisp. Sprinkle this and the chopped coriander over the dish and serve.

## ❧ SPICY COCONUT RICE ❧
*Nariyal ke chaawal*

*A*nother rice dish that is cooked mainly in the south, this delicious coconut-flavored rice tastes good with a hot curry and *poppadums.*

2 cups long-grain Patna rice
5 tablespoons oil or melted *ghee*
1 teaspoon mustard seeds
a few curry leaves
1 teaspoon split black beans or
    grams (*urad dal*)
1 onion
4 cloves garlic
1 teaspoon turmeric powder
1 teaspoon red chili powder
salt to taste
1 cup coconut milk (see page 28)
3 cups water
about 16 cashew nuts
1 fresh hot green chili pepper, for
    garnish

**SERVES** 6

**1** Wash the rice under cold running water and leave to soak in cold water for about 1 hour. Drain well.
**2** Heat 4 tablespoons oil or *ghee* in a heavy-based pan and add the mustard seeds, curry leaves and black beans or grams. Cook for about 5 minutes, shaking the pan frequently.
**3** Slice the onion and crush the garlic and add to the pan. Cook for about 5 minutes, stirring, then add the turmeric, chili powder, salt and coconut milk. Bring to a boil, then lower the heat and simmer for 5 minutes.
**4** Add the rice and water. Simmer gently, covered, until the rice is tender. Keep the pan covered until ready to serve.
**5** Fry the cashew nuts in the remaining oil or *ghee* until brown and crisp and sprinkle over the rice. Finely chop the chili pepper and sprinkle this over the rice, too. Serve at once.

## ❧ YELLOW RICE ❧
*Peeley chaawal*

*T*his delicious savory yellow rice is one of the traditional dishes to be served on *Basant Panchmi* – that is the day that heralds the spring each year in February. On this day everybody dresses in yellow and a "yellow" meal is served in which all the food – curries, rice and sweets – are a yellow color. Prepare it at other times of the year, too, though; it is good with a vegetable curry, a *raita* and some *poppadums.*

2 cups long-grain Patna rice
$\frac{1}{4}$ cup melted *ghee*
2 cloves
3 onions
4 cloves garlic
1 teaspoon turmeric powder
salt to taste
1 quart water
1 tablespoon oil

**SERVES** 6

**1** Wash the rice under cold running water and soak in cold water for 1 hour. Drain well.
**2** Heat the *ghee* in a heavy-based pan and add the cloves. Slice two of the onions and all the garlic and add them to the pan. Cook, stirring, for about 5 minutes, then add the turmeric, salt and rice.
**3** Add the water to the pan and cook, covered, on a low heat until the rice is tender and the water has been absorbed. Keep covered until ready to serve.
**4** Finely slice the remaining onion and fry in the oil until brown and crisp. Sprinkle over the rice just before serving.

## ❧ TOMATO RICE ❧
*Tamatar bhaat*

*T*omato rice is a popular brunch dish. It tastes good on its own.

2 cups long-grain Patna rice
6 tomatoes
2 onions
4 cloves garlic
¼ cup oil
1 teaspoon mustard seeds
1 teaspoon turmeric powder
salt to taste
1 teaspoon sugar
1 teaspoon red chili powder
1 fresh hot green chili pepper
1 inch piece fresh ginger root
1 quart water
a few coriander (cilantro) leaves,
    for garnish

SERVES 6

1 Wash the rice under cold running water and leave to soak in cold water for about 1 hour. Drain well.
2 Meanwhile, skin the tomatoes and reduce them to a purée in a blender. Mince the onions and garlic in a food processor.
3 Heat the oil in a heavy-based pan and add the mustard seeds. When they "pop," add the tomatoes, onions and garlic together with the turmeric, salt, sugar and chili powder. Finely slice the chili and ginger and add this too. Stir everything together and cook for about 5 minutes.
4 Add the rice and water. Simmer, covered, over a low heat until the water has been absorbed and the rice is tender. Keep covered until ready to serve.
5 Serve on a flat serving dish garnished with the coriander leaves.

## ❧ SPICED RICE WITH VEGETABLES AND DAL ❧
*Bisi bela*

*A* typical dish from Bangalore; serve it at lunchtime with yogurt and *poppadums*.

2 cups long-grain rice
4 tablespoons oil
2 dried hot red chili peppers
1 teaspoon coriander seeds
1 tablespoon dried shredded
    coconut
1 teaspoon split yellow chickpeas
    (*chana dal*)
1 teaspoon split black beans or
    grams (*urad dal*)
⅚ cup pigeon peas (*toor dal*)
5 cups water
1 eggplant
¾ cup peas, fresh or frozen
1 teaspoon turmeric powder
1 tablespoon melted *ghee*
a few curry leaves
salt to taste
½ cup tamarind water (see page 29)
melted *ghee* or butter, to serve

SERVES 6

1 Wash the rice under cold running water and soak for about 1 hour. Drain well.
2 Heat 1 tablespoon of the oil in a heavy-based pan and crumble in the chili peppers. Add the coriander seeds, coconut and the first two types of *dal*. Cook, stirring, until the *dals* are browned, then remove the mixture from the heat and grind it coarsely in a pestle and mortar or coffee grinder. Keep on one side.
3 Wash the pigeon peas and put in a pan with 1 cup water and the remaining oil. Simmer, covered, for about 30 minutes, then add the rice and remaining water. Chop the eggplant and add this together with the peas, turmeric powder and the ground cooked spices and *dals*. Simmer for 15 minutes.
4 Add the *ghee*, curry leaves, salt and tamarind water and stir to mix everything together well. Cook until the *dals* and rice are tender – the finished dish will be quite mushy.
5 Pour hot melted *ghee* or butter on the rice mixture just before serving.

# EGGS WITH RICE
### *Anda pullao*

2 cups Basmati or long-grain rice
8 hard-boiled eggs
$\frac{1}{4}$ cup oil or melted *ghee*
2 bay leaves
1 teaspoon whole *garam masala*
   (see page 29)
2 onions
4 cloves garlic
$\frac{1}{2}$ cup hot water
1 teaspoon turmeric powder
1 teaspoon red chili powder
2 teaspoons coriander powder
salt to taste
1 quart cold water
1 tablespoon raisins
GARNISH
2 onions
1 tablespoon oil

SERVES 6

1 Wash the rice under cold running water and leave to soak in cold water for 1 hour. Drain well.

2 Shell the eggs, then with a sharp knife, puncture one side of each hard-boiled egg to allow the curry flavors to penetrate inside. Gently fry the eggs in the oil or *ghee* for 4–5 minutes, turning frequently. Remove from the pan and put on one side.

3 Add the bay leaves and *garam masala* to the pan. Finely chop the onions and add them with the garlic cloves and hot water. Cook for about 5 minutes.

4 Add all the powdered spices together with the salt and drained rice. Add the cold water to the pan together with the eggs and raisins. Cook over a low heat until the liquid has been absorbed and the rice is tender. Transfer to a serving dish.

5 Prepare the garnish by slicing the onions and frying them in the oil until crisp. Sprinkle these over the eggs and rice.

MEAT PILAF (LEFT) AND SPICED RICE WITH VEGETABLES AND DAL (RIGHT) SERVED WITH PLAIN YOGURT.

## EGG AND MEATBALL RICE
*Ande aur kofte ki biryani*

*T*his is the same basic recipe as for *Hyderabadi gosht biryani* (see opposite), the difference being that it is made with ground meat instead of cubed meat and contains hard-boiled eggs.

2 cups Basmati rice
1 lb ground lamb or beef
2 teaspoons garlic purée or granules
2 teaspoons *garam masala* powder
salt to taste
oil for deep frying
$\frac{1}{4}$ teaspoon saffron
2 tablespoons milk
2 onions
1 tablespoon oil
1 fresh hot green chili pepper
6 hard-boiled eggs
juice of 2 lemons
$\frac{1}{2}$ cup chopped coriander (cilantro)

**SERVES 6**

1 Cook the rice as described on page 114. Put on one side.
2 Mix the ground meat with the garlic, *garam masala* and salt. Form into small round balls, slightly larger than walnuts.
3 Heat the oil for deep frying and fry the meatballs until browned. Drain on paper towels.
4 Soak the saffron in the milk. Finely slice the onions and fry in the 1 tablespoon oil until soft and lightly browned. Finely chop the chili pepper.
5 Shell the eggs and cut in half lengthwise.
6 Lightly grease a heavy-based pan and make layers of rice, meatballs, eggs, lemon juice, chopped coriander, saffron and milk, fried onions and chopped chili pepper. Cover the pan tightly and cook over a low heat for 30 minutes. Serve at once.

## MEAT PILAF
*Gosht ka pullao*

*T*his is my favorite rice and meat dish, particularly when cooked by my sister, Patsy.

2 cups Basmati, long-grain or Patna rice
1 lb lean boneless meat – lamb, pork, beef or chicken
4 onions
$\frac{1}{2}$ cup melted *ghee* or oil
salt to taste
$4\frac{1}{2}$ cups water
12 blanched almonds
6 green cardamoms
1 tablespoon raisins
$\frac{1}{2}$ cup milk
**GARNISH**
2 onions
1 tablespoon oil
1 teaspoon cumin seeds

**SERVES 6**

1 Wash the rice under cold running water and leave to soak in cold water for about 1 hour. Drain well. Meanwhile, cut the meat into small cubes and finely slice the onions.
2 Heat all but 1 tablespoon of the *ghee* or oil in a heavy-based pan and fry the onions until lightly browned. Add the meat and salt and cook, stirring, until the meat is browned.
3 Add the water to the pan and cook over a low heat until the meat is tender.
4 Slice the almonds and add to the pan with the cardamoms and raisins. Stir well, then add the rice, cover the pan and cook on a fairly high heat for about 15 minutes. Lower the heat and continue cooking until all the water has been absorbed.
5 Add the milk and simmer, covered, over a low heat for about 5 minutes. Remove from the heat, but leave the pan covered.
6 Prepare the garnish by slicing the onions finely and frying them in the oil until brown and crisp.
7 Heat the remaining *ghee* or oil and fry the cumin seeds for 1 minute. Sprinkle over the pilaf with the onions.

## CHICKEN RICE
### Murgi pullao

2 cups Basmati or long-grain rice
4 tomatoes
$\frac{1}{4}$ cup oil
2 bay leaves
1 teaspoon whole *garam masala*
 (see page 29)
2 onions
1 teaspoon turmeric powder
2 teaspoons red chili powder
salt to taste
6 chicken drumsticks
$4\frac{1}{4}$ cups water
GARNISH
2 onions
2 tablespoons oil

SERVES 6

1 Wash the rice under cold running water, and leave to soak in cold water for about 1 hour. Drain well.
2 Chop the tomatoes roughly.
3 Heat the oil in a heavy-based pan and add the bay leaves and *garam masala*. Finely chop the onions and add them with the turmeric and chili powders and salt. Cook for about 5 minutes, stirring.
4 Add the chicken drumsticks and tomatoes and mix everything together well. Cover the pan and cook on a low heat until the liquid has been absorbed.
5 Add the rice and water. Cover the pan again and cook for about 25 minutes until the liquid has been absorbed, the rice is tender and the chicken is cooked. Leave covered until ready to serve.
6 Just before serving, finely slice the onions for garnish and fry them in the oil until brown and crisp. Serve with a *raita*.

## MEAT WITH RICE
### Hyderabadi gosht biryani

*My* husband taught me how to cook this; Hyderabadis think they are the greatest cooks in the world! Serve the dish with tomato and onion *raita* (see page 134).

4 cups Basmati rice
2 quarts water
2 lb boneless lamb or beef
salt to taste
$\frac{1}{4}$ cup coarsely ground whole *garam masala* (see page 29)
$1\frac{1}{2}$ cups plain yogurt
$\frac{1}{4}$ teaspoon saffron
2 tablespoons milk
4 onions
2 tablespoons oil
1 cup melted *ghee*
juice of 4 lemons
$\frac{1}{2}$ cup chopped coriander (cilantro)
$\frac{1}{2}$ cup chopped mint

SERVES 8

1 Cook the rice as described on page 114 and put on one side.
2 Cut the meat into small cubes and gently cook in its own juices with the salt and *garam masala* in a covered heavy-based frying-pan. When the meat is tender turn off the heat, stir in the yogurt and leave the pan covered.
3 Soak the saffron in the milk. Slice the onions and fry them in the oil until soft and lightly browned.
4 Grease a heavy-based pan or flameproof casserole with a little *ghee*, and place a layer of meat in the bottom. Cover this with a layer of cooked rice and add 1 tablespoon *ghee*, 1 tablespoon lemon juice and a sprinkling of the saffron milk. Finally add some chopped coriander and mint and fried onions.
5 Repeat the layering of the ingredients until they have all been used. Cover the pan tightly and cook over a very low heat for about 30 minutes. Do not remove the lid until ready to serve.

# INDIAN BREADS

*I*ndian bread or *roti* is eaten at least twice a day in the northern part of India, where it, rather than rice, is the staple food. It is a form of flat, unleavened bread, generally made in a circle some 4–6 inches in diameter. A finer texture *roti*, called *phulka* or *chappati*, is also popular. Other types of *roti*, which you will find served in Indian restaurants the world over, are deep-fried *pooris*, greased *parathas*, tandoori roti, *naan*, etc. All vary slightly, but all are made fresh before every meal, are generally eaten with a curry and must be served hot. Serve brushed with melted *ghee* or butter.

In India, all these breads would be cooked on a hot heavy iron griddle called a *tava*. A heavy-based frying-pan can be used, but if you find you like these breads and cook them a lot, you may prefer to use a griddle.

## INDIAN BASIC BREAD
### Chappati or phulka

1¼ cups wholewheat flour
1 cup all-purpose flour
salt to taste
¾ cup water (approx)
¼ cup melted *ghee* or butter, to serve

YIELDS 12–14

1 Sift the two flours together into a large bowl and add the salt. Slowly pour in the water and mix into the flour to make a fairly soft dough. Add more water if necessary. Knead to make the dough pliable.
2 Wet your hands and knead the dough again. This binds the flours together thoroughly and makes the dough extra smooth. Wrap in foil and put in a cool place for 30 minutes.
3 Divide the dough into twelve to fourteen balls and roll each one on a floured surface to a circle about 5 inches in diameter.
4 Heat a heavy-based frying-pan or griddle on a medium heat. Cook the bread circles, one at a time, on the hot griddle for 1 minute. When small bubbles start appearing on the surface of the bread, flip the circle over.
5 Cook the second side for about 30 seconds, until the bread slides off the pan easily.
6 If cooking on gas, hold the *chappati* over the gas flame – the side which was cooked first should be over the flame – to puff it up. If cooking on electric or a solid burner, simply press the side which was cooked first hard with a folded kitchen towel. This will puff it up slightly. Place the cooked circles in a folded napkin and put onto a plate or into a bread basket to keep warm while you cook the remainder.
7 Serve with hot melted *ghee* or butter brushed over one side of the *chappati*.

CLOCKWISE FROM TOP LEFT: SEMOLINA POORIS, LEAVENED BAKED BREAD AND CORNMEAL PUNJABI BREAD.

## ❧ BAKED BREAD ❧
### *Tandoori roti*

*I*n India, this *roti* is usually made in a clay oven, but you can bake it quite successfully in an ordinary oven. Every street corner in Delhi has a *Tandoor waala*, where the bread is cooked. When we lived in Delhi, I used to send my little servant boy, Ramu, with the *roti* dough to the *Tandoor waala* for cooking. This was far and away the easiest way to get the *rotis* cooked. It cost almost nothing, and you got a free bowl of *dal* with an order of six *rotis* and above!

3½ cups wholewheat flour
salt to taste
¾ cup water (approx)
melted *ghee*, to serve

YIELDS 8

1 Sift the flour into a large bowl and add the salt. Slowly add the water and mix to a soft dough. Add more water if necessary.
2 Divide the dough into eight equal balls, then roll these out on a floured surface to circles 5 inches in diameter.
3 Sprinkle water on one side of the bread circles and stick them – this side down – onto baking sheets.
4 Bake in an oven heated to 375° for about 10 minutes.
5 Place under a hot broiler for 1 minute and serve hot with melted *ghee* poured on top.

## ❧ CHICKPEA FLOUR BREAD ❧
### *Besan ki roti*

*T*his is a tasty bread, made with a mixture of flour and spices. Look for chickpea flour in specialist grocers. Eat the bread with yogurt and pickles.

1¼ cups chickpea flour
1¾ cups wholewheat flour
salt to taste
1 teaspoon cumin seeds
1 onion
1 fresh hot green chili pepper
2 tablespoons chopped coriander
   (cilantro)
¾–1 cup water
½ cup melted *ghee* or corn oil

YIELDS 12–14

1 Sift the two flours together into a bowl and add the salt and cumin seeds. Finely chop the onion and chili pepper and mix these in too, together with the chopped coriander.
2 Slowly add the water and mix to a stiff dough. Add more water if necessary. Knead lightly, then divide into twelve to fourteen balls.
3 Roll out the balls on a floured surface to circles about 4 inches in diameter.
4 Heat a heavy-based frying-pan or griddle, brush the circles with melted *ghee* or oil and place on the pan. Cook until lightly browned on the underside, then brush the uncooked side with more melted *ghee* or oil, turn the bread over and cook the second side.
5 If you prefer, cook the bread without the *ghee* or oil and pour a little melted *ghee* over the bread before serving. Serve the bread hot.

## ❧ SAVORY BREAD ❧
### *Missi roti*

*A* tasty bread which is spicy and a bit salty – good for brunch or as a packed lunch. Eat it on its own or with some yogurt.

2¾ cups wholewheat flour
1¼ cups chickpea flour
salt to taste
2 tablespoons melted *ghee* or butter
1 teaspoon carom seeds or cumin seeds
1 onion
1 fresh hot green chili pepper
1 teaspoon red chili powder
1 tablespoon chopped coriander (cilantro)
¾ cup warm water (approx)
melted *ghee* or butter, to serve

YIELDS 12–14

1 Sift the two flours together into a bowl and add the salt with the melted *ghee* or butter and the carom or cumin seeds. Finely chop the onion and chili pepper and stir into the mixture with the red chili powder and chopped coriander.
2 Slowly add the water and mix to a stiff dough. Add more water if necessary. Knead gently to make the dough smooth, then divide it into twelve to fourteen balls.
3 Roll the balls out on a floured surface to circles about 5 inches in diameter.
4 Heat a heavy-based frying-pan or griddle and cook the bread circles for about 1 minute on one side. Flip them over and cook the other side for the same time.
5 Press a folded kitchen towel firmly onto the circles, and rotate the pan for 1 minute until they are brown and crispy. Remove from the pan and pour melted *ghee* or butter on one side. Make small incisions over the surface of the bread so that the *ghee* penetrates inside.
6 Stack the *rotis* in a pile and keep warm until they are all cooked and ready to serve.

## ❧ CORNMEAL PUNJABI BREAD ❧
### *Makki ki roti*

*T*his is a typical Punjabi bread, traditionally eaten with *Saag* which is dry curry made with spinach, mustard greens, cabbage and other vegetables, blended to a thick purée. It is usually eaten in the winter either for brunch or an early lunch. You will find that Indian restaurants around the world often serve this twin combination of *Makki ki roti* with *Saag*.

3½ cups cornmeal (*makki ka atta*)
salt to taste
½–¾ cup warm water (approx)
melted *ghee* or butter, to serve

YIELDS 12

1 Make a stiff dough with the cornmeal, salt and water and divide into twelve balls.
2 Roll out each ball on a floured surface to a circle about 4 inches in diameter – they will be a bit thicker than the usual *chappatis*.
3 Heat a heavy-based frying-pan or griddle and cook the bread circles on both sides until lightly browned. Take care when lifting – the bread will break easily.
4 Serve hot with melted *ghee* or butter.

# ⚬⚬ FRIED BREAD ⚬⚬
## *Bhatura*

*T*his is traditionally eaten as a twin combination of *Chana bhatura. Bhatura* is a fried bread, served at *Chaat* shops, that is Indian fast food shops. Good for when you are out shopping!

$2\frac{3}{4}$ cups all-purpose flour
salt to taste
1 teaspoon baking soda
1 egg
1 tablespoon sugar
$\frac{1}{4}$ cup plain yogurt
$\frac{1}{2}$ cup warm water (approx)
1 tablespoon melted *ghee*
1 cup oil for frying

YIELDS 10

1 Sift the flour, salt and baking soda into a large bowl. Beat the egg and add it to the flour with the sugar, yogurt and water. Mix to a fairly soft dough, adding more water if necessary.
2 Add the *ghee* and knead the dough until it is smooth and pliable. Put it back in the bowl, cover with a damp cloth and put in a warm place for about 4 hours to rise.
3 Knead the dough again and divide into ten balls. Roll out each one on a greased board to a circle about 4 inches in diameter.
4 Heat the oil in a deep frying-pan or wok and fry the *bhaturas*, one at a time, turning them so that they turn pale golden on both sides. Drain on paper towels and keep warm while you fry the remainder.

ABOVE: A CLOSE-UP VIEW OF *BHATURAS* COOKING IN HOT OIL.

LEFT: COOKED *POORIS* BEING LIFTED FROM A WOK OF HOT OIL. THE SMALL PORTABLE STOVE IS FUELED WITH COAL.

## ❧ FRIED BREAD TRIANGLES ❧
### *Parathas*

*Parathas* are very popular at breakfast time or for a packed lunch as they do not turn hard as they cool. They are also often eaten with yogurt in the morning; they are very filling and can keep you going through the day! They taste good with a dry vegetable curry or a pickle, or they can be stuffed with any mashed curried vegetables.

1¾ cups wholewheat flour
1⅓ cups all-purpose flour
salt to taste
1 teaspoon carom seeds
1 cup water (approx)
1 cup melted *ghee* or butter
   (approx)

YIELDS 8

1 Sift the two flours together into a bowl and add the salt and carom seeds. Slowly mix in the water to make a fairly soft dough. Add more water if necessary. Knead this well to make it pliable and smooth, then wrap it in foil and put in a cool place for about 30 minutes.

2 Divide the dough into eight balls and roll out to circles about 5 inches in diameter.

3 Brush the circles with melted *ghee* or butter on one side. Fold in half pressing the edges together. Brush one side of the semi-circle with melted *ghee* or butter and fold in half again to make a triangle. Now roll this triangle with a rolling pin to flatten it – the sides should be 4–5 inches.

4 Heat a heavy-based frying-pan or griddle and grease it lightly with a little of the melted *ghee* or butter. Put the *parathas* in the pan and cook for about 1 minute. Brush with melted *ghee* or butter and flip over. Brush the other side with melted *ghee* or butter and turn again. Cook for about 1 minute more, then remove from the pan and stack on a plate. Cover with foil and keep warm while you cook the remainder. Serve hot.

## ❧ SWEET BREAD ❧

### *Meetha paratha*

*T*ry this for breakfast served with yogurt. Children love it, too.

2¾ cups wholewheat flour
¾ cup all-purpose flour
¼ cup milk
¼ cup water (approx)
½ cup brown sugar
½ cup melted *ghee* for frying

YIELDS 12

1 Sift the two flours together into a bowl and stir in the milk. Gradually add the water and mix to form a stiff dough. Add more water if necessary.

2 Divide into twelve balls and roll out each one on a floured surface to a circle 3 inches in diameter.

3 Divide the sugar between the circles, placing it in the center of them. Bring the edges up over the top of the sugar.

4 Roll out the balls once more to circles about 4 inches in diameter.

5 Heat a heavy-based frying-pan or griddle and cook the circles on both sides lightly. Brush each one with 1 tablespoon melted *ghee* on both sides and cook for 2 minutes more turning once.

6 Keep warm stacked on a plate and serve hot.

# EGG BREAD
## *Egg or Omelette paratha*

EGG BATTER
4 eggs
1 teaspoon cumin seeds
1 onion
1 fresh hot green chili pepper
salt to taste
1 teaspoon red chili powder
DOUGH
2¾ cups wholewheat flour
1 teaspoon salt
½ cup water (approx)
½ cup oil

YIELDS 12–14

1  Beat the eggs and mix in the cumin seeds. Finely chop the onion. Seed the chili pepper and chop this finely too. Stir the onion and chili pepper into the eggs with the salt and red chili powder. Put this mixture on one side.
2  Make a stiff dough with the flour, salt and water. Divide this into twelve to fourteen balls and flatten each one slightly. Roll out to circles 5 inches in diameter.
3  Heat a little oil in a heavy-based frying-pan or griddle, and fry the bread circles lightly on both sides. Place a spoonful of the egg batter on the bread. When it has set, turn the circles over and place another spoonful of batter on top. Add more oil to the pan as necessary. Turn the bread once more when the batter has set to brown this side. Remove from the pan and keep warm while you cook the remainder in the same way.

# LEAVENED BAKED BREAD
## *Naan*

*Naan* originated in the north-west frontier borders of India and Pakistan where it was the *Pathans* who made the *naans* and the *tandoori* food popular. Moti Mahal Restaurant in old Delhi is the oldest *tandoori* restaurant in India. We used to go there as children and see the tall, fair, *salwar*-clad *Pathan* cooks make *naans* in the *tandoors*. Make them yourself in an ordinary oven.

3¾ cups all-purpose flour
1 teaspoon baking powder
½ teaspoon baking soda
1 teaspoon sugar
1 egg
6 tablespoons plain yogurt
3 tablespoons melted *ghee*
salt to taste
1 cup milk (approx)
1 tablespoon nigella or poppy seeds

YIELDS 6–8

1  Sift the flour, baking powder and baking soda into a bowl and mix well. Add all the remaining ingredients except the milk, nigella or poppy seeds and 1 tablespoon *ghee*. Mix everything together well.
2  Gradually add the milk to the flour mixture and knead lightly to form a soft dough. Cover the bowl with a damp cloth and put into a warm place to rise for 2 hours.
3  Knead the dough again and divide it into six to eight balls. Roll out these on a floured surface in one direction, so as to make an oval 6–8 inches long. Pull the dough with your hands to stretch it.
4  Wet the *naan* on one side with water and place it this side down on a baking sheet. Brush with the reserved melted *ghee* and sprinkle a few nigella or poppy seeds on top. Bake for 5–10 minutes in an oven heated to 400°.
5  An alternative way to cook the *naan* is to place it on a heated frying-pan or griddle. Cook on one side, then brush the uncooked side with melted *ghee*, sprinkle with the seeds and place under a hot broiler for about 5 minutes. Serve hot.

# SEMOLINA POORIS
### Sooji ki poori

*Semolina pooris* have a good flavor that goes well with a dry vegetable curry.

1⅓ cups plain flour
⅔ cup semolina flour
salt to taste
2 tablespoons melted *ghee*
½ teaspoon turmeric powder
½ teaspoon red chili powder
½–¾ cup water (approx)
1 cup oil for frying

YIELDS 16–20

1 Mix together the flour and semolina flour. Add the salt, melted *ghee* and the turmeric and red chili powders, then gradually mix in the water to make a soft dough.
2 Knead the dough to make it pliable, then divide into sixteen to twenty balls. Roll out each one on a floured surface to a 3 inch diameter circle.
3 Heat the oil for frying in a deep frying-pan or wok and fry the *pooris*, one at a time, until lightly browned on both sides. Keep warm while you fry the remainder. Serve hot.

# COCONUT POORIS
### Nariyal ki poori

¾ cup all-purpose flour
1¼ cups wholewheat flour
1 cup dried shredded coconut
salt to taste
1 teaspoon red chili powder
2 teaspoons sugar
2 tablespoons melted *ghee* or oil
½–¾ cup water (approx)
1 cup oil for frying

YIELDS 14–16

1 Mix the flours with the coconut in a bowl. Stir in all the remaining ingredients, except the oil, adding sufficient water to make a soft dough.
2 Divide into fourteen to sixteen equal balls, and flatten them slightly. Roll out each of the balls on a greased board to a 3 inch diameter circle.
3 Heat the oil for frying in a deep frying-pan or wok and fry the *pooris*, one at a time. Press each one down into the oil to brown it, then turn it over and cook on the other side. Drain on paper towels, and keep warm while you fry the remainder. You can serve these hot or cold.

# MILK POORIS
### Dookh ki poori

2¼ cups all-purpose flour
2 tablespoons sugar
1 teaspoon baking powder
1 tablespoon melted *ghee*
½ teaspoon cardamom powder
   (optional)
¾ cup milk (approx)
1 cup oil for frying

YIELDS 12–14

1 Sift the flour into a large bowl and add all the remaining ingredients, except the oil. Mix to a soft dough and put on one side for 30 minutes.
2 Divide the dough into twelve to fourteen equal balls, and flatten these slightly. Roll them out on a greased board to 3 inch diameter circles.
3 Heat the oil in a frying-pan or wok and fry the *pooris*, one at a time, turning to cook both sides evenly. Drain on paper towels and repeat until they are all cooked. Serve hot.

# YOGURT SALADS

Yogurt salads or *raitas* are the cooling agents of the curry. They go well with any curry, even a mild one, but they are essential with a spicy, hot dish. *Raitas* are always made from plain yogurt, which is then mixed with a variety of different ingredients. Try making your own yogurt for these salads; it is superior in taste to the commercial types and very easy to do. Simply heat 2 cups milk to body temperature – use a thermometer or test it with your little finger – then stir in 1 tablespoon live plain yogurt (this is for the culture). Put in a bowl – preferably one made of earthenware – cover with a clean dish towel and leave in a warm place overnight. In the morning, the yogurt should be ready for use. Keep in the refrigerator. All *raitas* taste better if they are sprinkled with roasted cumin seeds – either whole or powdered. It adds a bit of spice to the taste and aids the digestion. Roast the cumin seeds and leave them whole or grind to a powder, as you prefer (see page 28). Keep in a screw-top jar.

## CUCUMBER YOGURT SALAD
### *Kheere ka raita*

1¾ cups plain yogurt
2 cucumbers
1 teaspoon red chili powder
salt to taste
1 teaspoon salt
2 teaspoons raisins
1 teaspoon roasted cumin seeds
1 teaspoon dried mint, for garnish

SERVES 6

1  Lightly beat the yogurt.
2  Grate the cucumbers and put into a colander or sieve. Leave for about 30 minutes, then press out as much liquid as possible. Fluff up the cucumber with a fork and mix it thoroughly into the yogurt.
3  Stir in the red chili powder, salt, raisins and roasted cumin seeds. Place in a serving bowl and chill.
4  Serve with the mint sprinkled on top.

## SPINACH YOGURT SALAD
### *Paalak ka raita*

*T*his is a lovely green colored *raita*; it goes particularly well with hot buttered *chappatis*.

½ lb frozen spinach
1½ cups plain yogurt
1 onion
1 fresh hot green chili pepper
salt to taste
½ teaspoon red chili powder
1 teaspoon roasted cumin seeds
   (see page 28)

SERVES 6

1  Thaw the spinach completely and press out as much water as possible. Reduce to a purée in a blender.
2  Lightly beat the yogurt in a bowl. Finely chop the onion and green chili pepper and mix into the yogurt with the spinach, salt and red chili powder. Turn into a serving dish and chill until ready to serve.
3  Just before serving, sprinkle with the cumin seeds.

CLOCKWISE FROM TOP: BEET YOGURT SALAD, CARROT YOGURT SALAD AND SPINACH YOGURT SALAD.

## EGGPLANT YOGURT SALAD
### *Baigan ka raita*

1 large eggplant
1½ cups plain yogurt
salt to taste
1 teaspoon roasted cumin seeds
   (see page 28)
1 teaspoon coriander seeds
2 small dried hot red chili peppers
coriander (cilantro) leaves, for
   garnish

**SERVES 6**

1 Cook the eggplant in boiling water until tender, or by turning it over a naked flame until it turns completely black (this is the better method for this recipe). Peel the eggplant, and mash the flesh.
2 Lightly beat the yogurt and add the eggplant with the salt and roasted cumin seeds.
3 Roast the coriander seeds and red chili peppers in a dry frying-pan for 1 minute, then crush them finely in a pestle and mortar. Stir into the yogurt and chill until ready to serve.
4 Serve garnished with the coriander.

## CARROT YOGURT SALAD
### *Gajjar ka raita*

*C*arrot *raita* is tasty and has a pretty orange color. Try it with rice and a *dal* dish.

2 medium-sized carrots
1½ cups plain yogurt
1 scallion
1 fresh hot green chili pepper
salt to taste
1 teaspoon sugar
2 teaspoons oil
1 teaspoon mustard seeds

**SERVES 6**

1 Grate the carrots and steam them until quite tender.
2 Lightly beat the yogurt in a bowl and stir in the carrots.
3 Finely chop the scallion and green chili pepper and stir into the yogurt with the salt and sugar.
4 Heat the oil in a small frying-pan and add the mustard seeds. When they "pop," spoon them over the salad. Serve this *raita* at room temperature.

## BEET YOGURT SALAD
### *Chukandar ka raita*

*T*his *raita* is Jaipur pink! Serve it with two or three different colored salads at a party.

2 medium-sized cooked beets
1½ cups plain yogurt
1 teaspoon sugar
salt to taste
1 teaspoon red chili powder
1 teaspoon roasted cumin seeds
   (see page 28)
coriander (cilantro) leaves, for
   garnish

**SERVES 6**

1 Cut the beets into small cubes. Lightly beat the yogurt and gently fold the beets into it.
2 Add all the remaining ingredients except for the coriander and mix together gently. Chill until ready to serve.
3 Garnish with the coriander.

## CHICKPEA YOGURT SALAD
### Chane ka raita

*H*ere is an unusual but very nutritious salad.

1½ cups plain yogurt
10 oz can chickpeas
salt to taste
1 small onion
1 teaspoon red chili powder
1 teaspoon roasted cumin seeds
  (see page 28)
1 teaspoon sugar
1 scallion, for garnish

**SERVES 6**

1  Lightly beat the yogurt in a bowl.
2  Drain the chickpeas well and rinse them under cold running water. Drain again thoroughly, then add to the yogurt with salt to taste.
3  Finely chop the onion and add to the yogurt with the red chili powder and roasted cumin seeds. Stir in the sugar. Chill until ready to serve.
4  Garnish with the scallion, finely chopped.

## GRAPE YOGURT SALAD
### Angoor ka raita

*T*his lovely blend of grapes, honey and plain yogurt makes a very pretty salad.

1½ cups plain yogurt
1 cup seedless grapes
1 teaspoon honey
1 teaspoon sugar
salt to taste
½ teaspoon red chili powder
1 teaspoon roasted cumin seed
  powder (see page 28)

**SERVES 6**

1  Lightly beat the yogurt in a bowl. Wash and dry the grapes, discarding any that are soft.
2  Gently fold the grapes into the yogurt with all the remaining ingredients except for the cumin seed powder. Chill until ready to serve.
3  Sprinkle the cumin seed powder over the salad just before serving.

NOTE  If seedless grapes are not available, cut the seeded ones in half and deseed before mixing into the yogurt.

## BANANA YOGURT SALAD
### Kela ka raita

*A*nother sweet-flavored *raita*, which goes well with a fairly mild curry.

4 small bananas
1½ cups plain yogurt
1 tablespoon raisins
½ teaspoon salt
1 tablespoon sugar
½ teaspoon cardamom powder
  (optional)
½ teaspoon roasted cumin seed
  powder (see page 28)

**SERVES 6**

1  Peel the bananas and slice thinly.
2  Lightly beat the yogurt in a bowl, then gently stir in the bananas together with all the remaining ingredients except for the roasted cumin seed powder. Cover closely and chill until ready to serve.
3  Sprinkle with the cumin seed powder just before serving.

# CHUTNEYS AND PICKLES

Chutneys and pickles are always served with a curry meal. Chutneys could be described as "pungent relishes" and they are a must to serve with all deep-fried snacks. They can also be used as delicious dips to go with potato chips or crackers. Flavors of chutney vary in different parts of India; in the south, for example, they are generally made from coconut while in the north, mangoes are the most common ingredient. During the time of the British Raj, the British added sugar to chutneys, making them sweet and using them as an accompaniment to curry meals. By and large, most chutneys are hot, so only take a small quantity at first!

Chutneys are generally made to be eaten fresh with the snack or the meal. They will keep for three to four days, but should be kept in the refrigerator. Pickles on the other hand, are made in quite a different way, so that the ingredients are actually preserved. Most pickles need to "mature"

for a week or so before eating, and many will keep for up to a year, providing they are kept in airtight jars in a cool, dark place.

In India, almost anything can be pickled! Vegetables, fruits, meat and fish are all made into pickles and you will find a selection in every home. They make an ideal "hunger-filler" with a thick slice of bread, which can save you having to cook a meal or prepare a snack! Many pickles are oil-based and no water should come near the pickle jar in these instances, or the pickle will go rancid. Always pack them into screw-top jars and make sure the lid is screwed on firmly. For long storage, process in a boiling-waterbath.

The number of servings is not given in the recipes that follow, as how much chutney or pickle eaten at a meal will depend on the tastes of the people, and the kind of meal it is accompanying. The chutneys will be enough to accompany a curry meal for at least eight people; the pickles, in any event, you can eat whenever you feel like it.

## MANGO CHUTNEY
### Kairee ki chatni

Unripe green mangoes are used to make this chutney, so it either has to be made when mangoes are in season, or the green mangoes can be frozen after peeling and cutting them into small pieces. This chutney goes well with a dry vegetable curry and hot buttered *chappatis*.

1 green unripe mango
1 teaspoon coriander seeds
1 teaspoon cumin seeds
1 dried hot red chili pepper
1 fresh hot green chili pepper
½ cup water (approx)
salt to taste

1 Peel the mango and cut the flesh into cubes.
2 Roast the coriander and cumin seeds in a small dry frying-pan until well browned. Remove from the pan. Crush the dried red chili pepper and roast in the same pan.
3 Chop the green chili pepper finely.
4 Put all the ingredients in a blender or food processor and blend together thoroughly, adding more water if the chutney looks too dry. Turn into a bowl and serve.

**C**LOCKWISE FROM LEFT: HOT SWEET PLUM PICKLE, EGGPLANT PICKLE AND GUJRATI CHILI PICKLE.

## SWEET AND SOUR CHUTNEY
*Khatti meethi chatni*

6 tablespoons tomato ketchup
¼ cup tamarind water (see page 29)
1 teaspoon ground ginger
salt to taste
1 teaspoon garlic purée
1 teaspoon sugar
1 teaspoon red chili powder
1 tablespoon soy sauce
¼ cup water
1 tablespoon raisins

1  Place all the ingredients except for the raisins in a blender or food processor and blend together.
2  Wash the raisins and dry on paper towels. Stir into the chutney.

NOTE  Serve this chutney with fried snacks.

## RED CHILI CHUTNEY
*Lal mirchi ki chatni*

*T*his chutney is a specialty of Rajasthan. I remember we used to watch our servants eating it with very thick *chappatis* and beg them to give us some too! Now I always make it when I have any left-over cold *chappatis*. It is very hot – and a great favorite of Maharaja Bubbles. He eats it with his *shammi kebabs* (see page 37).

12 dried hot red chili peppers
1 cup water (approx)
salt to taste
1 teaspoon cumin seeds
6 cloves garlic
¼ cup plain yogurt

1  Soak the chili peppers in the water overnight.
2  The next day, put them with the water in a blender or food processor and add all the other ingredients except the yogurt. Blend until thoroughly mixed.
3  Stir this mixture into the yogurt. Turn into a serving dish and keep at room temperature until ready to serve.

## GREEN CHILI CHUTNEY
*Hari mirch ki chatni*

*T*his chutney is milder than the red chili chutney, but it is still very hot. Try it with a mild *dal*, boiled rice, *raita* and *poppadums*.

8 fresh hot green chili peppers
2 onions
salt to taste
1 teaspoon cumin seeds
1 tablespoon lemon juice
¼ cup water (approx)

1  Chop the green chili peppers and onions.
2  Put all the ingredients into a blender or food processor and blend thoroughly, adding more water if the mixture seems too thick. Keep the chutney in a plastic container in the refrigerator until required.

## TOMATO CHUTNEY
*Tamatar ki chatni*

1 tablespoon oil
1 teaspoon cumin seeds
1 onion
3 cloves garlic
1 inch piece fresh ginger root
$\frac{1}{2}$ teaspoon turmeric powder
1 teaspoon red chili powder
1 teaspoon coriander powder
salt to taste
2 teaspoons sugar
6 tomatoes

1 Heat the oil in a frying-pan and add the cumin seeds. Finely chop the onion and slice the garlic. Add to the pan and cook, stirring, for about 2 minutes.
2 Finely chop the ginger and add to the pan with the spices, some salt and the sugar. Cook for a few minutes.
3 Chop the tomatoes roughly and add to the pan. Stir, then cover and cook gently for 5–10 minutes, until the tomatoes are soft and everything is mixed together well. Serve the chutney hot with *dal*, rice and *poppadums*.

## COCONUT CHUTNEY
*Nariyal ya khopre ki chatni*

$\frac{1}{2}$ fresh coconut
2 fresh hot green chili peppers
1 inch piece fresh ginger root
2 cloves garlic
1 cup fresh coriander (cilantro)
1 teaspoon cumin seeds
salt to taste
1 teaspoon sugar
$\frac{1}{2}$ cup water (approx)
1 cup plain yogurt
1 tablespoon oil
1 teaspoon mustard seeds
a few curry leaves

1 Grate the flesh of the coconut, finely chop the chili peppers and crush the ginger and garlic. Wash the coriander, strip the leaves off the stem and chop finely.
2 Put all the ingredients except the oil, mustard seeds and curry leaves into a blender and blend together. Spoon into a glass serving bowl.
3 Heat the oil in a small frying-pan and add the mustard seeds and curry leaves. When the seeds begin to "pop," pour the mixture over the chutney. Gently mix it in with a spoon.

## TAMARIND CHUTNEY
*Imli ki chatni*

a walnut-sized piece of tamarind
   pulp
1 cup hot water
1 dried hot red chili pepper
3 cloves garlic
1 inch piece fresh ginger root
1 teaspoon cumin seeds
1 tablespoon brown sugar
2 teaspoons raisins

1 Soak the tamarind in the water for about 1 hour. Squeeze it and strain the liquid through a sieve into a bowl.
2 Grind the dried red chili pepper, garlic and ginger in a pestle and mortar or food processor. Roast the cumin seeds in a small dry frying-pan. Mix all these ingredients into the tamarind water.
3 Add the brown sugar and raisins and mix everything together thoroughly. If the mixture seems too thick, add a little cold water. Turn into a serving dish and chill before serving.

## FRESH CORIANDER CHUTNEY
*Hara dhaniya ki chatni*

*T*his is my favorite chutney, perhaps because I love the smell of fresh coriander. Wherever I am, I always grow my own fresh coriander in a shallow box. When I travel, my cook cuts the coriander leaves with scissors, washes them and then freezes them in a plastic bag so that, when I am home and cook a *dal* or curry, I just crush the bag and sprinkle some leaves into the dish; they taste and smell just like fresh!

$\frac{1}{4}$ lb bunch fresh coriander (cilantro)
1 fresh hot green chili pepper
2 cloves garlic
1 teaspoon cumin seeds
$\frac{1}{2}$ cup water (approx)
1 tablespoon lemon juice
1 tablespoon dried shredded
  coconut

1  Strip the coriander leaves off the stems, wash them, shake well to dry, then chop very finely. Finely chop the chili and crush the garlic.
2  Place all the ingredients in a blender or food processor and blend together. Keep refrigerated in a small covered plastic box, until required.

LADIES, DRESSED IN TRADITIONAL JAIPUR COLORS, SELLING FRESH TAMARIND AND BERRIES TO PASSERS-BY. ONE OF THE LADIES IS USING HER VEIL OR *AURNA* TO SHADE HER FACE COMPLETELY FROM THE SUN'S HEAT.

## ❧ FRESH MINT CHUTNEY ❧
*Podina ki chatni*

*M*int chutney is very popular in North India, where it is served almost daily at lunch time.
It goes well with *samosas* and *pakoras.*

¼ lb bunch fresh mint
2 onions
1 fresh hot green chili pepper
2 cloves garlic
salt to taste
1 teaspoon sugar
1 teaspoon red chili powder
1 tablespoon tamarind water (see
    page 29)
1 tablespoon lemon juice
1 teaspoon cumin seeds
½ cup water (approx)

**1** Strip the mint leaves from the stems, wash them, shake to dry, then chop finely. Finely chop the onions and green chili pepper and crush the garlic.
**2** Put all the ingredients together in a blender or food processor and blend to mix. Add more water if the mixture seems too thick. Turn into a serving dish.

## ❧ SHRIMP CHUTNEY ❧
*Jhinga chatni*

2 tablespoons dried shredded
    coconut
1 tablespoon dried shrimp
    (available from Indian and
    Chinese grocers)
1 small onion
1 teaspoon chili powder
salt to taste
1 teaspoon ground ginger
1 tablespoon lemon juice

**1** Roast the coconut in a dry pan until golden brown.
**2** Grind the shrimp to a powder in a coffee grinder or pestle and mortar.
**3** Chop the onion finely and add to the shrimp. Add all the remaining ingredients and blend together in a food processor. Transfer to a serving dish.

## ❧ SWEET AND SOUR MANGO PICKLE ❧
*Aam ka khatta meetha achaar*

1 lb green mangoes
2 tablespoons salt
6 tablespoons oil
2 teaspoons cumin seeds
1 teaspoon nigella seeds
2 teaspoons turmeric powder
2 teaspoons red chili powder
2 teaspoons fennel seed powder
2 teaspoons coriander powder
2⅓ cups brown sugar or *jaggery*

**1** Peel the mangoes and cut the flesh into cubes. Place in a bowl and sprinkle with the salt. Keep in a warm place – preferably in the sun for a day.
**2** Heat the oil in a frying-pan and add the cumin and nigella seeds. Cook for 1 minute, then add all the remaining spices and the sugar or *jaggery*, together with the mangoes and their liquid. Simmer for 5–10 minutes, then leave to cool completely.
**3** Put the mango mixture into a glass jar and keep on a sunny windowsill for two weeks before using.

## ❦ GRATED MANGO PICKLE ❦
### *Aam ke lacche ka achaar*

*H*ere is a pickle from the northern part of India. It tastes good with cold *chappatis* or pita bread.

2½ cups oil
2 teaspoons cumin seeds
1 teaspoon fenugreek seeds
2 teaspoons mustard seeds
2 teaspoons turmeric powder
2 teaspoons red chili powder
2 teaspoons fennel or anise seeds
1 tablespoon salt
1 lb green mangoes

1  Heat 2 tablespoons oil in a frying-pan or wok and add the cumin, fenugreek and mustard seeds. When they "pop" remove from the pan and grind in a spice or coffee grinder.
2  Add another 2 tablespoons oil to the pan and return the ground seeds together with the turmeric and chili powders, the fennel or anise seeds and the salt.
3  Peel the mangoes and grate the flesh. Add to the pan and cook gently, stirring frequently, for 10–15 minutes. Remove from the heat and leave to cool completely.
4  Put the remaining oil into a saucepan, heat it until it is very hot, then let it cool.
5  Put the cold mango mixture into a large jar and add the oil.
6  Cover the jar and leave on a sunny windowsill for at least one week before using.

## ❦ RAJASTHANI MANGO PICKLE ❦
### *Rajasthani aam ko achaar*

*T*his pickle, I remember, was made every summer in our backyard, by our maids. It was an all-day affair and we would sit on our chairs and watch the performance. Four or five people would be involved in the preparation as enough pickle was made at this one time for the whole year, plus enough extra to give to relatives who came to visit. The amount here is rather more manageable!

12 green unripe mangoes
1 tablespoon turmeric powder
2 tablespoons salt
8 dried hot red chili peppers
2 cups oil (approx)
2 teaspoons fennel or anise seeds
1 tablespoon nigella seeds
2 tablespoons mustard seeds
2 tablespoons cumin seeds

1  Wash the mangoes, but do not peel. Cut them into small square pieces, discarding the seeds, and place in a large bowl. Add the turmeric and salt.
2  Break off the ends of the chili peppers and empty out the seeds. Crush the remaining shells coarsely and put on one side.
3  Heat half the oil in a frying-pan or wok and add the fennel or anise, nigella, mustard and cumin seeds. When they "pop," drain the mangoes and add to the pan. Mix well.
4  Add the crushed red chili peppers and let the mixture simmer very gently for about 1 hour. Remove from the heat and cool.
5  Heat the remaining oil until it is very hot. Remove from the heat and let it cool completely.
6  When the mango mixture is cold, put it into a large, wide-necked jar and pour the cooled oil over it. If the oil does not cover the mangoes completely, heat a little more oil and let it cool, before pouring into the jar.
7  Cover the jar and let it stand for two weeks before using.

## SALTED LEMON PICKLE
*Dholva neebu*

*S*alted lemon pickle is a good one to keep always at hand, as it is a good cure for nausea. I have some whenever I feel sick – it was terrific when I was pregnant! The longer you keep it, incidentally, the better it tastes.

1 lb lemons
scant 1 cup rock salt or ordinary
  salt

**1** Wash and dry the lemons thoroughly, then cut into quarters but leave them joined at the bottom.
**2** Pack the salt into the slits, then pack the lemons into wide-necked jars. Pour any remaining salt over the lemons in the jars.
**3** Close the jars and put in a warm place – preferably on a sunny windowsill for at least six weeks. Shake the jar each day.
**4** The lemons will soften and change into a toffee brown color. Break off a quarter piece and eat it whenever you feel like it, or serve with a curry meal.

## SWEET LEMON PICKLE
*Neebu ka meetha achaar*

*S*weet lemon pickle goes very well with curries. Try it with *dal*, boiled rice and *poppadums*.

1 lb lemons or limes
2 tablespoons salt
20 cloves garlic
1¼ cups raisins
1 teaspoon red chili powder
1 inch piece fresh ginger root
2 cups malt vinegar
1⅓ cups brown sugar

**1** Cut the lemons or limes into quarters. Remove the seeds and put the quarters into a bowl.
**2** Sprinkle with the salt, then leave for three days, stirring the fruit at least once a day.
**3** Put the whole garlic cloves into a bowl with the raisins and red chili powder. Finely chop the ginger, and add this to the bowl, then pour in half the vinegar. Keep in the refrigerator for 24 hours.
**4** Remove the lemon or lime quarters from their bowl and chop into small pieces. Chop the raisin mixture finely and mix with the lemons or limes together with the remaining vinegar and the sugar.
**5** Tip this mixture into a saucepan, place over a low heat and simmer gently for about 1 hour, or until the liquid has thickened. Leave to cool completely.
**6** Spoon the pickle into jars, cover them and leave on a sunny windowsill for three days before using.

## EGG PICKLE
*Ande ka achaar*

*A* good pickle for dinner parties, this one seems to go well with everything.

6 lemons
1 inch piece fresh ginger root
1 fresh hot green chili pepper
1 teaspoon red chili powder
salt to taste
½ cup vegetable oil
12 hard-boiled eggs

1  Squeeze the juice from the lemons and thinly slice the ginger and chili pepper.
2  Mix these with the red chili powder, salt and oil.
3  Shell the hard-boiled eggs and cut them in half. Place in a large dish or jar. Pour the pickle mixture over them and keep, covered, in the refrigerator until required.

## GUJRATI CHILI PICKLE
*Gujrati mirch ka achaar*

*Q*uick to prepare, this pickle can be eaten right away. It tastes good with *pooris* or *chappatis*.

1 tablespoon sesame seeds
1 tablespoon cumin seed powder
16 fresh hot green chili peppers
1 cup oil
salt to taste
3 tablespoons lemon juice
1 teaspoon sugar

1  Roast the sesame seeds and cumin seed powder in a dry, heavy-based frying-pan until brown. Remove from the heat.
2  Wash the chili peppers and dry them on paper towels.
3  Heat the oil in a frying-pan or wok. Add the chili peppers and fry them for 2 minutes, then remove with a slotted spoon and drain on paper towels.
4  Put the chili peppers into a glass bowl and sprinkle with all the remaining ingredients. Let the pickle cool before serving.

## PEPPER AND GREEN TOMATO PICKLE
*Simla mirch aur hare tamatar ka achaar*

*T*his pickle is a bit like a curry, and tastes good with *chappatis* or *dal* and boiled rice.

1 lb green peppers
1 lb green tomatoes
6 onions
1 tablespoon salt
2⅓ cups brown sugar
1 tablespoon ground cloves
1 tablespoon ground cinnamon
2 cups vinegar

1  Slice the peppers, tomatoes and onions and put into a large bowl. Sprinkle with the salt and leave overnight.
2  The next day, drain the vegetables, squeezing out as much of the liquid as possible. Discard this and put the vegetables into a saucepan with the sugar, spices and vinegar. Mix well.
3  Place the pan on a low heat and simmer very gently, covered, for about 2 hours. Leave to cool completely.
4  Spoon the mixture into a wide-necked jar, cover and leave on the kitchen windowsill for one week before using.

# CAULIFLOWER, CARROT AND HORSERADISH SWEET PICKLE

### *Gobi-gajar-mooli ka meetha achaar*

*A* typical Punjabi pickle, this one is made in the winter when the three vegetables are in season.
It is a sweet pickle – very tasty with *chappatis*.

$\frac{1}{2}$ lb cauliflower
$\frac{1}{2}$ lb carrots
$\frac{1}{2}$ lb horseradish
1 tablespoon mustard seeds
2 teaspoons turmeric powder
2 teaspoons red chili powder
salt to taste
$\frac{2}{3}$ cup *jaggery* or brown sugar
$\frac{2}{3}$ cup malt vinegar

1 Cut the cauliflower into small florets and slice the carrots and horseradish into 2 inch strips. Wash these vegetables, then parboil them for about 5 minutes.
2 Drain the vegetables thoroughly and spread them out on a dish towel. Leave for 2–3 hours to dry, preferably under a fan or in the sun.
3 Put the vegetables into a bowl and add the spices and salt. Mix together.
4 Put the *jaggery* or brown sugar and vinegar into a saucepan, bring to a boil and stir until dissolved. Leave to cool.
5 Spoon the vegetables and spices into a wide-necked jar and pour the sweetened vinegar over them. Cover the jar and leave in a sunny place for at least one week before using.

**C**LOCKWISE FROM TOP: SALTED LEMON PICKLE, MANGO CHUTNEY AND FRESH CORIANDER CHUTNEY.

## EGGPLANT PICKLE
### *Baigan ka achaar*

1 lb eggplants
6 fresh hot green chili peppers
1 inch piece fresh ginger root
8 cloves garlic
$1\frac{1}{4}$ cups malt vinegar
1 teaspoon red chili powder
1 teaspoon turmeric powder
2 teaspoons ground ginger
1 cup oil
2 teaspoons cumin seeds
1 teaspoon fenugreek seeds
1 teaspoon salt
$\frac{1}{4}$ cup sugar

1  Wash the eggplants and green chili peppers, then dry them thoroughly on a dish towel. Discard the top ends and stalks from the eggplants and cut the remainder into 1 inch cubes. Slice the chili peppers in two lengthwise. Peel and finely slice the ginger.
2  Grind four cloves of garlic with $\frac{1}{4}$ cup vinegar, the red chili and turmeric powders and ground ginger, either in a pestle and mortar or a food processor. Put on one side.
3  Heat the oil in a frying-pan or wok and add the cumin and fenugreek seeds. Slice the remaining cloves of garlic and add to the pan. Stir to mix, then add the spice and vinegar paste.
4  Cook, stirring, for 5–10 minutes, then add the remaining vinegar, the salt and sugar. Mix well, and simmer gently for another 10 minutes.
5  Add the eggplants, chili peppers and ginger to the pan and cook until the eggplants are tender when pierced with a fork.
6  Leave the pickle to cool, then spoon it into a wide-necked jar. Keep on a sunny windowsill for two weeks before using.

## WILD BOAR OR PORK PICKLE
### *Suwar or soor ka achaar*

*I*n Rajasthan, this pickle would be made in the winter after a boar hunt.

2 lb boneless pork
1 cup oil for frying
3 large onions
12 cloves garlic
2 inch piece fresh ginger root
4 teaspoons red chili powder
2 lemons
$\frac{1}{2}$ cup malt vinegar
4 teaspoons cumin powder
1 tablespoon coriander powder
1 teaspoon cardamom powder
1 teaspoon ground cloves
1 teaspoon ground cinnamon
4 teaspoons salt
$1\frac{1}{2}$ cups mustard oil or vegetable oil
   (approx)

1  Cut the pork into small cubes. Heat the 1 cup oil in a frying-pan or wok and fry the pork pieces until lightly browned. Remove with a slotted spoon and drain on paper towels.
2  Mince the onions and garlic in a food processor and add to the oil. Fry until golden brown. Crush the ginger and add it with the red chili powder. Cook gently for 5 minutes more.
3  Squeeze the juice from the lemons and add to the pan with the vinegar. Cook for another 5 minutes, then add the meat, all the remaining spices and the salt. Cook for a further 10 minutes, then remove and cool.
4  Heat the mustard or vegetable oil in a saucepan, then let it cool. Put the cooled meat mixture into a large jar or jars and add enough of the cooled oil to cover it completely. If there is not enough oil, heat some more and let it cool before adding to the meat.
5  Cover the meat and leave for two days in the refrigerator before serving. Remove from the jar with a wooden spoon.

## HOT SWEET PLUM PICKLE
### *Aloo bukhare ka meetha achaar*

1 lb plums
20 cloves garlic
1 inch piece fresh ginger root
20 blanched almonds
1 tablespoon mustard seeds
2 cups malt vinegar
1¼ cups raisins
1 tablespoon red chili powder
1¾ cups brown sugar
1 teaspoon salt

1  Wash the plums, cut in half and remove the pits. Finely slice the garlic, ginger and almonds and crush the mustard seeds coarsely.
2  Put all these into a large saucepan with all the remaining ingredients. Simmer over a low heat for 1–1¾ hours, until the plums are thoroughly soft and the mixture has thickened.
3  Cool completely, then spoon into a glass jar. Keep for about two weeks before using.

## SWEET APPLE PICKLE
### *Meetha seb ka achaar*

16 unripe green apples
4 inch piece fresh ginger root
1¼ cups raisins
16 cloves garlic
1¾ cups brown sugar
2 cups malt vinegar
1 tablespoon mustard seeds
1 tablespoon salt
6 dried hot red chili peppers

1  Wash, peel and core the apples. Slice them roughly. Thinly slice the ginger and wash the raisins. Finely slice the garlic, put in a sieve and hold under cold running water, then dry on a paper towel.
2  Put the sugar and vinegar into a large saucepan and place on a low heat. Stir until the sugar has dissolved, then add the apples and raisins.
3  Simmer gently until the apples are tender. Leave to cool.
4  Add all the remaining ingredients to the pan, replace on the heat and simmer again for 30 minutes, until the mixture thickens slightly. Remove from the heat and stir well, then leave to cool completely.
5  Spoon into glass jars and leave at room temperature in the kitchen for three days before using.

## SWEET CARROT PICKLE
### *Gajjar murraba*

1 lb carrots
2 cups water
1 lb sugar
4 cloves
2 sticks cinnamon
4 whole cardamoms

1  Peel the carrots and cut into small cubes. Put in a heavy-based saucepan with the water and simmer until the carrots are tender. Drain, reserving the cooking liquid.
2  Add the sugar and all the spices to the reserved water, put it back into the pan and simmer gently, covered, for about 20 minutes.
3  Add the carrots and simmer the mixture until it thickens.
4  Cool the pickle completely, then spoon into jars.

# DESSERTS AND SWEETS

I ndian people have a very sweet tooth and consequently, desserts and sweets are a must at the end of a meal. By and large, these are very sweet and rich, made with dried fruits, various essences, lots of sugar, fresh fruits and nuts, different types of flour, and milk, cream or yogurt. Some are soaked in sugar syrups, while others are similar to toffee and marzipan. All festivals are celebrated with a mass of sweets. Housewives busy themselves for days in advance making sweets, and business at the sweet shops, which is always brisk, positively booms during festivals! At *Divali* – our biggest festival – sweets galore are made and eaten, relatives and friends exchanging gifts of sweets on this day, and all past mistakes and quarrels being forgiven and forgotten. We also offer sweets to our Gods in the temples.

## INDIAN TOFFEE I
### *Barfi*

*T*his is the most popular sweet of all in India. It is always made at *Divali* festival in November and given to friends and relatives as gifts. It can be bought in sweet shops, but try making this home-made one – it tastes really special!

2 cups sugar
1 cup water
1¼ cups milk powder
1 tablespoon blanched almonds

MAKES 20–24 SQUARES

1  Put the sugar and water into a pan and place over a medium heat. When the sugar has dissolved, bring the syrup to a boil and boil until the sugar starts to crystallize around the edges of the pan. This takes about 20 minutes. Put a teaspoon of the syrup onto a saucer and when it is cool enough to handle, test it to see if it will form threads between your thumb and index finger. This is called *teen taar ki chashni* and it indicates that the toffee will set as it goes cold. We always apply this test rather than boiling to a certain temperature.
2  Add the milk powder and stir it quickly so that it does not burn or go into lumps. Cook for 3–5 minutes, stirring all the time, until the mixture starts drying on the back of the wooden spoon as you lift it out of the pan.
3  Quickly pour the toffee onto a greased baking sheet. Press it evenly over the sheet using the back of the spoon.
4  Slice the almonds finely, sprinkle them over the toffee and press into the surface using the spoon. Cool until set, then cut into squares. Store in an airtight jar or tin.

CLOCKWISE FROM LEFT: CARDAMOM COOKIES, APPLE KHEER AND INDIAN TOFFEE I.

## INDIAN TOFFEE II
### *Doodh ki barfi*

*A*nother popular sweet to give as gifts at festivals. I devised this recipe in Nigeria.

4 cups sugar
2 cups water
½ teaspoon saffron
1 teaspoon warm milk
4 cups milk powder
2 tablespoons melted *ghee*
1 tablespoon shelled pistachio nuts
10 blanched almonds
1 teaspoon cardamom powder

**MAKES 40–50 SQUARES**

1 Put the sugar and water into a pan and set over a medium heat. When the sugar has dissolved, bring the syrup to a boil and boil until the sugar starts to crystallize around the sides of the pan. This takes about 20 minutes. Put a teaspoon of the syrup onto a saucer and when it is cool enough to handle, test it to see if it will form threads between your thumb and index finger. This is called *teen taar ki chashni* and it indicates that the toffee will set as it goes cold.
2 While the syrup is boiling, soak the saffron in the warm milk.
3 Stir the milk powder and saffron milk into the sugar syrup quickly when it has reached the stage described above. Stir briskly so that the milk does not go lumpy. Add the *ghee*, and let the mixture simmer for about 5 minutes more, until it comes together in a large lump.
4 Pour the toffee onto greased baking sheets and spread it evenly. Chop the pistachio nuts and almonds. Mix them with the cardamom powder, sprinkle over the top of the toffee and press into the surface with the back of a greased spoon.
5 Cool the toffee for about 20 minutes, preferably under a fan. Then cut into squares. Eat within a few days, or freeze until the toffee is required.

## SWEET FLOUR FRITTERS
### *Meetha pua*

*S*weet flour fritters are made on festival days and for large gatherings, as they are easy to prepare for a large number. They are like sweet *pakoras.*

2 cups wholewheat flour
1 cup sugar
⅔ cup plain yogurt
1 cup milk (approx)
1 tablespoon dried shredded
   coconut
1 teaspoon anise seeds
1 teaspoon cardamom seeds
2 cups melted *ghee* or oil for frying

**SERVES 6**

1 Sift the flour into a large bowl. Add the sugar and yogurt and mix well with your hands. Gradually add the milk together with the coconut and anise seeds. Crush the cardamom seeds and add them too, mixing everything together thoroughly.
2 Heat the *ghee* or oil in a frying-pan or wok and drop five to six spoonfuls of the mixture into it. Cook until evenly browned on both sides, then remove with a slotted spoon and drain on paper towels.
3 Repeat until all the *puas* are fried. Serve them hot or cold with whipped sweetened cream.

## SWEET RICE
### Zarda

*Zarda* is a typical Muslim dish, always cooked on Muslim festival days and for weddings and big parties. It is a sweet rice dish flavored with dried fruits and saffron.

2 tablespoons raisins
1 teaspoon saffron
1 tablespoon warm milk
2⅓ cups Basmati rice
1½ quarts water
¼ cup melted *ghee*
4 green cardamoms
1 small stick cinnamon
2 cloves
½ cup milk
1 cup sugar
1 tablespoon lemon juice
12 blanched almonds

SERVES 6

1 Put the raisins into a small bowl, cover with water and leave to soak. In a separate small bowl, soak the saffron in the warm milk.
2 Wash the rice thoroughly under cold running water, then put into a large pan with the water. Bring to a boil, then lower the heat and simmer gently until the rice is half cooked. Drain.
3 Heat the *ghee* in a large frying-pan and add the drained rice. Stir to coat the rice evenly in the *ghee*. Crush the cardamoms and add them to the rice with the cinnamon, cloves, milk and sugar. Simmer gently, covered, until the rice is tender.
4 Drain the raisins and add them to the pan with the lemon juice and saffron milk. Mix well and simmer, covered, for 5 minutes more. Remove from the heat, but leave it on the stove until ready to serve.
5 Spoon onto a flat serving dish. Slice the almonds and sprinkle them over the top.

## CHEESE BALLS IN MILK
### Ras malai

*T*his is a very popular sweet dish and you will find it on the menu of restaurants the world over. This recipe is a simplified version of the traditional one.

7½ cups milk
1 cup sugar
1 teaspoon green cardamoms
1 teaspoon saffron
1½ cups cottage cheese
¾ cup all-purpose flour
1 teaspoon rosewater or *kewra*
    essence
a few shelled pistachio nuts

SERVES 6

1 Put the milk into a large pan with the sugar. Crush the cardamoms and add to the pan with the saffron. Simmer the mixture over a medium heat until it has reduced by half and thickened slightly. Turn the heat down as low as possible under the pan.
2 Beat the cottage cheese and flour together, divide into six or eight portions and roll these into balls. Flatten each one slightly and drop them into the milk pan. Simmer for 10–15 minutes.
3 Remove the pan from the heat and carefully transfer into a serving bowl. Cool completely, then stir in the rosewater or *kewra* essence. Chill. Just before serving, slice the pistachio nuts and sprinkle over the top.

# FRIED MILK BALLS IN ROSE SUGAR SYRUP
### *Gulab jamun*

*A*nother festival sweet, these are everyone's favorite! They are very sticky, so be careful!
The best way to serve them is to drain them from the syrup, put on a plate and pierce each with
a wooden toothpick.

**MILK BALLS**
¾ cup all-purpose flour
1½ cups milk powder
1 tablespoon melted *ghee*
1 tablespoon baking powder
⅔ cup plain yogurt
½ cup milk (approx)
24 raisins
1 cup oil for frying
**SUGAR SYRUP**
1 cup water
2 cups sugar
4 green cardamoms
1 teaspoon rosewater
a pinch of saffron

**MAKES 24 BALLS**

1 Make the milk balls: mix together all the ingredients except the raisins and oil, to form a soft dough. Divide into 24 equal portions. Press a raisin into each portion and roll into small balls. Place on a plate and cover with a damp dish towel.
2 Prepare the sugar syrup: put the water and sugar into a pan and set over medium heat. When the sugar has dissolved, boil the syrup gently for about 20 minutes, until it thickens slightly. Crush the cardamoms and add to the syrup with the rosewater and saffron.
3 Heat the oil for frying in a frying-pan or wok and deep fry the milk balls a few at a time. Keep turning them over until they are an even brick-red color. Take them out and drop them into the sugar syrup.
4 Serve the milk balls straight from the syrup while they are still quite hot.

FRIED MILK BALLS IN ROSE SUGAR SYRUP.

154

## ❧ SEMOLINA PUDDING ❧
*Sooji ka halwa*

A popular pudding in all Indian homes – whenever there is a celebration or guests drop in, this nutritious pudding will be made.

2 cups water
1½ cups sugar
6 tablespoons *ghee*
1⅔ cups + 2 tablespoons semolina flour
1 tablespoon raisins
4 green cardamoms
10 blanched almonds, for decoration

SERVES 6

1  Put the water and sugar into a saucepan and set over medium heat. Stir until the sugar has dissolved, then bring to a boil. Remove from the heat.
2  Heat the *ghee* in a large frying-pan or wok and add the semolina. Stir-fry until it is evenly browned.
3  Add the raisins and stir to mix. Add the sugar syrup, and let the mixture simmer gently until all the water has been absorbed. Stir frequently, so that the mixture does not go lumpy.
4  Crush the cardamoms and add to the pudding. Continue simmering until the pudding is thick and the *ghee* is visible around the sides of the pan.
5  Turn out onto a flat plate. Slice the almonds and use to decorate. Serve warm.

## ❧ POPPY SEED PUDDING ❧
*Khus khus ka halwa*

A fried of mine, Manju Sarin, used to make this pudding every Tuesday and offer it to the Gods, as this was the day she fasted. I had never eaten the pudding before but it became a weekly ritual on Tuesdays, for about two years!

1½ cups poppy seeds
1 tablespoon raisins
⅞ cup (14 tablespoons) *ghee*
1½ cups milk
1½ cups sugar
2 green cardamoms
1 tablespoon dried shredded coconut
10 blanched almonds, for decoration

SERVES 6

1  Pick over the poppy seeds for any small pieces of grit, etc., then wash them. Put the raisins in a small bowl, cover with water and leave to soak.
2  Heat the *ghee* in a large frying-pan or wok and add the poppy seeds. Stir-fry them until they are lightly browned.
3  Add the milk and sugar. Simmer very gently until all the liquid has evaporated. Keep stirring all the time, or the mixture will stick to the pan.
4  Crush the cardamoms and add them to the pan with the drained raisins and the coconut. Stir to mix.
5  Turn the pudding out onto a serving plate. Slice the almonds and sprinkle them on top. Serve warm.

## ❧ CORNSTARCH PUDDING ❧
*Karachi or sohan halwa*

You will find this *halwa* sold in sweet shops, wrapped in colored paper. I learned to make it from a lady called Mrs. B. Singh who gave cooking lessons and who is also a cookbook writer. I was just recently married when I attended her classes, which ran for five weeks. They were great fun! The pudding tastes like Turkish Delight.

$1\frac{3}{4}$ cups sugar
$3\frac{1}{2}$ cups water
$\frac{1}{4}$ cup cornstarch
1 teaspoon yellow food coloring
1 tablespoon lemon juice
20 blanched almonds
10 cashew nuts
10 shelled pistachio nuts
2 cardamoms
1 teaspoon rosewater or vanilla extract
$\frac{2}{3}$ cup (10 tablespoons) *ghee*

**SERVES 6**

1  Put the sugar and 3 cups water into a large saucepan and set over a medium heat. Stir until the sugar has dissolved, then bring to a boil and boil for 5 minutes.
2  Remove from the heat and strain through a cheesecloth.
3  Mix the cornstarch to a smooth paste with the remaining water. Return the sugar syrup to the pan and set over a medium heat. Add the cornstarch mixture slowly, stirring all the time.
4  Add the yellow food coloring, then let the mixture simmer on a very low heat until it has thickened into one lump. Keep stirring continuously.
5  Add the lemon juice. Chop all the nuts and crush the cardamoms. Add to the mixture, reserving half the almonds, and stir to mix. Add the rosewater or vanilla extract.
6  Melt the *ghee* and add gradually to the pan, stirring all the time. Keep cooking, stirring until the *halwa* forms one lump again and the *ghee* has risen to the top. Remove from the heat.
7  Quickly pour the mixture onto a greased baking pan. Sprinkle the remaining almonds on top. Leave to set, then lightly grease the back of a large spoon and use to press the almonds into the surface of the *halwa*. Serve cut into squares or diamond shapes.

## ❧ CARDAMOM COOKIES ❧
*Naan khatai*

We always used to buy these cookies from the bread man who came to the house on his bicycle with a large tin box attached to the back of his bike. He had all sorts of goodies in it, but since *naan khatais* were the cheapest, we could buy the most of these! They just melt in your mouth.

$2\frac{1}{4}$ cups all-purpose flour
$1\frac{1}{3}$ cups semolina flour
$1\frac{3}{4}$ cups sugar
1 cup + 6 tablespoons *ghee*, melted
1 teaspoon cardamom powder

**MAKES 20–24 COOKIES**

1  Sift the flour and mix with all the remaining ingredients to make a pliable dough.
2  Roll the mixture into small balls. Place these on a greased baking sheet and flatten them slightly.
3  Bake the cookies in an oven heated to 350° for 20–25 minutes, until pale golden. Keep checking to make sure they do not burn.

## VERMICELLI PUDDING
*Seviyan*

*A* traditional Muslim dish, this one is always served on the *Idd* Festival. It can be cooked in a sugar syrup as here or boiled in milk. It is very quick to make. You can buy silver *varak* leaves at Indian grocers if you want to decorate the pudding in traditional manner.

½ lb vermicelli
6 tablespoons *ghee*
1 cup water
½ cup sugar
a pinch of saffron powder
1 tablespoon warm water
12 blanched almonds
1 tablespoon raisins
½ teaspoon cardamom powder
6 shelled pistachio nuts
2 silver *varak* leaves, for decoration
  (optional)

SERVES 6

1  Break the vermicelli into 2 inch lengths.
2  Heat the *ghee* in a frying-pan or wok and stir-fry the vermicelli until golden brown. Remove the pan from the heat.
3  Put the water and sugar into another pan and place on a medium heat until the sugar has dissolved.
4  Pour this syrup over the vermicelli and return the pan to the heat. Cook gently until all the liquid has evaporated.
5  While the vermicelli is cooking, dissolve the saffron in the warm water and slice the almonds. Add these to the pan with the raisins and cardamom powder and stir everything together well.
6  Turn the pudding into a serving dish. Slice the pistachio nuts and sprinkle over the top. Decorate the pudding with the silver *varak*, if using.

## CORN PUDDING
*Makki ka halwa*

*T*his is a delicious pudding which we make when fresh corn is in season. You can use canned or frozen whole kernel corn if fresh is unavailable.

6–8 fresh ears of corn
6 tablespoons *ghee*
1 cup water
1 cup milk
1 cup sugar
1 tablespoon raisins
2 green cardamoms
10 blanched almonds, for
  decoration

SERVES 6

1  Shuck the corn, then grate the kernels off the cobs. Alternatively, scrape off the kernels with a knife, then grind finely in a food processor.
2  Heat the *ghee* in a frying-pan or wok and add the corn. Stir-fry it until it is evenly golden in color, then add the water and milk and let the mixture simmer until it thickens.
3  Add the sugar and raisins. Crush the cardamoms and add them too. Continue simmering the mixture until all the liquid has been absorbed and the *ghee* is visible around the top of the pan.
4  Continue cooking very gently for 5 minutes more, stirring all the time or the mixture will stick to the pan.
5  Spoon into a serving dish. Slice the almonds and use to decorate. Serve the pudding hot.

# MANGO KHEER
*Aam ki kheer*

1 lb ripe fresh or canned mangoes
3½ cups milk
1 cup sugar
½ teaspoon rosewater
12 shelled pistachio nuts, for
   decoration

SERVES 6

1  Peel the fresh mangoes; purée the flesh in a blender.
2  Put the milk into a large saucepan and bring it to a boil. Add the mango purée, and cook over medium heat, stirring. When the milk and mango are well mixed, add the sugar.
3  Let the mixture simmer, stirring frequently, until it thickens slightly. Add the rosewater and remove the pan from the heat.
4  Cool slightly, then turn into a serving dish and leave to cool. Slice the pistachio nuts and sprinkle them over the pudding just before serving.

# ORANGE KHEER
*Naarangi ki kheer*

3 oranges
1 cup sugar
3 tablespoons melted *ghee*
8 blanched almonds
1 tablespoon raisins
⅔ cup semolina flour
2 green cardamoms
3½ cups milk

SERVES 6

1  Squeeze the juice from the oranges and mix it with the sugar.
2  Heat the *ghee* in a frying-pan or wok. Slice the almonds and add to the pan with the raisins. Stir-fry for 1 minute, then add the semolina and continue stirring until the semolina is evenly browned.
3  Crush the cardamoms and add to the pan with the milk. Simmer the mixture until it thickens.
4  Add the orange juice and sugar mixture and simmer for 5–10 minutes more, until the pudding has thickened again. Serve hot or cold.

# APPLE KHEER
*Seb ki kheer*

¾ lb sweet apples
4 tablespoons melted *ghee*
5 cups milk
1 cup sugar
10 blanched almonds
2 green cardamons
1 tablespoon raisins

SERVES 6

1  Peel the apples and grate them into a pan of cold water. Bring to a boil and simmer for 5 minutes, then drain, pressing out as much water from the apples as possible.
2  Heat the *ghee* in a frying-pan or wok and add the apples. Stir-fry them until golden. Remove from the heat.
3  Bring the milk to a boil in another pan and add the apples. Cook gently, stirring, until thick. Stir in the sugar.
4  Slice the almonds and crush the cardamoms. Add to the pan with the raisins and continue cooking until the mixture is thick and creamy.
5  Turn into a serving dish and serve hot or cold with *naan khatai* (see page 156).

## ❧ TAPIOCA KHEER ❧
### *Sabudaana ki kheer*

*T*his was a great favorite of mine whenever I was ill as a child. In fact, it was the only food we were allowed if we were ill! It looks like tiny transparent pearls floating in milk.

1 tablespoon raisins
1 cup pearl tapioca
3 cups milk
1 cup water
½ cup sugar
2 green cardamoms
a pinch of saffron powder
6 blanched almonds

SERVES 6

1 Wash the raisins, put them in a small bowl and cover with water. Leave to soak.
2 Put the tapioca in a sieve and wash it under cold running water. Put it into the saucepan with the milk and water and cook on a medium heat until it is soft. Stir in the sugar.
3 Crush the cardamoms and add to the pan with the saffron and the drained raisins. Stir to mix, then simmer until the mixture is the consistency of oatmeal.
4 Turn it into a serving bowl. Slice the almonds and sprinkle them over the top. Serve warm.

AT THIS SHOP FRESHLY MADE SWEETS AND ASSORTED SAVORY SNACKS ARE BEING SOLD.

# ❧ MANGO ICE CREAM ❧
### *Aam ki ice cream*

2 large mangoes
¼ cup custard powder or cornstarch
3½ cups cold milk
½ cup sugar
¾ cup heavy cream

SERVES 6

1  Peel the mangoes and purée the flesh in a blender.
2  Mix the custard powder or cornstarch to a smooth paste with a little of the milk and stir this into the remaining milk with the sugar.
3  Pour the custard mixture into a large saucepan and place over a medium heat. Cook until the custard has thickened, stirring all the time to keep it smooth.
4  Remove from the heat and place the pan in a large bowl of cold water to cool it quickly. Stir frequently to prevent a skin forming.
5  When the custard is cold, stir in the cream and the mango purée. Pour into a rigid freezer container and freeze for 30 minutes.
6  Whip the ice cream with a fork until it is smooth, then return to the freezer and freeze until firm.

# ❧ YOGURT DESSERT I ❧
### *Shrikhand*

2 cups plain yogurt
1 cup sugar
2 tablespoons blanched almonds
1 tablespoon pistachio nuts
a pinch of ground cinnamon
a pinch of grated nutmeg
1 teaspoon cardamom powder
½ teaspoon saffron powder
1 tablespoon raisins

SERVES 6–8

1  Suspend the yogurt in a damp cheesecloth over a large bowl. When most of the watery liquid has dripped out, squeeze the bag to remove the remainder.
2  Empty the yogurt in the cloth into a bowl and stir in the sugar. Slice the almonds and pistachio nuts and stir them in with all the remaining ingredients.
3  Mix well, then spoon into individual serving bowls. Chill well before serving.

# ❧ YOGURT DESSERT II ❧
### *Badaam ka shrikhand*

2 cups plain yogurt
1 tablespoon raisins
⅔ cup sugar
½ cup ground almonds
1 teaspoon cardamom powder
12 shelled pistachio nuts
12 blanched almonds

SERVES 6

1  Suspend the yogurt in a piece of cheesecloth over a large bowl and let it drip for about 1 hour.
2  While the yogurt is dripping, put the raisins in a small bowl and cover them with water. Leave to soak.
3  Turn the yogurt in the cloth into a bowl and stir in the sugar, ground almonds and cardamom powder. Drain the raisins and slice the pistachio nuts and almonds. Add these to the yogurt and stir to mix evenly.
4  Turn into a serving dish and chill until required.

## ❧ SWEET BREAD PUDDING ❧
*Shahi tukri*

2 cups milk
1 teaspoon saffron
1¾ cups *ghee*
12 slices white bread
1¾ cups sugar
1 cup water
½ cup *khoa* (see page 28) or heavy
   cream
2 tablespoons shelled pistachio nuts

SERVES 6

1 Put the milk and saffron in a saucepan and bring to a boil. Take off the heat and leave to cool completely.
2 Heat the *ghee* in a large frying-pan and fry the slices of bread until golden on both sides. Drain them, and put to soak in the saffron milk.
3 In a separate pan dissolve the sugar in the water, then simmer over medium heat for about 15 minutes.
4 Put the soaked bread and milk into a large rectangular ovenproof dish and pour the sugar syrup evenly over it. Dot the *khoa* or cream on top of the bread, then bake the pudding for 10–15 minutes in an oven heated to 375°.
5 Slice the pistachio nuts and sprinkle them over the pudding. Serve hot.

## ❧ GROUND RICE PUDDING ❧
*Phirni*

*Phirni* pudding is always made at the Royal Palace in Jaipur on the festival of *Sharad Purnima* in October. This festival is celebrated on a bright moonlit night and the Rajmata always has a dinner party. We are all expected to wear pale pink *poshaks*, and there is lots of singing and dancing. This pudding is made and put in earthenware bowls, then it is placed out of doors in the moonlight under a net. There it is left until the next morning, when, it is believed, the moonbeams will have turned it into nectar! Eating it for breakfast was a great treat when we were children, but you can serve it at dinner parties, too. Chill it well.

5 cups milk
1 cup rice flour
1 cup water
2 cups sugar
1 teaspoon black cardamom seeds
1 tablespoon raisins
12 blanched almonds
1 teaspoon rosewater
12 shelled pistachio nuts, for
   decoration

SERVES 6

1 Bring the milk to a boil in a large saucepan. Meanwhile, mix the rice flour with the water. Add to the boiling milk, stirring well, then simmer for 10 minutes, stirring all the time.
2 Add the sugar, cardamom seeds and raisins. Stir well. Slice the almonds and stir them in too, with the rosewater. Keep simmering until the mixture turns thick and creamy.
3 Spoon the pudding into individual serving bowls. Slice the pistachio nuts and sprinkle on top. Chill before serving.

# DRINKS AND SHAKES

M ost drinks in India are served to produce some special effect on the human body or mind – either to cool or to heat, to stimulate or to tranquilize. Many drinks are recommended as an antidote to sun-stroke – ever a danger in the hot Indian sun. All herbs, fruits, nuts and spices have their own special effect on the body and mind, and much use of this knowledge is made in Indian cuisine. Yogurt has a cooling effect and is often used as the base of a drink. Other drinks have a fruit base and will be laced with an essence for extra flavor. In all cases, quantities do not have to be measured accurately.

## FRESH LIME JUICE
### *Nimboo paani or shikanji*

*T*his is a very good thirst-quenching and refreshing drink, made popular during the time of the British Raj in India. *Nimboo paani* was as much part of the summer as the "uniform" of khaki shorts and khaki *topi* (hat).

4 limes or lemons
6 glasses cold water
3 tablespoons sugar
1 teaspoon salt
ice cubes

SERVES 6

1 Squeeze the juice from the limes or lemons and mix it with the water, sugar and salt.
2 Stir thoroughly, then strain the mixture into a glass serving jug.
3 Fill the glasses with ice cubes and pour the fruit juice mixture onto them.

## SWEET YOGURT SHAKE
### *Meethi lassi*

*L*assi is a yogurt-based drink, very good for digestion and to counteract the summer heat. It is a staple drink of Punjab and every morning the Punjabis will drink a glass of *lassi* at breakfast, served in a very tall glass.

1½ cups plain yogurt
3 cups cold water
3 tablespoons sugar
a few drops rosewater
ice cubes (optional)

SERVES 6

1 Mix all the ingredients except the ice cubes together in a blender.
2 Pour the frothy mixture into tall glasses, and add some ice if you like. Alternatively, you could chill the *lassi* before serving, but give it a good stir before pouring into glasses.

FRESH LIME JUICE (LEFT) AND SWEET YOGURT SHAKE (RIGHT).

## ❧ SALTY YOGURT SHAKE ❧
*Namkeen lassi*

*T*his is a slightly salty shake, normally drunk at lunchtime in the summer months of June and July, where in Delhi, for example, the temperature is generally over 100°F! *Namkeen lassi* is said to help in avoiding sun-stroke. A large jug of this drink is a common sight on luncheon tables.

1½ cups plain yogurt
3 cups cold water
salt to taste
2 teaspoons roasted cumin seed
    powder (see page 28)

SERVES 6

1 Mix all the ingredients together in a blender.
2 Pour into a large jug and put on the lunch table.

NOTE Some people add finely chopped onions to this *lassi* as this is said to counteract the heat still further – try it!

## ❧ MANGO MILK SHAKE ❧
*Aam ka shake*

*T*his milk shake is made from ripe mangoes and is a great favorite with children. Serve it at brunch or lunch, with wafer cookies.

6 ripe mangoes
½ cup sugar
4 glasses cold milk
lots of crushed ice

SERVES 6

1 Peel the mangoes and cut the flesh into small pieces. Purée in a blender with the sugar and milk.
2 Serve the shake in tall glasses, filled with crushed ice. Put a straw in each glass.

## ❧ ORANGE SHERBET ❧
*Santare ka sharbat*

*M*ake a batch of this and keep it in bottles to use like a soft drink.

12 oranges
1¾ cups sugar
6 glasses cold water

1 Squeeze the juice from the oranges.
2 Put the sugar and water into a large saucepan and set over medium heat. When the sugar has dissolved, let the syrup boil gently for about 10 minutes.
3 Add the orange juice to the syrup and simmer for another 10–15 minutes. Remove from the heat and cool completely.
4 When the orange syrup is cold, pour it into screw-top bottles. Keep them in the refrigerator.
5 To serve, put about 1½ inches of the syrup into a tall glass and fill up with icy cold water. Stir before serving.

## ❧ BANANA MILK SHAKE ❧
### *Kele ka shake*

*B*anana milk shake is a great favorite of my youngest twin daughter – Roshika. It is good for Sunday breakfast with pancakes or *dosas* – very nourishing and filling!

4 ripe bananas
½ cup sugar
4 glasses cold milk
1 teaspoon vanilla extract

SERVES 6

1  Peel the bananas and cut into small pieces. Purée in a blender with all the other ingredients.
2  Chill in the refrigerator until ready to serve, then blend the drink again, so that it is well mixed and frothy.

## ❧ SUGAR CANE DRINK ❧
### *Ganne ka ras*

*T*his is a refreshing drink that is good for the digestion and especially recommended for hepatitis or jaundice sufferers. It is sold at every street corner in carts in India. Sugar cane juice can be bought in Indian grocery stores.

1 inch piece fresh ginger root
4 glasses sugar cane juice
2 lemons
salt to taste
a dash of black pepper
crushed ice

SERVES 6

1  Grind the ginger smoothly with a little water in a pestle and mortar. Strain and reserve the liquid.
2  Put the ginger water into a blender with the sugar cane juice. Squeeze the juice from the lemons and add it to the blender goblet with the salt and pepper. Blend everything together in the machine.
3  Fill tall glasses with crushed ice and pour the suar cane drink over it.

## ❧ SPICED TEA ❧
### *Masala chai*

*S*piced tea is very popular in Bombay, where it is always given to visitors. The family only have it as a special treat on Sundays!

2 oz ground ginger
1 oz whole black peppercorns
1 oz green cardamom seeds
½ oz cloves
pot of brewed tea
milk and sugar, for serving

SERVES 6

1  Grind the four spices together in a spice or coffee grinder. Put into a screw-top jar.
2  Add ½ teaspoon of this *masala* to the pot of tea.
3  Stir the tea and serve with milk and sugar. Keep the remaining *masala* in the jar for future use.

# A WEDDING FEAST

Weddings are a cause of rejoicing and festivity the world over, but in few places do the ceremonies last as long as they do in India! Several days before the wedding, relatives will come to the bride's parents' house – where the actual wedding ceremony will be held – to perform various rituals involving the bride. These are all a traditional part of the whole and the performing of them is very important. Come the day of the wedding itself, the ceremony will last at least three hours – and then there is the feasting afterwards! The next day, the bride and groom return to her parents' house for more traditional ceremonies and still more feasting!

Red, orange and pink are the colors considered auspicious for ladies to wear at weddings in Rajasthan, and the bride will wear red on her wedding day. In the days beforehand, she will wear orange – as when she emerges from the sacred *pooja* (prayer) room of the house, with her female relatives and a small boy in attendance. Then, and during these days before the wedding, she keeps a dagger constantly to hand. This is a relic from bygone days when brides-to-be kept such a weapon with them because attack from the enemy was likely. The dagger was to kill themselves, not to wield at the assailants.

The day before the wedding, the bride's feet and hands are painted in intricate patterns with henna by a professional painter. Then, immediately before the wedding, tradition demands she should wash her hair and tie it on top of her head without drying it, before covering it with her wedding veils. This has to be done even if she has a temperature of 102° as my daughter, Shivina, had on her wedding day!

The bridegroom arrives amid much pomp and style. Bhawani – Shivina's groom – rode to our house on an elephant beautifully decorated with colorful painted patterns on its head and draped with luxurious trappings. The male relatives accompany the groom on foot, and Bhawani was also accompanied by lantern bearers (most weddings take place at 7 o'clock in the evening) and a brass band. The groom receives presents from the bride's father as he arrives at the house,

MANJU'S ELDEST DAUGHTER, SHIVINA, AND SON-IN-LAW, BHAWANI, IN THEIR WEDDING ATTIRE. THE BRIDE'S HANDS ARE PAINTED WITH HENNA.

Preparations in the form of various traditional ceremonies begin two weeks before the actual wedding. Here two relatives of Shivina's are grinding barley and turmeric into a paste, which will then be put on the bride-to-be's hands and feet to cleanse them.

and the bride's mother presses a *teeka* on his forehead.

And for the feasting – you may imagine that this is an important part of the occasion! Huge dishes of curry and its accompaniments are prepared, for the guests sit down to an elaborate feast after the ceremony. There would be at least four meat curry dishes (providing the hosts are not vegetarians, of course) and at least one fish one. Then the usual vegetable, rice, bread, *dal* and *raita* accompaniments would be served too.

Special sweets are prepared for afterwards. The bride and groom feed each other, and then each guest also offers them a mouthful.

The recipes that follow are all ones that might be prepared for a wedding feast – or indeed for any festive occasion. If you are planning a special event, try serving some of these – they are all very special. Each recipe serves six people as it stands; make larger quantities if you are planning a big party. Many of the dishes – the meat curries in particular – could be made ahead and frozen.

## ❧ LAMB CURRY ❧
### *Gosht pasanda*

6 onions
8 cloves garlic
4 fresh hot green chili peppers
1 inch piece fresh ginger root
2 cups water
salt to taste
1 teaspoon turmeric powder
$\frac{1}{2}$ teaspoon black pepper
2 teaspoons chopped coriander
(cilantro) or mint
2 lb boneless lamb from the leg
$\frac{1}{4}$ cup oil
12 blanched almonds
juice of 2 lemons
2 teaspoons *garam masala* powder

SERVES 6

1  Put three of the onions into a food processor with the garlic, chili peppers and ginger and grind together.
2  Put this onion mixture into a large saucepan with the water, salt, turmeric powder, black pepper and coriander or mint.
3  Cut the lamb into 3 inch long thin slices and add to the pan. Set over medium heat and cook gently, stirring occasionally, until the meat is tender. Remove from the heat.
4  Finely slice the remaining onions. Heat the oil in a large frying-pan and fry the onions until brown and crisp. Remove with a slotted spoon and keep on one side.
5  Remove the pieces of meat from the saucepan using tongs and add them to the oil in the frying-pan. Grind the almonds in a pestle and mortar or a coffee grinder and add to the meat. Cook for about 10 minutes, stirring frequently.
6  Add the lemon juice and *garam masala* powder to the meat together with the boiled spicy onion mixture. Stir thoroughly, then add the fried sliced onions. Cook gently until the sauce is thick – for about 10 minutes more.

## ❧ BARBECUED LEG OF LAMB ❧
### *Tandoori raan*

*T*his is the Indian version of roast leg of lamb! My sister, Madhu, often cooks this dish for friends.

1 inch piece fresh ginger root
6 cloves garlic
2 onions
1 fresh hot red chili pepper
salt to taste
1 tablespoon *garam masala*
powder
3 cups plain yogurt
1 leg of lamb, weighing about 4 lb
juice of $\frac{1}{2}$ lemon
GARNISH
lemon and lime slices
mint sprigs

SERVES 6

1  Put the ginger, garlic, onions, red chili pepper, salt and *garam masala* into a food processor and blend to a paste. Mix this with the yogurt.
2  Prick the leg of lamb all over with a fork, then pour the yogurt mixture over it. Leave to marinate for at least 4 hours.
3  Either put the lamb in a large wok with a lid and cook over medium heat for about 45 minutes, turning frequently, or put it into a roasting pan and cook for the same time in an oven heated to 375°.
4  After this, either cook the lamb on a barbecue for another 20–30 minutes, or place it under a hot broiler for this time so that the outside gets brown and crisp.
5  Just before serving, squeeze the lemon juice over the lamb. Serve garnished with lemon and lime slices and mint sprigs.

## WHITE MEAT CURRY
*Rajasthani safed gosht or maas*

12 onions
2 tablespoons poppy seeds
½ fresh coconut
20 blanched almonds or cashew nuts
2 inch piece fresh ginger root
10 cloves garlic
2 lb boneless meat – lamb or pork
5 tablespoons oil
2 teaspoons whole *garam masala*
   (see page 29)
1 tablespoon coriander seeds
4 fresh hot red chili peppers
2 cups plain yogurt
salt to taste
3 cups milk
½ cup hot water

SERVES 6

1  Chop two of the onions finely and grate the remaining ten. Put the poppy seeds, fresh coconut flesh, almonds or cashews, ginger and garlic into a food processor with a splash of water and grind to a thick paste. Cut the meat into bite-sized pieces.
2  Heat the oil in a large frying-pan and add the two chopped onions. Fry for 5 minutes over a high heat, stirring frequently.
3  Lower the heat and add the grated onions, the meat, the ground paste mixture, the whole *garam masala*, coriander seeds, chili peppers, yogurt and salt. Stir well and cook gently until all the liquid has been absorbed and the oil has separated out from the mixture.
4  Add the milk and hot water and stir well. Simmer for 15–20 minutes more, until the meat is tender and most of the liquid has been absorbed.
5  Serve with hot buttered *chappatis* and a *raita*.

## MOGHUL SHREDDED CHICKEN CURRY
*Murg mokul*

1 lb boneless chicken breasts,
   skinned
1 large and 1 small onion
⅓ cup golden raisins
½ cup *ghee*
1 tablespoon cumin seeds
2 cloves garlic
1 inch piece fresh ginger root
1 tablespoon red chili powder
1 teaspoon turmeric powder
1 tablespoon oil
1 cup cashew nuts
¼ cup blanched almonds
⅔ cup dried shredded coconut
7 tablespoons water
¼ cup plain yogurt
salt to taste
2 tablespoons heavy cream
GARNISH
1 small onion
1 tablespoon oil
1 small fresh hot green chili pepper
1 small fresh hot red chili pepper
a few blanched almonds

SERVES 6

1  Steam the chicken breasts for about 20 minutes, then shred them very finely. While the chicken is cooking, chop the large onion finely. Put the raisins into a small bowl, cover with water and leave to soak.
2  Heat the *ghee* in a heavy-based pan and add the cumin seeds. Cook for 1 minute, then add the chopped onion and cook, stirring occasionally, until soft.
3  Meanwhile, grind the garlic and ginger to a paste in a pestle and mortar and add it to the pan with the red chili and turmeric powders. Stir well.
4  Finely chop the remaining small onion and fry in the oil until brown. Put in a food processor with the cashew nuts, almonds and coconut and grind to a paste. Add to the pan and cook for about 3 minutes, stirring, then add the water. Stir well, then cook over low heat for about 5 minutes.
5  Beat the yogurt until smooth. Drain the raisins. Add these to the pan with some salt and simmer for 10 minutes.
6  Add the finely shredded chicken and cook for 7–10 minutes.
7  Meanwhile, prepare the garnish. Slice the onion finely and fry in the oil until brown and crisp. Cut the green and red chili peppers and the almonds into fine strips.
8  Stir the cream into the chicken and spoon into a serving dish. Garnish with the onion, chilies and almonds.

## SPICY BARBECUED CHICKEN
### Tikka murgi

1 lb boneless chicken
2 teaspoons garlic granules
2 teaspoons ground ginger
1 teaspoon red chili powder
2 teaspoons *garam masala* powder
salt to taste
2 tablespoons oil
juice of 3 lemons

SERVES 4

1 Cut the chicken into 1 inch cubes. Put into a shallow dish.
2 Thoroughly mix together all the remaining ingredients and spoon over the chicken, turning to coat it evenly with the marinade. Leave in a cool place for at least 4 hours.
3 Grease four skewers and thread the chicken onto them.
4 Cook over a charcoal barbecue for the best taste, or under a hot broiler, turning to cook the meat evenly, until it is cooked through. It should be slightly charred on the outside.

## WHOLE STUFFED CHICKEN
### Murg-mussallam II

*A* very rich and special dish similar to the recipe on page 74.

2 tablespoons poppy seeds
1 tablespoon whole *garam masala*
    (see page 29)
1 teaspoon cumin seeds
12 onions
$\frac{1}{4}$ cup oil
$\frac{1}{2}$ fresh coconut
1 inch piece fresh ginger root
a slice of green raw papaya
    (optional)
salt to taste
a pinch of grated nutmeg
1 cup plain yogurt
1 chicken, weighing 4–5 lb
2 hard-boiled eggs
$\frac{1}{2}$ cup melted *ghee* or oil
10 cloves garlic
$\frac{1}{2}$ cup water
a few raisins and blanched almonds
a pinch of saffron powder
dash of *kewra* essence or rosewater
2 leaves of edible silver *karak*
    (optional)

SERVES 6

1 In a small heavy-based pan roast the poppy seeds, whole *garam masala* and cumin seeds separately. Then grind the *garam masala* with the cumin adding a dash of water – use a spice or coffee grinder or a pestle and mortar. Put on one side.
2 Finely slice four of the onions and fry in the $\frac{1}{4}$ cup oil until soft and lightly browned. Grate the coconut and ginger.
3 Place the fried onions, coconut, poppy seeds, ginger, papaya (if using), salt and nutmeg in a food processor and blend together. Stir in the yogurt.
4 Stuff the chicken with this spicy mixture together with the shelled hard-boiled eggs (leave them whole). Tie the legs and vent end of the chicken together tightly with string to close the opening.
5 Prick the outside of the chicken with a fork and rub the ground roasted *garam masala* and cumin into the skin.
6 Mince the remaining onions in a food processor. Heat the *ghee* or oil in a large, deep, heavy-based saucepan and fry the onions until soft. Crush the garlic and add to the pan with the water. Place the chicken on top, then cover the pan and cook over a low heat, turning the chicken from time to time so that it cooks evenly. When you turn the chicken, stir the onions so that they do not stick and burn.
7 When the chicken is cooked, add the raisins and almonds, saffron and a few drops of *kewra* essence or rosewater to the onion mixture.
8 Serve the chicken on a bed of rice with the fried onion mixture around it. Decorate with silver *karak* if using.

# CHICKEN CURRY
### *Murgi curry*

6 onions
$\frac{1}{4}$ cup oil
2 bay leaves
1 teaspoon whole *garam masala*
   (see page 29)
1 cup hot water
6 cloves garlic
$\frac{1}{2}$ cup water
1 teaspoon turmeric powder
2 teaspoons red chili powder
4 teaspoons coriander powder
2 tablespoons tomato paste
$1\frac{1}{2}$ lb boneless chicken
salt to taste
$\frac{1}{2}$ lb fresh bulk spinach (optional)
juice of 2 lemons
1 teaspoon *garam masala* powder
chopped coriander (cilantro), for
   garnish

SERVES 6

1 Mince the onions in a food processor. Heat the oil in a heavy-based pan and add the bay leaves and whole *garam masala*. Stir, then add the onion. Cook for a few minutes, then add half the hot water and let the mixture simmer gently.
2 Crush the garlic. Mix the water and turmeric, red chili and coriander powders together to form a paste.
3 When the liquid in the pan has almost evaporated and the onion mixture is thick, stir in the garlic and the spicy paste. Add the tomato paste.
4 Cut the chicken meat into bite-sized pieces. When the oil has separated out from the onion mixture, add the chicken and salt. Add the remaining hot water and the spinach, if using. Simmer over a low heat until the chicken is tender.
5 Remove from the heat, but leave on the stove for about 15 minutes to let the flavors blend.
6 Turn the curry into a serving dish and pour over the lemon juice. Sprinkle with the *garam masala* powder and coriander.

ABOVE: THE ROYAL WEDDING OF MAHARAJ JAI SINGH, YOUNGER BROTHER OF MAHARAJA "BUBBLES," WAS HELD WITHIN A WEEK OF SHIVINA'S WEDDING. HERE HE ACCEPTS A CUSTOMARY GIFT.

RIGHT: AFTER HER WEDDING, SHIVINA RECEIVES ASSISTANCE FROM HER RELATIVES IN REMOVING HER MANY ITEMS OF JEWELRY. SOME OF THESE WILL HAVE BEEN A PRESENT FROM HER NEW HUSBAND.

# PARTRIDGE CURRY
## *Teetar curry*

3 partridges
½ cup oil
1 teaspoon whole *garam masala*
   (see page 29)
4 onions
12 cloves garlic
2 tomatoes
1 teaspoon turmeric powder
2 teaspoons red chili powder
4 teaspoons coriander powder
salt to taste
1 cup plain yogurt
½ cup boiling water
1 inch piece fresh ginger root
a pinch of saffron powder

**SERVES 6**

1  Cut the partridges into quarters – poultry shears are the best thing to use for this – then prick the flesh all over with a fork.
2  Heat half the oil in a frying-pan and add the *garam masala*. Quickly add the partridge pieces and brown them on both sides. Then lower the heat and cook gently until the partridge pieces are tender. Remove from the oil and put on one side.
3  Meanwhile, mince the onions and garlic together in a food processor and chop the tomatoes.
4  Add the rest of the oil to the frying-pan and cook the minced onions and garlic until golden brown. Add the turmeric, red chili and coriander powders, together with the salt and chopped tomatoes. Cook for 5 minutes, stirring all the time.
5  Return the cooked partridge pieces to the pan with the yogurt and boiling water. Cover the pan and cook on a low heat for 10 minutes.
6  Crush the ginger and add to the pan with the saffron. Stir well, then remove the pan from the heat and keep covered until ready to serve.
7  Serve with hot buttered *chappatis* or plain boiled rice.

# FISH CURRY WITH CREAM AND SAFFRON
## *Machhali malai kesar ki*

1 lb white fish fillet
4 onions
4 cloves garlic
1 inch piece fresh ginger root
¼ cup oil
salt to taste
1 teaspoon turmeric powder
2 teaspoons red chili powder
4 teaspoons coriander powder
1–2 tablespoons water
2 teaspoons raisins
a pinch of saffron powder
1 cup plain yogurt
1 teaspoon *garam masala* powder
¼ cup hot water
¼ cup heavy cream

**SERVES 6**

1  Skin the fish and cut it into 2 inch pieces, discarding all bones. Finely chop the onions, garlic and ginger.
2  Heat the oil and fry the onions, garlic and ginger. Add the salt and all the spices together with the water. Cook until the oil separates out, then add the raisins and saffron. Stir to mix well and cook for 1 minute.
3  Add the fish, yogurt, *garam masala* powder and hot water. Simmer the mixture very gently, covered, until the fish is tender. Stir in the cream, heat gently without boiling and serve.

NOTE  If you prefer you can cook this in an oven heated to 375° for about 25 minutes. Serve the fish with saffron rice (see page 177).

## CURRIED PEAS AND INDIAN CHEESE
### *Matar paneer nakhuda*

*A*n exotic dish which is good for a dinner party too.

¾ lb *paneer* (see page 28)
½ cup oil
2 onions
6 cloves garlic
1 inch piece fresh ginger root
½ cup hot water
1 teaspoon turmeric powder
1 teaspoon red chili powder
2 teaspoons coriander powder
3 tomatoes or 2 tablespoons tomato
   paste
1⅔ cups peas, fresh or frozen
salt to taste
1 cup plain yogurt
1 teaspoon *garam masala* powder
½ cup heavy cream

**Serves** 6

1 Cut the cheese into 1 inch squares. Heat the oil in a frying-pan or wok and fry the cheese squares until pale golden. Remove with a slotted spoon and put on one side.
2 Finely chop the onions, garlic and ginger. Fry in the oil used for the cheese until the onions are soft and golden. Add the hot water and simmer for 5 minutes.
3 Add the spices and stir to mix. Chop the tomatoes, if using fresh, and add to the pan, or add the tomato paste. Stir again to mix, then add the peas, salt, yogurt and *garam masala* powder.
4 Cover the pan and cook gently until the liquid is absorbed. Add the fried cheese and cook for 5 minutes more.
5 When ready to serve, stir in the cream and serve at once.

## CURRIED TOMATOES
### *Tamatar dilbahar*

6 tomatoes
2 cloves garlic
1 onion
1 inch piece fresh ginger root
2 tablespoons oil
1 teaspoon cumin seeds
1 teaspoon turmeric powder
1 teaspoon red chili powder
1 teaspoon coriander powder
salt to taste
1 teaspoon sugar
¼ lb *paneer* (see page 28)
2 tablespoons grated Cheddar
   cheese
chopped coriander (cilantro), for
   garnish

**Serves** 6

1 Cut a slice off the tops of the tomatoes and discard. Scoop out the insides of the tomatoes, chop the pulp and reserve. Rinse out the tomatoes and leave them upside down on paper towels to drain.
2 Finely chop the garlic, onion and ginger. Heat the oil in a frying-pan and add the cumin seeds, garlic, onion and ginger. Fry, stirring, for 5 minutes.
3 Add the tomato pulp to the pan together with all the spices and the salt and sugar. Simmer for 5–10 minutes.
4 Dice the *paneer* into the pan and simmer for another 5 minutes or until the mixture is thick. Remove from the heat.
5 Spoon the mixture into the tomato shells. If there is any left over arrange it around the tomatoes on a heatproof serving dish.
6 Sprinkle the Cheddar cheese over the tomatoes. Place under a hot broiler until the cheese has melted and is bubbling. Serve at once, sprinkled with the coriander.

CLOCKWISE FROM TOP LEFT: CHUTNEYS WITH TOMATO AND ONION YOGURT SALAD, BARBECUED LEG OF LAMB,

PEAS FRIED RICE, *NAAN*, FISH CURRY WITH CREAM AND SAFFRON AND SAFFRON RICE AND CURRIED TOMATOES.

## ❧ DRY POTATO CURRY ❧
*Poori wale aloo*

1 lb potatoes
1 onion
2 cloves garlic
1 inch piece fresh ginger root
1 fresh hot green chili pepper
2 tablespoons oil
1 teaspoon mustard seeds
1 teaspoon turmeric powder
1 teaspoon red chili powder
salt to taste
1 tablespoon lemon juice
1 teaspoon roasted cumin seed
  powder (see page 28)
chopped coriander (cilantro), for
  garnish.

**SERVES 6**

1  Cook the potatoes until just tender in boiling water. Drain and cut into cubes.
2  Finely slice the onion, garlic and ginger and chop the chili pepper.
3  Heat the oil in a frying-pan or wok and add the mustard seeds. When they "pop," add the onion, garlic and ginger. Cook, stirring, for 5 minutes.
4  Add the potatoes, chopped chili pepper, turmeric and red chili powders and the salt. Mix well, then cook gently, stirring, for another 5 minutes.
5  Remove from the heat and stir in the lemon juice. Mix well and spoon into a serving dish. Sprinkle with the roasted cumin seed powder and chopped coriander and serve with *pooris* (see page 133).

## ❧ LENTIL FRITTERS IN YOGURT ❧
*Dahi baras*

*Dahi baras* are a very popular snack in North India. They are delicious, particularly when eaten with tamarind chutney (see page 141).

BARAS
2 cups split black beans or grams
  (*urad dal*)
1 tablespoon cashew nuts
1 inch piece fresh ginger root
½ teaspoon red chili powder
1 teaspoon cumin seeds
salt to taste
a pinch of asafetida
1 tablespoon raisins
2 cups oil for frying
YOGURT SAUCE
4 cups plain yogurt
salt to taste
2 teaspoons sugar
1 teaspoon roasted cumin seed
  powder (see page 28)
1 teaspoon red chili powder
1 teaspoon dried mint

**SERVES 6**

1  Soak the black beans or grams in cold water overnight. Drain them the following day and grind to a smooth paste in a blender or food processor.
2  Finely chop the cashew nuts and ginger and add to the *dal* paste with all the remaining *bara* ingredients except for the oil. Mix well – it will be quite a dry mixture, but do not add any water.
3  Heat the oil in a frying-pan or wok and drop four to five spoonfuls of the paste into it at a time. Cook until lightly browned on both sides.
4  Place a large bowl of cold water by the stove. Remove the *baras* with a slotted spoon when they are cooked and drop them into the water.
5  When all the *baras* are cooked, gently squeeze the water out of them by pressing them between the palms of your hands. Arrange in a circle in a shallow dish.
6  Make the yogurt sauce: beat the yogurt lightly and add the salt and sugar. Pour this over the *baras*, then sprinkle the roasted cumin powder, the red chili powder and the dried mint over the yogurt to form a "tricolor" pattern. Chill well before serving.

## ❧ PEAS FRIED RICE ❧
### Matar pullao

*I* always order this rice in my favorite restaurant – "Niros" – in Jaipur. It is one of the best restaurants in the world!

2 cups Basmati rice
¼ cup melted *ghee* or oil
1 teaspoon cumin seeds
4 cloves
8 black peppercorns
salt to taste
1 tablespoon raisins
¾ cup peas, fresh or frozen
1 quart water (approx)

SERVES 6

1 Wash the rice under cold running water. Soak in cold water for about 1 hour. Drain well.
2 Heat the *ghee* or oil in a heavy-based saucepan and add the cumin seeds, cloves and peppercorns. Fry for 1–2 minutes, stirring, then add the rice. Stir to mix and to coat the grains evenly in the oil.
3 Add the salt, raisins and peas and stir to mix. Add the water and cook over a medium heat until all the water has been absorbed. Stir with a fork to separate the grains. Leave, covered, on the stove, off the heat, until ready to serve.

## ❧ SAFFRON RICE ❧
### Kesar ka pullao

2 cups Basmati or long-grain rice
5 tablespoons melted *ghee*
1 teaspoon cumin seeds
4 cloves
3 onions
1 inch piece fresh ginger root
1 fresh hot green chili pepper
½ teaspoon saffron
1 tablespoon warm milk
salt to taste
12 blanched almonds, sliced
1 tablespoon raisins
1 cup coconut milk (see page 28)
4 green cardamoms
1 quart water
1 tablespoon oil

SERVES 6

1 Wash the rice under cold running water. Soak in cold water for about 1 hour. Drain well.
2 Heat the *ghee* in a heavy-based pan and add the cumin seeds and cloves. Finely slice two of the onions, the ginger and chili pepper and add to the pan. Cook, stirring, for about 5 minutes.
3 Add all the remaining ingredients, except for the remaining onion and the oil. Cook gently over a low heat until the water has been absorbed and the rice is tender. Leave the pan covered until ready to serve.
4 Slice the remaining onion and fry it in the oil until brown and crisp. Sprinkle over the rice and serve.

## ❧ LAYERED CHAPPATI ❧
### *Parat ki roti*

$1\frac{3}{4}$ cups wholewheat flour
$1\frac{1}{2}$ cups all-purpose flour
salt to taste
$\frac{1}{4}$ cup milk
$\frac{3}{4}$ cup melted *ghee* (approx)
1 cup water (approx)

SERVES 6

1 Sift the wholewheat flour into a bowl with $1\frac{1}{4}$ cups all-purpose flour. Add the salt, milk and 2 tablespoons melted *ghee*. Add sufficient water to make into a stiff dough.
2 Turn the dough onto a floured board. Knead until smooth.
3 Break off small pieces of dough and roll out into circles, about 3 inches in diameter. Brush one circle with a little melted *ghee* and sprinkle with a little of the reserved all-purpose flour.
4 Place a second circle on top of the first one, brush with more *ghee* and sprinkle with a little more flour. Place a third circle on top and press down firmly.
5 Heat a heavy-based frying-pan or griddle and grease it lightly. Place the layered *roti* in the pan and cook on both sides until lightly browned.
6 Pour a little melted *ghee* over the surface of the *roti* and spread it evenly. Turn the *roti* over and pour a little more *ghee* onto the other side, spreading it evenly again.
7 Remove from the pan and keep warm while you cook the remainder of the *roti* in the same way. Serve cut into quarters.

THROUGHOUT THE WEDDING CEREMONY, THE PRIEST (AT THE RIGHT OF THE PICTURE) CHANTS *MANTRAS*. DURING THE CEREMONY, THE BRIDE AND GROOM WALK SEVEN TIMES AROUND THE SACRED FIRE.

# ❧ SPICED FESTIVE RICE ❧
## *Kabooli*

*I* had this dish at my mother's friend's house in Jaipur. It is a tasty and filling vegetarian rice dish that looks colorful and is quite easy to prepare. Serve it with *poppadums*, pickles and chutneys for a complete meal or as part of a special feast or dinner party.

2 cups Basmati rice
1 quart water
2 onions
6 cloves garlic
6 tablespoons melted *ghee*
1 teaspoon turmeric powder
1 teaspoon red chili powder
2 teaspoons coriander powder
salt to taste
1 cup plain yogurt
1 cup oil
4 slices of bread
2 potatoes
½ small cauliflower
1 teaspoon dried mint
1 teaspoon *garam masala* powder
2 tablespoons lemon juice
1 tablespoon raisins, soaked in
    water, drained
20 blanched almonds, sliced
½ teaspoon green food coloring
½ teaspoon yellow food coloring
1 tablespoon melted butter
½ cup buttermilk
chopped coriander (cilantro), for
    garnish

SERVES 6

1 Wash the rice under cold running water and leave to soak in cold water for about 1 hour. Drain well. Cook the rice, covered, in the water. Separate the grains lightly with a fork, then leave on one side.

2 Mince the onions and garlic in a food processor and fry them in the *ghee* for 5 minutes. Add the turmeric, chili and coriander powders with the salt and yogurt. Simmer for 5–10 minutes, stirring occasionally. Remove from the heat and keep on one side.

3 Heat the oil in a deep frying-pan or wok. Cut the slices of bread into four triangles each and fry these until golden brown. Remove from the pan and drain on paper towels.

4 Cut the potatoes into cubes and the cauliflower into small florets. Fry these vegetables in the hot oil until golden brown. Remove and drain on paper towels. Mix with the bread triangles.

5 Mix the mint, *garam masala*, lemon juice and the fried bread and vegetables with the cooked onion and spices. Stir in the raisins and almonds.

6 Divide the boiled rice into three portions. Color one portion green with the green food coloring and one portion yellow. Leave the remaining third white.

7 Brush a deep glass dish with the melted butter. Place the green rice in an even layer over the bottom and top it with a third of the spicy vegetable and bread mixture. Cover with the white rice, then another layer of the spicy vegetable mixture. Top with the yellow rice and cover this with the remaining spicy vegetable mixture.

8 Make a well in the center of the rice and pour the buttermilk into it. Garnish with chopped coriander and serve at once.

# DAL BREAD
*Daal ki poori*

*A* filling and particularly nutritious bread, this one has a stuffing of *dal*. Any kind of *dal* can be used – my favorite in this instance is *chana dal*.

⅔ cup split yellow chickpeas (*chana dal*)
1 fresh hot green chili pepper
4 cloves garlic
1 cup + 1 tablespoon oil
1 teaspoon cumin seeds
salt to taste
1¾ cups water (approx)
2 tablespoons sugar
2¾ cups wholewheat flour
¾ cups all-purpose flour

MAKES 12–16

1 Soak the *dal* overnight in cold water. Drain the next day.
2 Finely chop the chili pepper and garlic. Heat 1 tablespoon oil in a frying-pan and add the chili pepper and garlic, together with the cumin seeds. Fry, stirring, for 1 minute.
3 Add the drained *dal*, with the salt, 1 cup water and the sugar. Cook gently until the *dal* is tender, adding more water if necessary.
4 Remove from the heat and leave to cool, then grind to a paste in a food processor.
5 Sift the two flours together into a bowl and add sufficient of the remaining water to make a pliable dough. Knead until smooth.
6 Divide the dough into twelve to sixteen pieces, roll into balls, then flatten each one slightly.
7 Roll out the balls on a greased board to circles about 3 inches in diameter. Place a spoonful of the *dal* mixture on top of each one. Dampen the edges of each circle and fold over the *dal* to make a semi-circle.
8 Heat the remaining oil in a frying-pan and fry the *dal pooris* one at a time. Drain on paper towels and keep warm in a dish covered with foil until ready to serve.

# DEEP FRIED BREAD
*Poori*

1¾ cups wholewheat flour
1 cup all-purpose flour
salt to taste
2 tablespoons oil
1 cup water (approx)
2 cups oil for frying

MAKES 20

1 Sift the two flours together and add the salt and 2 tablespoons oil. Mix well, then gradually add sufficient water to make a stiff dough.
2 Put the dough on one side, covered, for 30 minutes.
3 Grease a board with oil and put the remainder of the oil on to heat in a frying-pan or wok.
4 Divide the dough into small pieces the size of a golf ball, roll them into rounds, then flatten them slightly.
5 Roll out each ball into a thin circle about 4 inches in diameter and drop one by one into the hot oil. Press them down with a slotted spoon – this makes them puff up.
6 Flip the *pooris* over and cook on the other side for 30 seconds. Remove with a slotted spoon and drain on paper towels. Keep warm while you fry the remainder in the same way.

## TOMATO AND ONION YOGURT SALAD
*Cachumber ka raita*

1½ cups plain yogurt
2 tomatoes
1 onion
1 fresh hot green chili pepper
2 tablespoons chopped coriander
    (cilantro)
1 teaspoon red chili powder
salt to taste
1 teaspoon roasted cumin seed
    powder (see page 28)

SERVES 6

1  Put the yogurt into a bowl and beat it lightly.
2  Finely chop the tomatoes, onion and green chili pepper. Stir these into the yogurt with the chopped coriander.
3  Add the chili powder and salt. Mix well and chill the *raita*.
4  Sprinkle the cumin powder on the *raita* just before serving.

## TOMATO PICKLE
*Tamatar ka achaar*

1 lb tomatoes
1 cup sugar
½ cup water
2 bay leaves
salt to taste
½ cup malt vinegar
⅔ cup raisins
12 blanched almonds
1 teaspoon nigella seeds
6 cloves garlic
½ teaspoon saffron powder
    (optional)

1  Blanch the tomatoes in boiling water and peel off the skins. Then cut into quarters. Put on one side.
2  Put the sugar into a saucepan with the water and bay leaves and simmer gently for 10 minutes.
3  Add the tomatoes and cook gently until the tomatoes are thoroughly softened.
4  Add all the remaining ingredients and mix well. Simmer for 10–15 minutes more, until the ingredients are well mixed. Remove from the heat and leave to cool completely.
5  Spoon into a screw-top jar and keep in the refrigerator until required.

## MANGO AND JAGGERY PICKLE
*Aam aur gur ka achaar*

*T*his is a sweet pickle that tastes very good with *chappatis* or *parathas*. It can be made with raw apples instead of mangoes.

14 oz *jaggery*
1½ cups water
12 unripe green mangoes
1 tablespoon anise seeds
1 teaspoon nigella seeds
salt to taste
1 teaspoon red chili powder

1  Put the *jaggery* and water in a pan and cook over a low heat, stirring frequently, for 15–20 minutes.
2  Meanwhile, peel the mangoes and cut the flesh into cubes.
3  When the mixture in the saucepan has thickened slightly, add the mangoes with all the other ingredients. Stir well and simmer gently until the mango pieces are soft, and the syrup is really thick.
4  Remove from the heat and leave to cool before transferring to a glass jar. This pickle can be eaten immediately.

## ❧ CHICKPEA FLOUR PUDDING ❧
### *Besan ka halwa*

*A* very rich pudding, so serve this one in small quantities. It can have quite a laxative effect!

⅔ cup melted *ghee*
2½ cups chickpea or gram flour
1½ cups hot water
1 cup milk
1 cup sugar
1 tablespoon raisins
1 tablespoon cashew nuts
2 green cardamoms
1 teaspoon rosewater
dried shredded coconut, for
    decoration

SERVES 6

**1** Heat the *ghee* in a frying-pan or wok and sift the flour into it. Stir-fry it until it turns brown.
**2** Stir in the hot water and milk and keep stirring to keep the mixture smooth. Add the sugar and raisins.
**3** Chop the cashew nuts and crush the cardamoms and stir them into the mixture, with the rosewater. Keep stirring, so that lumps do not form.
**4** When the liquid has been absorbed and the *ghee* is visible around the *halwa*, remove the pan from the heat and turn the pudding into a serving dish. Decorate with dried shredded coconut.

## ❧ SWEET RICE ❧
### *Meetha zarda pullao*

*T*his is a Muslim and Rajasthani specialty, which is traditionally prepared for the bride and bridegroom at a wedding.

2 cups long-grain rice
1 quart water
1 teaspoon yellow food coloring
1½ cups sugar
½ cup melted *ghee*
2 tablespoons raisins
2 tablespoons blanched almonds
2 large cardamoms

SERVES 6

**1** Wash the rice under cold running water and drain well. Put it into a saucepan with the water, the yellow food coloring and the sugar.
**2** Cook over a low heat until almost all the water has been absorbed, then add the *ghee* and stir in the raisins.
**3** Slice the almonds finely and add to the pan. Remove the cardamom seeds from the pods and add them to the pan too. Cook for 5–10 minutes, then remove from the heat, but leave the pan sitting on the stove, covered, for about 30 minutes before serving.

CLOCKWISE FROM TOP LEFT: SWEET RICE, CARROT PUDDING AND SWEET OAT PUDDING.

## ❧ SWEET OAT PUDDING ❧
### *Laapsi*

*T*his is a typical Rajasthani dish, and is made on all festive occasions, particularly weddings, christenings or birthday celebrations. The host and hostess feed it by hand to all relatives and friends just before the meal. At a wedding the bridge and bridgegroom feed this as the first mouthful to each other. As you can see, it is considered to be an auspicious dish!

1 cup *ghee*
3⅔ cups rolled oats or broken wheat
5 cups water
2 teaspoons anise seeds
1¾ cups sugar
4 black cardamoms
1 teaspoon saffron
2 tablespoons dried shredded
  coconut
¼ cup cooked rice, for garnish

**1** Heat the *ghee* in a frying-pan or wok and stir-fry the oats or wheat until golden brown.
**2** Add 3 cups water and bring to simmering point. Add the anise seeds, stir, then remove from the heat.
**3** Put the sugar and remaining water in a separate pan. Remove the seeds from the cardamom pods and add to the pan with the saffron. Set over medium heat and when the sugar has dissolved, simmer gently for 20–25 minutes.
**4** Pour this syrup over the oats and simmer gently until the oats are tender, all the water has been absorbed and the *ghee* comes to the top of the pudding. Keep stirring all the time.
**5** Arrange in a circle on a plate and sprinkle the coconut on top. Place the rice in the center – this is supposed to bring prosperity and good luck!

## ❧ CARROT PUDDING ❧
### *Gajjar ka halwa*

*C*arrot pudding is a great favorite of my second daughter – Rupina. I remember how, as children, we were all given a little cup of this every morning with breakfast – it was delicious. It is usually made in the winter when the carrots are in season and it is generally served hot.

1 lb carrots
1½ quarts milk
1 cup sugar
1 tablespoon raisins
6 tablespoons melted *ghee*
½ teaspoon saffron
2 green cardamoms
10 blanched almonds
2 sheets of edible silver paper
  (optional)

SERVES 6

**1** Peel and grate the carrots. Put the milk into a large saucepan and bring to a boil. Add the carrots and simmer very gently until all the liquid has evaporated and the carrots have turned creamy.
**2** Add the sugar and raisins and continue simmering gently until the mixture has thickened. Stir in the *ghee*.
**3** Dissolve the saffron in 1 teaspoon warm water and crush the cardamoms. Add these to the pan and continue cooking, stirring all the time, until the *ghee* has been absorbed into the carrots and the pudding comes away from the sides of the pan. Remove from the heat when the *ghee* comes to the surface.
**4** Slice the almonds finely. Turn the *halwa* out onto a glass serving dish and sprinkle with the almonds. Decorate with the silver paper, if using.

# INDEX

Page numbers in *italics* refer to photographs of the dishes.

## ACKNOWLEDGEMENTS

STYLIST
Nova Pilbeam

PICTURE CREDITS
Duncan Brown p. 26, 118, 142
Alan Duns p. 22–23
Paul Grater p. 31, 34, 39, 43, 46, 51, 54, 59, 62, 67, 70, 79, 82, 91, 94, 102, 107, 110, 115, 122, 127, 135, 139, 147, 151, 163, 174, 183
Fran Jones p. 10–11, 46 bottom, 130, 159
Fred Mancini p.154
Rebecca New p. 27
Gopal Varma p. 15, 16, 19, 86, 166, 167, 171
Zul p. 46 top, 99
All other photographs are from Manju Shivraj Singh's private collection.